Karl Llewellyn's Dueling Canons in Perspective

Karl Llewellyn's Dueling Canons in Perspective

Michael Sinclair

VANDEPLAS PUBLISHING, LLC

UNITED STATES OF AMERICA

Karl Llewellyn's Dueling Canons in Perspective
Sinclair, Michael

Published by:

Vandeplas Publishing, LLC – May 2014

801 International Parkway, 5th Floor
Lake Mary, FL. 32746
USA

www.vandeplaspublishing.com

ISBN 978-1-60042-185-3

For my wife, Karen

TABLE OF CONTENTS

CONTENTS vii

PREFACE ix

ACKNOWLEDGEMENTS xii

1: INTRODUCTION 1
- What is a canon of construction? 2
- Three basic principles 5
- What follows 7

2: PAIRS ONE TO FOURTEEN 11
- Pair 1 11
- Pair 2 17
- Pair 3 23
- Pair 4 29
- Pair 5 35
- Pair 6 39
- Pair 7 45
- Pairs 8, 9, and 10 51
- Pair 11 65
- Pair 12 75
- Pair 13 81
- Pair 14 85

3: INTERIM ASSESSMENT 91

4: PAIRS FIFTEEN TO TWENTY-EIGHT 95
- Pair 15 95
- Pair 16 101
- Pair 17 105
- Pair 18 111
- Pair 19 115
- Pair 20 119
- Pair 21 129
- Pair 22 135
- Pair 23 141
- Pair 24 147
- Pair 25 153
- Pair 26 157
- Pair 27 161
- Pair 28 165

5: CONCLUSION 171

BIBLIOGRAPHY 177

INDEX 183

PREFACE

In 1950, Karl N. Llewellyn, one of the foremost legal thinkers in the United States, wrote "[I]n the field of statutory construction ..., there are "correct," unchallengeable rules of "how to read" which lead in happily variant directions."[1] The "unchallengeable rules of 'how to read'" to which he refers are called "canons of construction." To demonstrate his thesis he appended a list of twenty-eight pairs of canons, "thrusts" and "parries" leading, he said, "in happily variant directions." The list, known as "dueling canons," quickly became famous and hugely influential. It is the subject of this book.

Before the work that led to this book, I simply accepted Llewellyn's thesis as a given, as did everyone else that I knew or knew of. In my Statutory Interpretation course I introduced students to it with a couple of its examples at the beginning of the classes on canons. At the time, I used also to teach commercial law and payment systems, the law for which was conceived by Llewellyn, whom I greatly admired, so I gave no thought to looking further into his famous demolition of hitherto received wisdom. In about 1992 I thought of working through some of the pairs, spelling out the justifications for their "thrusts" and "parries," and bringing their judicial exemplars up to date; it would make a good summer project, research intensive and unexciting but worthwhile. Many canons are useful —indeed some, like "*Expressio unius est exclusio alterius*" (Thrust #20) are essential —so I did wonder if I might find ways out of some of Llewellyn's "fiendishly deconstructive"[2] antinomies. But there are few kudos for reworking someone else's project, the work would be unexciting, and I had other interesting projects to get on with, so it took me about ten years actually to get started. I had little idea what I was getting into: The list simply fails to produce the promised antinomies; it is poorly researched, and very commonly the thrusts and parries have little or no claim to canonical status. Overall it simply fails to provide support for Llewellyn's thesis.

I started from the top, Pair One, and worked through the first seven pairs in my first summer on the project. In only one pair did the thrust and parry lead in different directions and in that one, Pair Five, the thrust, far from being canonical, seemed to have been made up for the purpose. Still, I thought, later pairs would be better, more antagonistic. After Pair Fourteen I was ready to give up. Llewellyn, a hero of realist jurisprudence whose approach to many subjects I followed in both teaching and research, had fallen from his pedestal and I was not up for kicking

---

[1] Karl N. Llewellyn, "*Remarks on the Theory of Appellate Decision and the rules or Canons of about how Statutes are to be Construed,*" 3 VANDERBILT L.REV. 395, 399 (1950).

[2] Daniel A. Farber, *The Inevitability of Practical Reason: Statutes, Formalism, and the Rule of Law*, 45 VAND. L. REV. 533, 535 (1992).

at the pieces. But the work, especially spelling out the reasoning supporting each canon, had proven both interesting and instructive, and should be completed, for better or for worse. I'm glad I persisted. Readers may judge the wisdom of that decision for themselves. The project taught me a great amount about statutes and their interpretation and application, not only benefitting myself but also improving my class teaching and course materials.

The basic work was first published in a series of articles, first in the New York Law School Law Review, then on the Social Science Research Network, under the serial titles "“Only a Sith Thinks Like That”: Llewellyn's “Dueling Canons,” Pairs … to … ."[3] The pre-colon title of the articles, *"Only a Sith Thinks Like That,"* was not a success: I have never met a reader who caught the point. I could have used "Manichean" rather than "Sith," but thought the title "*Manichean thinking:…*" would have worked for very few. Conceiving the social and moral universe as black or white, with no shades of gray, is called "Manichean," after an ancient Persian religion (founded by one Mani, hence the name) which held that the universe was controlled by two opposing forces, good and evil. The word "Manichean" came to be used for reasoning that presupposes only categorical extremes, black and white, no intermediate shades. I thought, probably wrongly, that more people would now know of Siths, the totalitarian bad guys of the *Star Wars* movie sextet, and also Manichean thinkers.[4] Implicit in the title is that Llewellyn's list, as reasoning, rests on the Manichean fallacy, a fallacy we try to rid students of in their first semester.

Canons –accepted rules of interpretation —are of jurisprudentially interesting status. They are not rules of law, as are statutes, but depend for authority on their acceptance and wisdom. Acceptance is an empirical matter: it requires a reasonable period of consistent judicial application; if judges reject a proposed "wise saw" it is not a canon. Wisdom in law is a matter of values, morals, politics, social efficiency and sometimes even expediency, all ethical predicates. But philosophers have long assured us that one cannot mix the empirical and the ethical, the "is" and the "ought." Do canons suffer by trying to establish a combination of both modes of

---

[3] "“Only a Sith Thinks Like That”: Llewellyn's “Dueling Canons,” One to Seven" 50 NEW YORK LAW SCHOOL LAW REVIEW 919-92 (2006); "“Only a Sith Thinks Like That”: Llewellyn's “Dueling Canons,” Eight to Twelve," 51 NEW YORK LAW SCHOOL LAW REVIEW 1003-1054 (2006-07)) SSRN: http://ssrn.com/abstract=902853; "“Only a Sith Thinks Like That”: Llewellyn's “Dueling Canons,” Thirteen to Sixteen," 53 NEW YORK LAW SCHOOL LAW REVIEW 953-993 (2008-09))SSRN: http://ssrn.com/abstract=1337057; "“Only a Sith Thinks Like That”: Llewellyn's “Dueling Canons,” Seventeen to Twenty," SSRN: http://ssrn.com/abstract=1387503, fall 2008; "“Only a Sith Thinks Like That”: Llewellyn's “Dueling Canons,” Twenty-one to Twenty-four," SSRN: http://ssrn.com/abstract=1557831, January, 2010; "“Only a Sith Thinks Like That”: Llewellyn's “Dueling Canons,” Twenty-five to Twenty-eight," SSRN: http://ssrn.com/abstract=1682164, September, 2010 (the last two with Adam Schlusselberg).

[4] In Episode III of the "*Star Wars*" sextet (really the final installment, the third part of the three part "prequel," the series having begun with Episode IV), just before talented and erstwhile nice kid Anakin Skywalker turns into bad-guy Darth Vader he says to his mentor Obi-Wan Kenobe, near-quoting President George W. Bush, "If you're not with me, you're my enemy." Kenobe replied "Anakin, only a Sith thinks like that!"

justification? The "Principle of Sufficient Reason" —commonly attributed to Leibniz, "no state of affairs can obtain, and no statement can be true unless there is sufficient reason why it should not be otherwise."[5] —I believe resolves the dilemma. If a principle has seen consistent judicial use over a reasonable period of time and in a variety of circumstances, that is if it has proven adaptive to the needs of the society, then it must have a sound justification based in the values of that society. This operational axiom works to bridge the moral and empirical underpinnings of canons of construction. More simply, were an interpretive principle not justifiable in our legal society it would not be used and not be a canon, or if used in a different time (*e.g.*, Statutes in derogation of the common law are to be strictly construed" (Thrust #2)) it would fall into desuetude and no longer be a canon. On this reasoning I investigated not only Llewellyn's case law support for his pairs —and when it failed found alternative cases —but also offer justifications for those justifiable. In this aspect the book goes beyond its primary result of showing the invalidity of Llewellyn's thesis, *viz*, there are unchallengeable rules of statutory interpretation "which lead in happily variant directions."

Llewellyn wrote a short article, and the argument for which it is remembered, namely his "contradictory canons" thesis and the list of twenty-eight pairs to demonstrate it, occupied only some four to five pages; I have taken a whole book to discredit it. Isn't there an unjustifed disproportionality to that? A bulldozer weeding the rose bed? If Llewellyn's thesis is as wrong as I have argued, shouldn't that be apparent in rather fewer words?

Yes, maybe it should. But if one is going to say that a renowned and hugely influential argument by one of the greatest figures in twentieth century jurisprudence is pretty much wall to wall nonsense, one had better be on solid ground and establish that ground very thoroughly. That is what I have aimed at in this protracted argument in contradiction of the great man's famous thesis. And along the way I have learned much about canons of statutory interpretation, bench-marks of judicial experience and recorded wisdom, and the reasons justifying their ubiquity and longevity. Explaining canons may not have been my primary objective, but I hope that it will be found a useful and perhaps even interesting side benefit of this exercise.

---

[5] Gottfried Wilhelm Leibniz (1646-1716) MONADOLOGY ¶31 (1714).

ACKNOWLEDGEMENTS

Jethro Lieberman suggested that I turn this project into a book, an idea that had not occurred to me; I thank him for this and for his encouragement. New York Law School provided generous support in Summer Faculty Research Fellowships and research assistance. I thank my research assistants for this project, Jessica Ventarola[6] on Pairs One through Twelve and Adam Schlusselberg[7] on the remainder; both were helpful beyond my expectations. Indeed, the original treatment of the last eight pairs, Pairs ##21 to 28, were published jointly on the Social Science Research Network[8] and Adam Schlusselberg was the primary author of the analyses of Pairs Twenty-One and Twenty-Two. I should also like to thank friends and fellow faculty members for their support and wisdom, especially Jim Brook, John Murphy, Ross Sandler, and Silvy Singh, my secretary for the twenty years before my retirement. My wife Karen, to whom I dedicate this book, has been unfailing in her faith and support and also in her careful editorial scrutiny of drafts.

---

[6] J.D. 2007, New York Law School.

[7] J.D. 2009, New York Law School.

[8] Adam Schlusselberg and Michael Sinclair, "“Only a Sith Thinks Like That”: Llewellyn’s “Dueling Canons,” Twenty-one to Twenty-four,” SSRN: http://ssrn.com/abstract=1557831, January, 2010; "“Only a Sith Thinks Like That”: Llewellyn’s “Dueling Canons,” Twenty-five to Twenty-eight,” SSRN: http://ssrn.com/abstract=1682164, September, 2010.

1: *Introduction*

> [I]n the field of statutory construction …, there are "correct," unchallengeable rules of "how to read" which lead in happily variant directions.[1]

With that, in 1950, the redoubtable Karl N. Llewellyn launched the most famous of all attacks on canons of construction —rules for applying a statute —a list of twenty-eight pairs of canons, each pair a "thrust" and a "parry" having opposite effect. Academic theorists widely considered this "fiendishly deconstructive"[2] list devastating to the legitimacy of canons, and for almost half a century research on canons virtually ceased.[3] In 1992, more than forty years after its publication, an academic symposium gave Llewellyn's critique uniform approval,[4] and as recently as 2010 a new textbook for first year law students treated it as authoritative.[5] Yet all this went by without any detailed examination of the validity or contrariety of Llewellyn's renowned pairings.[6]

This book is an evaluation of Llewellyn's thesis that to every canon there is an equal and opposite canon. It takes each pair in turn and holds it up to scrutiny, examines the justifications, the cases Llewellyn provides in illustration and, where necessary, provides further cases. My initial hypothesis was that Llewellyn's pairings might not prove so devastatingly inconsistent, that the justifications and conditions for proper use of members of a pair might deflate the dramatic

---

[1] Karl N. Llewellyn, *Remarks on the Theory of Appellate Decision and the rules or Canons of about how Statutes are to be Construed,* 3 VANDERBILT L.REV. 395, 399 (1950)("*Canons*").

[2] Daniel A. Farber, "*The Inevitability of Practical Reason: Statutes, Formalism, and the Rule of Law,*" 45 VAND.L.REV. 533, 535 (1992).

[3] John F. Manning, *Legal Realism and the Canons' Revival*, 5 THE GREEN BAG 2nd 283, 283-84 (2002)("Karl Llewellyn largely persuaded two generations of academics that the canons of construction were not to be taken seriously. . . . [His] critique of the canons is one of the most influential realist works of the last century."); *similarly*, James J. Brudney and Corey Ditslear, *Canons of Construction and the Elusive Quest for Neutral Reasoning*, 58 VAND.L.REV. 1, 8 (2005)("Professor Karl Llewellyn's classic critique, which listed a counter-canon for each of twenty-eight canons, highlighted what he viewed as the canons' radical indeterminacy.").Jonathon R. Macey & Geoffrey P.Miller, *The Canons of Statutory Construction and Judicial Preferences*, 45 VAND.L.REV. 647, 647 (1992)(Llewellyn "derailed" "intellectual debate about the canons for almost a quarter of a century.").

[4] SYMPOSIUM: A REEVALUATION OF THE CANONS OF STATUTORY INTERPRETATION, 45 VAND.L.REV. 529 *et seq*. (1992).

[5] John F. Manning and Matthew C. Stephenson, LEGISLATION AND REGULATION, 223 (2010).

[6] *See* Michael Sinclair, *Only a Sith Thinks Like That": Llewellyn's "Dueling Canons," One to Seven*, 50 N.Y.L. SCH. L. Rev. 919 (2005–06).

effect of the prima facie contrariety. After all, even if academics disapproved, judges and lawyers had continued to find canons helpful in statutory reasoning. It was a long and sometimes tedious project. Llewellyn merely listed pairs of formulae with footnoted authority in treatises and judicial opinions; I found and spelled out all those details. This, then, is a book length review of an appendix to an article; but what an appendix and what an impact it has had!

The unavoidable conclusion of this project is that Llewellyn's thesis and its justificatory list fail even a superficial examination: the list contains no real contradictions, nor even inconsistencies of significance; on even a cursory scrutiny it is hard to see it as a list of genuine canons. This is a very great disappointment, a realization that at first makes one feel sick at heart. Llewellyn was a very bright star in my jurisprudential pantheon, for the twentieth century perhaps matched only by Lon Fuller and maybe H.L.A. Hart. *Canons* is his best known article and has been called a monument not only of statutory interpretation but of legal realist scholarship.[7] Perhaps, it might be excused as a throw-away, dashed off under time pressure;[8] but if so, why did Llewellyn repeat the list as an appendix to his book, *The Common Law Tradition-Deciding Appeals*.[9] These are very strong conclusions that require their own justification; and, along the way, there proved to be much of interest about canons to be unearthed.

What is a canon of construction?

Canons are wise saws that have proven helpful in applying the written words of statutes to particular factual situations.[10] They are not law, nor do they claim to be universally binding, but they should have significance greater than a mere cliché. One might see them as having compulsive weight somewhere between homespun sayings and general truths of science or mathematics: "*Expressio unius est exclusio alterius*" carries more weight than "A stitch in time saves nine" but less than "Every even number is the sum of two primes."[11]

---

[7] John F. Manning, *Legal Realism and the Canons' Revival*, 5 THE GREEN BAG 2nd 283, 283-84 (2002)("[Llewellyn's] critique of the canons is one of the most influential realist works of the last century.")

[8] Professor Manning offers this excuse: "Interestingly, Llewellyn's discussion of the canons comes at the end of his piece, and appears to have been added almost as an afterthought. Although we can never know, perhaps Professor Llewellyn had the familiar experience of finally confronting a symposium deadline, and sent his research assistant to check out a 'hunch' that Llewellyn had long held. Such experiences usually yield less success." John F. Manning, *Legal Realism and the Canons' Revival*, 5 GREEN BAG 2d 283, 283 n.3 (2002).

[9] Karl N. Llewellyn, THE COMMON LAW TRADITION—DECIDING APPEALS, 521-28 (1960)(Under the caption "Canons on Statutes." There he attributes the list to Charles Driscoll, explicitly claiming only the introductory paragraphs for himself.)

[10] *See* Michael Sinclair, TRADITIONAL TOOLS OF STATUTORY INTERPRETATION (Vandeplas Publishing, 2013) Ch.s 5 and 6.

[11] "Goldbach's Conjecture." Goldbach suggested it in a letter to Euler dated June 17, 1742. It has never been either proven or disproven although it has been verified up to 10^{14}.

Although one ought not demand a formulation of statute-like determinacy, some stability or limit on variety in expression, some *canonical form*, is necessary.[12] Second, a canon should have a sufficient frequency of application to have been used, tested, and contested over time in a decent variety of circumstances on a decent variety of cases. Only thus can a principle achieve the sort of acceptance needed to make it useable without further ado. For example, the self-translating Latin maxim "*expressio unius est exclusio alterius*" is a paradigmatic canon: it is a stable verbal formula showing no variation in Latin and little in its occasional translations,[13] and it finds common application in cases. But despite coming, like statutes and unlike precedents, in verbal formulae, canons are not law. They have authority only in virtue of their wisdom and justification; they do not have the commanding power of statutes or precedents. A judge who declines to use a potentially applicable canon is not for that reason alone at fault, as she would be were she to ignore an applicable statute or reject a precedent without distinguishing it. Yet perhaps the mark of the true canon is that cites are not necessary, the formula itself carrying sufficient interpretive authority.

Canons depend for their application on their wisdom and justifications. But wisdom alone is unsatisfying: we like to have an explanation for why a wise saw is wise, why it is accepted or acceded to so easily, not just in statutory interpretation, but everywhere. So justification is critical. Llewellyn himself said so: "Plainly, to make any canon take hold in a particular instance, the construction contended for must be sold, essentially, by means other than the use of the canon."[14] When the reasoning underlying a canon —the sales pitch supporting it —does not hold or the conditions presupposed by that reasoning do not obtain, then the canon should not be used. A canon, then, looks more like a formulaic summary of the end result of a process of reasoning, but a process sufficiently commonplace to justify a canonical formula.

Most general criticisms of canons treat them as fixed, unconditional, formulaic rules, to be applied mindlessly at every opportunity.[15] It is *ignoratio elenchi* —"knocking down a straw man I never set up" —common enough in jurisprudence but still a fallacy and hardly a valid or even useful strategy. Yet scholars of statutory construction have been arguing for an increase in rigidity, in formalism in the use of canons, for example that every judge should adopt and follow

---

[12] William Eskridge compiled a list of some ninety six "canons" used by the Supreme Court between 1986 and 1991. If one follows Eskridge's example, a canon is any verbal formulation relating to interpretation, although not necessarily a canonical formulation. But surely that is too broad a meaning to be of use. William N. Eskridge, Jr., *DYNAMIC* STATUTORY INTERPRETATION, 323-28 (1994).

[13] As in Thrust #20: "Expression of one thing excludes another." *Canons* at 405.

[14] *Canons, supra* at 401. To do Llewellyn justice, one should see his list of dueling canons not as a devastating deconstruction but as a demonstration of this thesis.

[15] *See, e.g.*, Reed Dickerson, THE INTERPRETATION AND APPLICATION OF STATUTES 234 (1975).

a fixed interpretive doctrine,[16] or for a restatement as an authoritative formulation of permissible rules of interpretation,[17] or, in the extreme, for the adoption of statute-like rules of interpretation.[18] A collateral effect of close examination of Llewellyn's pairs of canons is to demonstrate these arguments fundamentally misguided, that any attempt to rigidify or formalize canons and their use should fail in theory and in practice.

It is useful to classify canons into two bags, "substantive" and "linguistic," although perhaps better words would be "endogenous" and "exogenous" respectively. The classification is based on the source of justification: "Linguistic canons" are those whose justifications come from outside peculiarly legal process, most often from the communicative function of statutes, hence "linguistic." "Substantive canons" are all the rest, which means simply that their justifications are found elsewhere, mostly in the principle of legislative supremacy and the grab-bag we call "policy." They are hardly different from those settled rules of common law —"The rule of Foakes v. Beer," "The Rule in Shelley's Case" —naming a particular *ratio decidendi*, with the insecure force of *stare dictis* rather than *stare decisis*. Thus one might expect substantive canons to be more tenuous, more easily refuted by judicial argument than linguistic canons.

Substantive canons can have a confusing variety of justifications so depend more often on a history of prior use, on *stare dictis*, than do linguistic canons. They also come with variable compulsive strengths —from convenient or advisable tie-breakers, as for example the antiquated exhortation to construe statutes in derogation of the common law narrowly, to the "avoidance canon," at least in its strong form, telling a judge to interpret a statute as constitutional if such an interpretation is available. Justice Scalia calls them "a thumb of indeterminate weight" and "dice-loading rules,"[19] (perhaps an unfortunate metaphor, reminding one too much of Rabelais' Judge Bridlegoose,[20] but for many substantive maxims, reasonably apt.)

Statutes are our legislatures' only official means of communicating control data to the governed. This simple fact grounds a very strong presumption in interpreting statutes: the legislature intended its use of language to be intelligible to the governed, thus to follow the usual constraints of syntax, semantics, and pragmatics, the three aspects of linguistics.[21] Syntax is about how kinds of words —nouns, verbs, adjectives, prepositions etc. —fit together to make

---

[16] Adrien Vermeule, "*Interpretive Choice*," 75 N.Y.U.L.REV. 74 (2000); I have argued that the reasoning on which Vermeule's thesis is based is fallacious; Sinclair, "*The Proper Treatment of "Interpretive Choice" in Statutory Decision-Making*," 45 N.Y.L.S.L.REV. 389 (2002).

[17] Gary E. O'Connor, "*Restatement (First) of Statutory Interpretation*," 7 N.Y.U.J.OF LEGISLATION & PUBLIC POLICY 333 (2003-04).

[18] Nicholas Quinn Rosenkranz, "*Federal Rules of Statutory Interpretation*," 115 HARV.L.REV. 2085 (2002).

[19] Antonin Scalia, A MATTER OF INTERPRETATION: FEDERAL COURTS AND THE LAW, 28 (Princeton U.P., Princeton, 1997).

[20] Francois Rabelais, GARGANTUA AND PANTAGRUEL Bk.3, Ch.39 (1546)(Judge Bridlegoose decided cases with a small pair of dice.)

[21] The source usually cited as the origin of this classification is Morris, *Foundations of the Theory of Signs*, 1 INTERNATIONAL ENCYCLOPEDIA OF UNIFIED SCIENCE 79, 87 (1938).

sentences. Generally we presume the syntactic propriety of a statute, and that a court will respect that syntax, although, as for example in *X-Citement Video*,[22] a supreme court being final can ignore the usual rules if sufficiently motivated. Semantics is about the meanings of words, the conditions for their proper application to the world. Much litigated interpretation is about semantics. Following the presumption that the legislature has used ordinary words with their ordinary meanings (unless otherwise stipulated), one of the most elementary and pervasive canons of construction tells us to "Use ordinary meanings" in interpreting a statute.

Pragmatics is the least familiar branch of linguistics. It is about the relation of the use of words to the context of their use. The simplest examples are the use of *indexical* words, such as personal pronouns: "*I* am hungry," "*That* is gross." Unless you know who the speaker is in a use of the first example, and unless you know to what the speaker is referring in the second example, you cannot tell the meaning of these sentences. But pragmatics also covers more complicated relationships between text and context of use, and these provide important justifications for some canons. It is reasonable to presume that the legislature wishes to communicate fairly — *felicitously* is pragmatics' term of art —and not deceptively or duplicitously; indeed it is a presumption more reasonable of legislation than of ordinary human discourse. Felicity conditions, based on the seminal work of the English philosopher H. P. Grice, (first publically presented in 1967 as the William James Lectures at Harvard University[23]), underpin some of most useful and most controversial canons.

Three basic principles.

Legislative intent is the key to statutory interpretation. Absent an intent to legislate, to make law, the legislature would not produce "a working instrument of government ...[but] merely ... a collection of English words."[24] If the statute is clear as enacted, then it must be applied without further ado as it is the legislature's only official expression of its intent. However, if the application of the statute to the case at hand is less than perfectly clear, we should

---

22 *United States v. X-Citement Video, Inc.*, 513 U.S.64 (1994).

23 The English philosopher H.P.Grice, introduced the mode of analysis in his William James Lectures at Harvard University in 1967, widely disseminated in mimeograph and subsequently published in anthologies, usually under the title "*Logic and Conversation*;" for example, P. Cole and J. Morgan, SYNTAX AND SEMANTICS: SPEECH ACTS 41 (1975); since 1989, Paul Grice, STUDIES IN THE WAY OF WORDS 24 (1989). For the application of this theory to law *see, e.g.* Sinclair, *Law and Language: The role of Pragmatics in Statutory Interpretation* 46 U.PITT.L.REV. 373 (1985); Geoffrey Miller, *Pragmatics and the Maxims of Interpretation*, 1990 WISCONSIN L. REV. 1179 (1990).

24 *United States v. Dotterweich*, 320 U.S. 277, 280 (1943) *per* Frankfurter, J. ("The purposes of this legislation thus touch phases of the lives and health of people which, in the circumstances of modern industrialism, are largely beyond self-protection. Regard for these purposes should infuse construction of the legislation if it is to be treated as a working instrument of government and not merely as a collection of English words.") "Intent" and "purpose" and "will" are sometimes given slightly different meanings, "purpose" being said to be at a higher level of generality. Very seldom does anything hang on the distinction.

interpret it as intended by the legislature that enacted it rather than, say, as a judge might prefer.[25] This has been recited innumerable times in as many ways. For example, our revered fourth chief justice, Chief Justice Marshall, in 1824 wrote that the judge's aim is to "give effect to the will of the Legislature."[26] One of our finest federal circuit court judges, ex-Chief Judge Patricia Wald of the D.C.Circuit, writes "When a statute comes before me to be interpreted, I want first and foremost to get the interpretation right. By that, I mean simply this: *I want to advance rather than impede or frustrate the will of Congress.*"[27]

Two further principles, legislative supremacy and the necessity of notice, follow as subsidiaries of the primary rule of giving effect to the intent of the legislature, but are sufficiently pervasive and foundational to warrant independent accounting. Legislative supremacy is a requirement of our form of democracy, embodied in the very first provision of the federal Constitution: "All legislative powers herein granted shall be vested in a Congress of the United States … ."[28] The judiciary may have the last word as to the meaning and application of a statute to a case,[29] but it is nevertheless constrained by the intent of the legislature as expressed in the words of the statute; for the judiciary to subvert that legislative intent would be an exercise of power, not of right, a usurpation of the legislature's law making supremacy, a wrong.[30] In day to day judicial practice, legislative supremacy means that if the legislature and the judge disagree as to the wisest decision, the legislature must prevail, the judge must defer.

From the viewpoint of the governed, it is abhorrent to be required to follow a rule of which one could not have notice. Lon L. Fuller:

> Certainly there can be no rational ground for asserting that a man can have a moral obligation to obey a legal rule that does not exist, or is kept secret from

---

[25] There has long been a quasi-debate over whether there can be such a thing as legislative intent. It was raised and disposed of in the earliest treatise on statutory interpretation, the sixteenth century *Discourse upon the Exposicion & Understandinge of Statutes*, *see* Samuel E. Thorne, A DISCOURSE ON THE STATUTES, 103 *ff*, 151 (1942) but still occasionally raises its head. *See, e.g.* William Eskridge, *DYNAMIC* STATUTORY INTERPRETATION 14-25 (1994); Michael Sinclair, TRADITIONAL TOOLS OF STATUTORY INTERPRETATION (Vandeplas Publishing, 2013) Ch.1; Steven D. Smith, LAW'S QUANDARY, 135-40 (2004).

[26] *Osburn v. Bank of the United States*, 22 U.S. (9 Wheat.) 738, 866 (1824)

[27] Patricia M. Wald, *The Sizzling Sleeper: The Use of Legislative History in Construing Statutes in the 1988-89 Term of the United States Supreme Court*, 39 AMERICAN U. L. REV. 277, 301 (1990), emphasis in original. *See also,* Justice Stephen Breyer, *The Uses of Legislative History in Interpreting Statutes*, 65 S.CAL.L.REV. 845 (1992)(similar); *NBD Bank v. Bennett*, 67 F.3d 629, 633 (7th Cir. 1995), *per* Easterbrook, J. (similar). Some writers have stipulated distinctions between the words "intent", "purpose", and "will" as applied to legislatures; however, as there is no such refinement in common currency, in this context the words are better treated as synonymous.

[28] United States' Constitution, Art.1, sec.1.

[29] *Marbury v. Madison*, 5 U.S. (1 Cranch) 137, 177 (1803) (*per* Marshall, C.J.).

[30] It wasn't always so. As late as 1610, Lord Coke was able to say, in *Dr. Bonham's Case* [*The Case of the College of Physicians*, 8 Co. 114a, 2 Brownl. 255 (C.P. 1610)] that a statute contrary to the common law was "utterly void."

> him, or that came into existence only after he had acted . . . or [that] changed every minute.[31]

As a moral principle this is self-evident, but it has also been held a condition of legal responsibility for about as long as we have had legal philosophy, from Demosthenes in the fourth century B.C.E. through St. Thomas Aquinas, John Locke, Jeremy Bentham, to the twentieth century United States' Supreme Court.[32] The Supreme Court founded the principle in the due process requirement of the Constitution's Fifth Amendment: "Ingrained in our concept of due process is the requirement of notice."[33]

These two principles, legislative supremacy and the necessity of notice, do not always pull in the same direction. When they are in accord interpretive questions do not arise: the meaning of the statute is plain to its audiences —the governed, and the courts; that is the normal situation. But when these principles do not accord, when the intent of the legislature is not the same as the apparent meaning of the statute, or when the meaning of the statute is unclear, under-determinate, or morally abhorrent, then the ordinary reader in the target audience would not know how to behave according to this statutory law and we have a question of statutory interpretation. Thus statutory interpretation issues arise in cases where these fundamental principles are in tension.

To emphasize plain meaning and the ordinary reader's response to a statute is to shift power to the judiciary, to de-emphasize legislative supremacy, and so minimize the over-arching goal of implementing legislative intent. Conversely, arguments emphasizing legislative supremacy favor the search for legislative intent but reduce the reader's right to notice of laws limiting his or her choices of action. Justifications for canons rest on these elements as they play out in the practical business of governance and communication.

What follows

The conflict between the principles of legislative supremacy and the necessity of notice is commonly expressed in "The Plain Meaning Rule," roughly, that if the statute is clear, unambiguous and determinate, and not absurd or manifestly unjust as applied to the facts at hand,

---

[31] Lon Fuller, THE MORALITY OF LAW, 38-39 (1964).

[32] Demosthenes' "Speech against Timokrates," XXIV DEMOSTHENES, 371 (350 B.C.E.)(J.H.Vince, trans., Loeb Classical Library, 1935)St. Thomas Aquinas, SUMMA THEOLOGICA, Question 90, Articles 1 and 3 (1273); John Locke, SECOND TREATISE ON GOVERNMENT, " 56, 136 (1690); William Blackstone, 1 COMMENTARIES ON THE LAWS OF ENGLAND, 45-46 (4th American edition, George Chase, ed., 1938); Jeremy Bentham, *Of Promulgation of the Laws*," 1 WORKS 155 (Bowring, ed. 1859); Lon L. Fuller, THE MORALITY OF LAW, 34-35,39(1964); *Lambert v. California*, 355 U.S. 225 (1957); *Grayned v. City of Rockford*, 408 U.S. 104, 108 (1972).

[33] *Lambert v. California*, 355 U.S. 225, 228 (1957).

then interpretation is out of place, the court may look no further.[34] It is not so much a canon of construction as a condition on construction: unless one or both of its conditions obtains, no interpretive questions arise. It is on Llewellyn's list as Pair #12; it should have been number one, as unless the meaning is not plain one does not need interpretation, whether by the application of a canon or otherwise. Nevertheless in the following it keeps its place at number twelve.

The structure of the following is straightforward. I shall treat the pairs of canons *seriatum*, first the thrust, then the parry. In *Canons*, Llewellyn gives only his statement of each of the canons in a pair, two or more secondary sources, and a case for each member of the pair; nothing more. I follow that pattern, with the secondary sources first as these sometimes give explanations. Llewellyn relies on four secondary sources, the Sutherland treatise, *Statutory Construction*, in its 1904 edition,[35] Corpus Juris *Statutes* from 1932,[36] Black's *Handbook on the Construction and Interpretation of Laws*, 1911,[37] and *Ruling Case Law*,[38] 1929, a treatise that has faded from fashion. Unlike Black, Sutherland, or *CORPUS JURIS*, Llewellyn's more favored secondary sources, *R.C.L.* tends to be discursive, offering more by way explanation and criticism, and, for a treatise, some very stylish writing.

After a general introduction to the thrust or parry of the pair, I brief Llewellyn's cited case and examine how it supports the cannon. Where Llewellyn's cases are not quite adequate as support, or support the canon in only one of its aspects, I provide further illustrative cases. Out of respect for the justifiedly high regard in which Llewellyn is held, I make no attempt to be "wise after the fact;" I have used and relied on only materials available in 1950. Bringing the list of canons up to date is another project.

In some cases, one is forced to query whether Llewellyn's choice of dueling thrust and parry should properly be called "canons."[39] Unfortunately this detracts greatly from the rhetorical force of the list as argument, and severely undermines the claim that canons may be chosen to suit one's ends, whatever they may be. But it is an aspect of Llewellyn's *Canons* that must be addressed.

After analyzing both thrust and parry, I offer a "Resolution" or not, according as the conflict is genuine or pseudo. Where necessary, I add a subsection labeled "Comment." It is

---

[34] Michael Sinclair, TRADITIONAL TOOLS OF STATUTORY INTERPRETATION (Vandeplas Publishing, 2013) Ch. 3.

[35] Sutherland, J.G., STATUTORY CONSTRUCTION (2nd ed., 1904)("Sutherland '04")

[36] 59 CORPUS JURIS (1932)("CORPUS JURIS" or just "C.J.").

[37] Black, HANDBOOK ON THE CONSTRUCTION AND INTERPRETATION OF LAWS (2nd ed., 1911)("Black").

[38] 25 RULING CASE LAW *Statutes*, (1929)("*R.C.L.*").

[39] I recently heard one of our must eminent jurists refer to "Statutes in derogation of the common law are to be construed narrowly" as "a maxim of the common law." "It is," he continued, "you can find it on Llewellyn's list in the Vanderbilt Law Review." If being on Llewellyn's list in *Canons* is a criterion for being a canon, then of course we can have no ground for raising this question.

essential to keep in view that, as eminent legal historian Willard Hurst wrote: "A rule of construction [is] only an aid to fulfilling the legislative intent; as such it [is] always rebuttable by more specific matter from the statutory text or from legislative history."[40] Accordingly, inconsistency or inconcinnity between canons will be in terms of their facilitating the determination of legislative intent. Legislative intent and its determinants thus provide the arena and the scorecards for Llewellyn's dueling pairs of canons.

At half way, after Pair #14, there is an interlude. It was at this point in the initial project that I felt inescapably the poverty of Llewellyn's list as a ground for his thesis that "in the field of statutory construction ..., there are "correct," unchallengeable rules of "how to read" which lead in happily variant directions."[41] It was a heart-sinking moment, and certainly colored the completion of the project. An interim assessment thus seemed necessary. At the end there comes, naturally, a concluding chapter.

---

[40] James Willard Hurst, DEALING WITH STATUTES 56-57 (1982).
[41] "*Canons*" 3 VANDERBILT L.REV. at 399.

2: *PAIRS ONE TO FOURTEEN*

Pair One

THRUST: "A statute cannot go beyond its text."
PARRY: "To effect its purpose a statute may be implemented beyond its text."[1]

Thrust #1: "A statute cannot go beyond its text."

This is not the familiar "Statutes in derogation of the common law will be construed narrowly;" Llewellyn saved that for his second pair. Thrust #1 would be applicable in either of two situations: (i) when two statutes converge as to some requirement, one may not be construed so broadly as to encroach upon the other; (ii) when the common law is neutral, a statute may not be applied by judicial construction beyond its terms.

The secondary sources Llewellyn offers express this principle more elaborately than he does. Sutherland, always concerned with legislative intent as the touchstone of interpretation, begins "There can be no intent of a statute not expressed in its words," but then progressively weakens this formulation, from not giving "a statute a meaning repugnant to its terms" to a weak version of the plain meaning rule.[2] Corpus Juris is less helpful, being equally supportive of Parry #1:

> Necessary implications and intendments from the language employed in a statute may be resorted to to ascertain the legislative intent where the statute is not explicit, but they can never be permitted to contradict the expressed intent of the statute or to defeat its purpose.[3]

Llewellyn's cites one case, *First Nat'l Bank of Webster Springs v. DeBerriz*,[4] which illustrates the first of the applicable situations, the extension of a statute into the domain of another statute (West Virginia, 1921): "[T]here is a presumption against legislative intent in the enactment of one law to innovate upon, limit or alter another."[5]

---

1 *Canons* at 401.
2 Sutherland '04, §388, 745-47.
3 59 CORPUS JURIS §575 "e. Implications and Inferences.", 972-73 (1932).
4 87 W. Va. 477; 105 S.E. 900 (W.Va., 1921)
5 87 W.Va. at 480-81, repeated on the next page, 482: "[T] here is a presumption against legislative intent in the enactment of one statute to encroach upon another, having different subject matter, further than is absolutely necessary to the accomplishment of the purpose of the act."

Two statutes potentially overlapped in the case, creating a possible inconsistency by implication although not explicitly. §7 of Ch.139 of the West Virginia Code provided for court action to enforce judicial liens against real property when the debtor's personal property proved insufficient.[6] §7 of Ch.86 of the West Virginia Code provided

> When the personal estate of a decedent is insufficient for the payment of his debts, his executor or administrator may commence and prosecute a suit in equity to subject his real estate to the payment thereof as provided in this article.[7]

Further,

> If such suit be not brought within six months after the qualification of such executor or administrator, any creditor of such decedent, whether he has obtained a judgment at law for his claims or not, may institute and prosecute such suit on behalf of himself and the other creditors of such decedent, in which the personal representative, surviving wife or husband, heirs and devisees, if any, of the decedent shall be made defendants.[8]

Clearly the implication is that a creditor of the decedent must allow the decedent's personal representative six months before commencing suit on the debt. Does that implication extend to the action, already commenced, to enforce a judgment lien against the decedent's property?

The West Virginia supreme court held that it did not. "There is no express statutory inhibition of the prosecution of a judgment lien suit, after the death of the judgment debtor, nor any statute expressly staying prosecution thereof." Nor was a six month stay of action a necessary implication of §7 of Ch.86 as it spoke only in terms of general creditors: it "pertains to general debts, not judgment lien debts for which provision is made by chapter 139 of the Code. The two subjects are wholly different, although related." Generally, "implication cannot prevail over a clear and positive express provision."[9]

A clash of the two statutes could thus be avoided, and so ought to be. Especially is this so as "[i]t cannot be assumed that the Legislature was ignorant of this all pervading and fundamental principle. Presumptively, its members were familiar with it, and, not having provided otherwise, they must be taken to have intended it to operate in proceedings instituted under these two statutes."[10]

The reasoning here is impeccable: one should not find contradictions between statutes if one can avoid it; whether realistically or not, we must presume legislatures would not intentionally impose inconsistent constraints on our behavior, whether in everyday life or in legal procedures.

---

6 It is now W.Va.Code §38-3-9 (2004). Chapter 139 "deal[t] with general debts and ma[d]e provision for payment thereof." 87 W.Va. at 481.

7 It is now W.Va.Code §44-8-7 (2004).

8 Id

9 87 W.Va. at 480-82.

10 87 W.Va. at 483.

Had Llewellyn really intended more than this first application, he chose not to illustrate it. He might have, with the oft-cited Supreme Court decision in *Dewey v. United States*.[11] At issue was the prize money to be paid United States naval officers and men for the defeat of Spanish naval ships in the battle of Manila Bay. The statute provided for a sum "of one hundred dollars, if the enemy's vessel was of inferior force, and of two hundred dollars if of equal or superior force, to be divided among the officers and crew in the same manner as prize money." The individual Spanish vessels sunk or captured were of inferior force, but they were more numerous, carried more men, and further "[t]he enemy's vessels were supported by land batteries and by mines and torpedoes in the entrance to Manila Bay and in the bay itself, and some of those in the bay exploded during the action." Thus, wrote Justice Harlan, "We are asked to construe the words in the present statute 'one hundred dollars, if the enemy's vessel is of inferior force, and two hundred dollars if of equal or superior force'": Was it confined to consideration of the individual vessels or might it take into account the entire opposing force including enemy "land batteries, mines and torpedoes?" Notwithstanding that it had "not forgotten the skill and heroism displayed by the distinguished commander of our fleet in the battle of Manila, as well as by the officers and sailors acting under his orders," the Court refused the latter interpretation.

> We cannot do that without going far beyond the obvious import of the words employed by Congress. Of course, our duty is to give effect to the will of Congress touching this matter. But we must ascertain that will from the words Congress has chosen to employ … we are not at liberty to hold that it proceeded upon the broad basis suggested, when it expressly declared that the amount of its bounty shall depend upon the question whether "the enemy's vessel" -- not the enemy's vessel and the land batteries, mines and torpedoes, by which it was supported -- was of inferior or of equal or superior force.[12]

Despite being highly motivated, and being given a useful legal argument by Chief Justice Fuller in dissent,[13] the majority thus kept strictly to the statutory text. It's a good illustration of the general version of Thrust #1, without another statute in contention.

Notice that Justice Harlan does not rely on the recitation of a canon in making the argument. He builds his argument on a more fundamental principle, itself resting on the democratic principle of legislative supremacy, *viz*, that a court must ascertain and give effect to the intent of the legislature, as expressed in "the words Congress has chosen to employ."[14] As Sutherland put it succinctly in 1904, "The intention is not something evinced *dehors* the statute; it

---

[11] 178 U.S. 510 (1900).
[12] 178 U.S. 511-20.
[13] "Indeed, the words of the statute, if literally construed, might be limited to engagements of single vessels on each side, yet as to this the principal opinion correctly applies a liberal construction, and any other would be preposterous. But if a liberal construction be proper at all, why not altogether?" 178 U.S. at 523. (Joined by Justices White and McKenna.)
[14] 178 U.S. at 520.

is to be learned from it … ."[15]

Parry #1: "To effect its purpose a statute may be implemented beyond its text."

In *First Nat'l Bank of Webster Springs v. DeBerriz*, Ms. DeBerriz argued that a suspension of the bank's suit on its judgment lien was implied by §7 of Ch.86, but failed to convince the court that such an implication was required in light of its inconsistency with §7 of Ch.139 of the West Virginia Code. What if §7 of Ch.139 had not been there? The court recited "A necessary implication within the meaning of the law is one that is so strong in its probability that the contrary thereof cannot reasonably be supposed."[16] But for the legislative restriction, it might well have found such an implication. This is what Llewellyn contemplates in Parry #1, as shown by his illustrative case, *Dooley v. Penn.R.R.* District Judge Booth: "It is elementary that what is implied in a statute is as much a part of it as what is expressed."[17] Llewellyn's only secondary source, C.J. *Statutes*, agrees, but with equivocation: "That which is implied in a statute is as much a part of it as that which is expressed. A statutory grant of a power or a right carries with it, by implication, everything necessary to carry out the power or right and make it effectual and complete, but powers specifically conferred cannot be extended by implication."[18]

Dooley v. Penn.R.R. was about the United States' President's control over the railroad under a war powers statute:

> The President, in time of war, is empowered, through the Secretary of War, to take possession and assume control of any system or systems of transportation, or any part thereof, … for the transfer and transportation of troops, war material and equipment, or for such other purposes connected with the emergency as may be needful or desirable.[19]

Did this give the President the power to avoid by proclamation a creditor of the railroad's garnishment of "traffic balances" owed the railroad? Of course it did: "It is also elementary that, when a power is conferred by statute, everything necessary to carry out the power and make it effectual and complete will be implied."[20]

Thus the statute is extended beyond its express terms to cover actions without which it could not achieve its purpose. If it could not "take possession and assume control" of a railroad's property, including moneys owed it, then the administration could not exercise the power authorized under the President's proclamation.

This form of argument is, strictly speaking, not about implication but presupposition, a.k.a.

---

15 Sutherland '04, §586, 1077.
16 87 W.Va. at 481
17 250 F. 142, 143 (D.Minn., 1918).
18 59 CORPUS JURIS §575, 973, citing, *inter alia*, *Dooley v. Penn.R.R., supra.*
19 Act of Aug. 29, 1916, ch. 418, Pub. L. No. 64-242, 39 Stat. 645.
20 250 F. at 143.

"pragmatic implicature": their argument is that the statute could not make any sense, could never apply, unless such-and-such also applied. How could the federal administration take control of a railroad if it could not take control of its assets, including debts owed it? If the power presupposed does not clash with another statutory mandate, the decision is easy.

A straightforward example of Parry #1 as Llewellyn formulated it is the Supreme Court's 1868 decision in *Silver v. Ladd*.[21] The Donation Act (1850) provided, *inter alia*:

> There shall be, and hereby is, granted to every white settler or occupant of the public lands ... above the age of eighteen years ... who shall have resided upon and cultivated the same for four consecutive years, ..., the quantity of ... 320 acres of land, if a single *man*, and if a married *man* the quantity of ... 640 acres; one-half to himself and the other half to his *wife*, to be held in her own right.

Elizabeth Thomas, 20 years a widow, and her adult unmarried son went to Oregon, built a house on the dividing line between two 320 acre sections, and cultivated both. At the appropriate time donation certificates —patents to the tracts —were issued Mrs. Thomas and her son, one 320 acre section each. But a year later, Mrs. Thomas' certificate was revoked. She sued and lost in the Oregon courts, which followed Thrust #1 in sticking to the text of the statute. The Supreme Court decided for Mrs. Thomas, arguing that there was a societal need to encourage the determination and perseverance in the face of hardship and danger that were necessary to pioneer the land, and that this was the purpose of the statute. The case is often held up as an example of an expansion of the scope of a statute by Plowden's method of implementing the equity of the statute,[22] *i.e.* an example of Parry #1. With respect to the values and qualities the statute sought to reward, *viz* courage and perseverance, Mrs. Thomas was indistinguishable from a married woman or person of the male persuasion; thus granting her the land gave effect to the legislative purpose.[23]

Resolution:

There is no clash between the first version of Thrust #1 ("[T]here is a presumption against legislative intent in the enactment of one law to innovate upon, limit or alter another."[24]) as illustrated by *First Nat'l Bank of Webster Springs v. DeBerriz*, on the one hand and Parry #1 as expounded in the secondary sources cited and illustrated in *Dooley v. Penn. R.R.* on the other. We must assume a legislature would not intentionally enact an inconsistency and so, if possible, we interpret prima facie conflicting statutes sufficiently narrowly to avoid one's encroaching upon the other: Thrust #1. On the other hand, where a statute would be meaningless without some prerequisite power, we must presume the legislature also presupposed that power, in the

---

[21] 74 U.S. (7 Wall.) 219 (1868).
[22] *See Eyston v. Studd*, 2 Plow. 459, 75 Eng.Rep. 688 (1574).
[23] Id at 225-26.
[24] 87 W.Va. at 480-81

absence of some clear statutory indication to the contrary (such as a statute): Parry #1.

If we take the more general version of Thrust #1 —*viz*, when the common law is neutral, a statute may not be applied by judicial construction beyond its terms —as illustrated by *Dewey v. United States*, and contrast that with Parry #1 in its most general form —*viz*, that "...what is implied in a statute is as much a part of it as what is expressed," —as illustrated by *Silver v. Ladd*, we may indeed have a clash. In both cases the Court had a strong motivation to find a broader interpretation than the terms of the statute appeared to warrant. In this respect there appear to be only two relevant distinctions. First, in *Silver v. Ladd* the Court found no reason to believe that Congress had contemplated the situation at issue, thus no grounds to infer it intended to exclude the widow from its beneficial purpose. By contrast, in *Dewey* Justice Harlan wrote that Congress must have been aware of exactly the situation at issue. Second, in *Silver v. Ladd* to deny the widow Thomas her land would have been to discriminate against widows as compared to married women, something not contemplated elsewhere in the act and unlikely unless stated expressly. In *Dewey* there was no parallel discrimination consequent upon denying an expansive reading of the statute: brave officers and men would merely be compensated at half the rate they sought. Thus legislative intent, as inferred from the context of enactment won out in both cases.

It is only because we find the parsimony to the heroes who so brilliantly fought and won the battle of Manila Bay distasteful that we might wish for a more generous interpretation in *Dewey*. Yet *Silver v. Ladd* might also have met with a parsimonious interpretation, albeit with more difficulty than in *Dewey*. "Surely," one can almost hear the righteous opinion, "the legislature should be more careful in its choice of words; Mrs. Thomas' loss is a small price for sending such a message to congress. As a court we find law, not make it, and we do not have the power to grant 320 acres of Oregon to Mrs. Thomas when the legislature has not seen fit to do so."

Thus, with some effort, we can show a difference between Thrust #1 and Parry #1, and a difference that might not be dissolved by exploration of the context. It just requires a determined refusal to implement apparent legislative intent, and a willingness to accept the frustration of that intent and an unpalatable deprivation to one who acted in reasonable reliance on a sensible interpretation.

Are we really dealing with canons in Pair One? Why, one might ask, did we not find anything of the form Llewellyn uses in any of the cases or secondary sources that he cites?

Pair Two

THRUST: "Statutes in derogation of the common law will not be extended by construction."
PARRY: "Such acts will be liberally construed if their nature is remedial."[1]

Thrust #2: "Statutes in derogation of the common law will not be extended by construction."

We need have no doubt as to the stature of Thrust #2 as a canon; it was for long one of the most familiar, although usually expressed as an exhortation to strict construction. For example, the 1874 Supreme Court: "[s]tatutes passed in derogation of the common law … should be construed strictly."[2] This made a lot of sense in the days when there was a general belief in a supreme set of organizing values, mutually consistent and unchangeable, and encapsulated in the common law, the "brooding omnipresence in the sky."[3]

By the twentieth century the canon had fallen from grace along with the belief that "an a priori guarantee of the proposition that a total harmony of true values is somewhere to be found."[4] Both Sutherland, Llewellyn's first secondary source, in 1904 and Black, his second, in 1911, weaken the canon by allowing for extending the scope of a statute's derogation of common law to implications from its language, nature, or purpose.[5] Black argued that Thrust #2 had lost all vitality, that it "no longer has any foundation in reason" and should be modified or abandoned.[6]

If Thrust #2 has any continuing force, it is on its alternate justification, the principle of the necessity of notice. Common law draws its power from reason, and gives notice by the standards of decency current in society.[7] Thus a statute in accord with common standards of behavior need not be narrowly construed. But one that seeks to change behavior or to penalize a common practice needs active publicity and should not be construed beyond the scope thus

---

1 *Canons* at 401.
2 *Ross v. Jones*, 89 U.S. (2 Wall.) 576, 591 (1875).
3 *Guaranty Trust v. York*, 326 U.S. 99, 113 (1945)(Frankfurter, J.).
4 Isaiah Berlin, *Two Concepts of Liberty*, THE PROPER STUDY OF MANKIND 191, 238 (Hardy and Hausheer, ed.s, 1997).
5 Sutherland, §573, 1058-59; Black, §113, 367, both with, of course, numerous cites at each point.
6 Black, above at 368 with cites showing courts were in general agreement.
7 Charles Breitel, *The Lawmakers*, 65 COLUM.L.REV. 749, 772 (1965); Sinclair, TRADITIONAL TOOLS OF STATUTORY INTERPRETATION, above, Ch.2.

publicized —that is, it should be strictly construed.[8] The requirement of notice, determined by the nature of the behavior in question and how one engaged in it ordinarily knows the standards required, provides a much better and more discriminating ground for Thrust #2 in the modern world than does the old "brooding omnipresence in the sky."

Llewellyn supports Thrust #2 with *Devers v. City of Scranton*[9] from the 1932 Pennsylvania Supreme Court. One of Scranton's fire trucks, allegedly negligently driven, had "run down and killed" plaintiff Devers' son. At common law a municipality could not be liable for damages it caused in carrying out its governmental functions —health, safety, and welfare. So if Devers had any chance, it had to be under a statute, *viz,* "Every county, city, borough, incorporated town or township within this Commonwealth, employing any person, shall be jointly and severally liable with such person for any damages caused by the negligence of such person while operating a motor vehicle upon the highway in the course of their employment."[10] But what is a motor vehicle for this purpose? The statute tells: "motor vehicles" includes "every vehicle ... which is self-propelled, except tractors, power shovels, road rollers, agricultural machinery, and vehicles which move upon or are guided by a track, or travel through the air." Very good, but what is a vehicle for this purpose? "Vehicle" means "every device in, upon, or by which any person or property is or may be transported or drawn upon a public highway" with a list of exceptions similar to that in the definition of "motor vehicle". Thus the court could decide against Devers: "We are clearly of the opinion that a fire truck is not a device intended for the transportation of persons or property upon the public highway." That is indeed a narrow construction. But "In construing a statute which changes or is in derogation of the common law, the letter of the act is to be strictly considered;" after all, "it is not to be presumed the legislature intended to make any innovation upon the common law, further than the case absolutely requires."[11] In the 1932 Pennsylvania Supreme Court, it appears the common law of sovereign immunity along with the old cliché, Thrust #2, still held sway.

What was the 1932 Pennsylvania Court thinking? That the driver operated the truck with notice of his employer's freedom from liability for his negligence? That his employer paid less attention to hiring and training than it otherwise might have because of its freedom from liability for the driver's negligence? Hardly. But the court no doubt felt a general background support for

---

[8] "The citizen is entitled to unequivocal warning before conduct on his part, which is not *malum in se*, can be made the occasion of a deprivation of his liberty or property." *People v. Phyfe*, 136 N.Y. 554, 559, 32 N.E. 978, 979 (1893).

[9] 308 Pa.13, 161 A. 540 (1932).

[10] §619, art.6, of the Act of May 1, 1929, P.L. 905 (75 PS §212), the Vehicle Code. 161 A. at 541.

[11] §102 (75 PS §2); 161 A. at 542, cites omitted. It had perhaps a better argument. The legislature had amended the section specifically to provide liability if the negligent driver was a "member of a *volunteer* fire company", **id** (emphasis supplied), and this driver was in a professional fire company. "[H]ad the Legislature intended to fix liability upon municipalities for the negligence of the *paid* employees ... it would have so stated specifically as it did in the case of volunteer fire companies." **Id** (emphasis in original); an example of *expressio unius est exclusio alterius*.

the principles —dubious though we might now find them —underlying sovereign immunity and the inroads that could be made upon it by tort liability. No doubt the City of Scranton's insurer was also gratified.

Parry #2: "Such acts will be liberally construed if their nature is remedial."

This too is a maxim with a long history. A hint of it occurs in 1584 in the celebrated *Heydon's Case*: "[E]quity will aid remedial laws though penal... ."[12] Having restated Thrust #2, Sutherland immediately says "statutes may be remedial, and then they must, except as antagonized by other rules of construction, be liberally construed."[13] *Corpus Juris* recites Parry #2 to include also the converse, excluding a case within the letter of the statute but not the intent.[14]

Two questions stand out: What counts as remedial? And what is it to construe a statute liberally? In answering the first question, both secondary sources paraphrase *Heydon's Case*'s first steps:

> 1st. What was the common law before the making of the Act.
> 2nd. What was the mischief and defect for which the common law did not provide.
> 3rd. What remedy the Parliament hath resolved and appointed to cure the disease of the commonwealth.[15]

If the statute is seen not as imposing a restriction or right or duty on the common law but in fixing it so as to cover a new situation or an otherwise unforeseen problem, then it is remedial, "[a]nd it is the duty of judges so to construe the statute as to suppress the mischief and advance the remedy."[16] That is the essence of what treatise writers mean by 'construe liberally': "... to

---

12 *Heydon's Case*, 30 Co. 7a, 7b, 76 Eng.Rep. 637, 638 n.B (Exch. 1584).

13 Sutherland (1904) §574, p.1061. Llewellyn cites §§573-575. As an illustration to Parry #2 Sutherland gives "A statute legitimating bastards should be liberally construed. *Beall v. Beall*, 8 Ga. 210."

14 59 CORPUS JURIS §657, p.1109. It illustrates with the well known torts case, *Gorris v. Scott*, L.R.9 Exch. 125 (1874), where, in violation of the Contagious Diseases Act, the defendant shipowner had failed to build pens to segregate stock being transported; the animals were lost overboard in a storm, thus "the damage is of such a nature as was not contemplated at all by the statute, and as to which it was not intended to confer any benefit on the plaintiffs." Id.

15 The famously quotable interpretive method is completed by:

> And, 4th. The true reason of the remedy; and then the office of all the Judges is always to make such construction as shall suppress the mischief, and advance the remedy, and to suppress subtle inventions and evasions for continuance of the mischief, *pro privato commodo*, and to add force and life to the cure and remedy, according to the true intent of the makers of the Act, *pro bono publico*.

3 Co. at 7b, 76 Eng.Rep. at 637-38. Justice Frankfurter wrote: "The well known resolutions in *Heydon's Case*, have the flavor of Elizabethan English but they express the substance of a current volume of U.S.Reports as to the considerations relevant to statutory interpretation." Felix Frankfurter, *Some Reflections on the Reading of Statutes*, 47 COLUM.L.REV. 528, 541 (1947). That remains valid today.

16 Sutherland (1904) at §583, 1074. Sutherland would exclude penal statutes; id at §584, 1074.

construe a statute liberally or according to its equity is nothing more than to give effect to it according to the intention of the law-maker, as indicated by its terms and purposes."[17]

Becker v. Brown,[18] (Nebraska, 1902) Llewellyn's example, is not especially well chosen to illustrate Parry #2. It is a complicated dispute over priority between liens on cattle, and was resolved before the opinion added a reference to Parry #2. An agister is a person who feeds and takes care of any kind of live stock, as, for example, in preparing them for sale —that is, a bailee of cattle. An ordinary bailee's common law possessory lien would lose its perfection along with possession. In a cattle producing economy it would be, and would be known by supreme court justices to be essential that the general rule for bailments be modified for cattle, so that a statutory "agister's lien," though unperfected, should take priority over a contractual lien perfected after the agister's surrender of possession: at the appropriate time cattle must be sent to market; delays to resolve legal disputes would destroy their value. Thus "we think that by our statute the legislature plainly indicated an intent to do something more than to extend to agisters the common-law lien of a bailee for hire."[19] Parry #2 is tagged on at the end, seemingly as an afterthought, "The statute is remedial in its character, and in accordance with familiar rule, it should receive a liberal construction for the purpose of effectuating its object."[20]

Resolution:

Prima facie there is no clash between Thrust #2 and Parry #2. The condition on Parry #2, "...if their nature is remedial," separates its application to special cases, not covered by Thrust #2. Thrust #2 tells us that if a statute should impose some innovation on the "robe without seam" that is the common law, the judiciary should minimize its effect. But should there be a tear in that fabric, then a statute to patch, mend, stitch up, in a word to remedy that flaw should be construed as liberally as needed to make it effective.

That is nice and idealistic, but much too prima facie. Look, for example, at Llewellyn's illustrative cases. *Devers v. City of Scranton* could as easily have gone the other way and illustrated Parry #2. The common law gave sovereign immunity to the defendant city: was the statute in derogation of that just and wise law? or was it stitching up a rent, newly apparent in the otherwise perfect fabric? Sovereign immunity arose in an historic era in which governmental functions were fewer and did not include the use of motor vehicles. Much changed with the introduction of motor vehicles, including the felt propriety of governmental immunity from responsibility for its drivers. But the common law had trouble with its precedents, so firmly in

---

[17] Id at §589, 1085. *See also* Black at §113, 378-79.

[18] 65 Neb. 264, 91 N.W. 178 (1902)

[19] Id, 65 Neb. at 268, 91 Neb. at 179; a contractual lien perfected prior to the agister's taking temporary possession of the cattle –the role of bailee – would, of course, keep its priority as the agister could readily discover it; *Marseilles Mfg. Co. v. Morgan*, 12 Neb. 66, 10 N.W. 462 (1881).

[20] Id, 65 Neb. at 269, 91 Neb. at 180.

place, albeit an antiquated place. Wasn't this statute, perhaps, designed to remedy that maladaptivity? One could understand excepting a fire fighting vehicle on the grounds that it served a governmental function fraught with hazards known for centuries, but hardly on the ground that it was not a vehicle (even as statutorily defined.) But as it is reported, the court was not interested in rationality, only in the wooden, unthinking application of a cliché.

You cannot make quite the same argument for symmetrical application of the agister's lien statute in *Becker v. Brown*. The common law bailee's lien did not take into account the peculiar time sensitivity of cattle fattening and marketing. In a state economically dependent on agriculture that was a significant problem necessitating a legislative remedy. Had the court interpreted the statute narrowly, it would have made the statutory agister's lien no different from the common law bailee's lien: that is, it would have interpreted the legislature as doing nothing in enacting the statute, a violation not only of common sense and legislative supremacy, but also of Thrust #16: "Every word and clause must be given effect."

In a very pretty case Llewellyn might have used for either thrust or parry the 1818 Massachusetts Supremes decided with common sense, the principle of notice, and legislative intent.[21] "The question presented in this case is more curious than difficult": was a swine once butchered still a swine or was it distinguishable as pork, thus not exempt from execution by the sheriff under the statute construed strictly? C.J.Parker: "It is said that statutes, made in derogation of the common law, are to be construed strictly. This is true; but they are also to be construed sensibly, and with a view to the object aimed at by the legislature." The purpose of the statute was to protect the very poor by allowing a family one cow and one swine exempt from process; that purpose would not be served if the family could not slaughter and eat their pig.

There are two points to draw. First, if a court wishes, it can often pick either of Thrust or Parry #2 and by brute force produce its choice of outcome. Misused in this way, the two canons are indeed contraries. But this is no more than an indictment of mindless, mechanical decision making.[22] Second, when faced with a statute inconsistent with the common law, whether a judge applies Thrust #2 or Parry #2 depends very greatly on whether the judge sees the statute as solving a problem in the common law or imposing legislatively upon it. Mechanics' liens, when first introduced, met with different opinions as to their status, remedial or in derogation of the common law. The Michigan the Supreme Court:

> [T]his court has repeatedly declared in substance that these acts are innovations upon the common law over the rights of property by permitting the institution of private charges on property without or against the owner's assent and without any judicial or other official sanction, and by authorizing an enforcement of such

---

[21] *Gibson v. Jenney*, 15 Mass. 205, 206 (1818).

[22] Postmodern viewpoint epistemology --"[M]any of the truths we cling to depend greatly on our own point of view.", Obi-Wan Kenobi to Luke Skywalker, *Star Wars VI: The Return of the Jedi* (1983) – doesn't help; it is a denial of rationality, justifying any outcome at the whim of the judge.

> charges by unusual and summary methods, and that the provisions of these enactments cannot be extended in their operation and effect beyond the plain and fair sense of the terms…[23]

Right next door, the Ohio Supreme Court:

> Looking thus at the object of the statute, and perceiving it to be one of an equitable character and beneficent tendency, section seven being directory of the mode of securing the object of the statute, the same ought to be liberally construed, for the furtherance and attainment of such object.[24]

What do you think? Was it a defect in the common law in need of remedy that the laborer had no way "to secure … his hire or reward for the construction or repair which he had made"?[25] Or was it an innovation upon the common law power of the purchaser of the work to retain the benefit but avoid paying for it? To the judiciary of the time, few if any of whom had experience selling repair or construction services, that might not have been as transparent as it seems to us today.

Llewellyn is correct that this pair of canons cannot solve such a question. A judge who uses one or other without explaining the ground on which she does so has not switched on her brain. Explaining the ground requires answering *Heydon's Case*'s first questions, that is, explaining the purpose for enacting the statute at the time it was enacted. For "[a] statute merely declaring a rule, with no purpose or objective, is nonsense."[26]

Legislatures, whether reorganizing or changing the common law, have sometimes included in a statute a provision preempting the possibility of subversion of their intent by either Thrust or Parry #2. For example, the Uniform Commercial Code in its very first provision of consequence it says: "This act shall be liberally construed and applied to promote its underlying purposes and policies."[27] In view of the number of moves they put on the ossified common law of contract they were replacing, Llewellyn and his fellow code drafters were wise to include this provision.[28]

Finally, Llewellyn did not include the rule of lenity ("Criminal statutes are to be construed narrowly") in his list of dueling pairs, perhaps because it is a special instance of Thrust #2 or might even be subsumed under Thrust #1. He should have, if only for completeness. It is as hoary an old canon as we have, and often disputed.[29]

---

[23] *Wagar v. Briscoe*, 38 Mich. 587, 592 (1878); accord *Wade v. Reitz*, 18 Ind. 307 (1862).

[24] *Thomas v. Huesman*, 10 Ohio St. 152, 156 (1859).

[25] The purpose of the mechanic's lien statute "…was to secure to the laborer his hire or reward for the construction or repair which he had made." Id.

[26] *Canons* at 400.

[27] U.C.C. §1-102(1)

[28] Eugene F. Mooney, *Old Kontract Principles and Karl's New Kode: An Essay on the Jurisprudence of Our New Commercial Law*, 11 Vill. L. Rev. 213, 235 (1966).

[29] It is quoted as settled in 1584 as a footnote in *Heydon's Case*, *supra*, but with an equivocation about legislative intent.

Pair Three

> **THRUST**: "Statutes are to be read in the light of the common law and a statute affirming a common law rule is to be construed in accordance with the common law."
> **PARRY**: "The common law gives way to a statute which is inconsistent with it and when a statute is designed as a revision of a whole body of law applicable to a given subject it supersedes the common law."[30]

Thrust #3: "Statutes are to be read in the light of the common law and a statute affirming a common law rule is to be construed in accordance with the common law."

There is a certain accolade value to calling a string of words a canon; not just any old sentence about interpretation, even of suitable pomposity, warrants it. Thrust #3 doesn't deserve this elevation. It is scarcely more than a restatement of the justificatory thinking underlying Pairs 1 and 2, a corollary to Thrust #2. It is not surprising that secondary sources for it are so few. *R.C.L.*, in the cited §280 under the caption "Presumption Against Change of Common Law," says "it is rather to be presumed that no change in the common law was intended, unless the language employed clearly indicates such an intent."[31] Of course: given the conceptual status of the common law —as pure, immutable, and universal —that dominated legal thinking through a good part of the nineteenth century, it could hardly be otherwise.

Thrust #3 comes from *R.C.L.*, not in the section cited, §280, but the preceding section, §279; whether a statute accords with or is in derogation of the common law, it tells us,

> it must be read in light of the common law in force at the time of its enactment; for, as has been said, to know what the common law was before the making of the statute, whereby it may be seen whether the statute was introductory of a new law or only affirmative of the common law, is the very lock and key to set open the windows of the statute.[32]

In other words, *Heydon's Case*'s first two questions. Where the statute restates the common law, "affirm[s] a common law rule," then of course it is to be read "in accordance with the common law." Both the legislature and judicial preference agree; why should any judge construe differently. The contrary situation, where the statute innovates on the common law, is the explicit domain of Thrust #2.

---

[30] *Canons* at 401.
[31] 25 R.C.L. *Statutes* §280, 1054.
[32] 25 R.C.L. *Statutes* §279, 1053-54.

Bandfield v. Bandfield, Lllewellyn's case in support of Thrust #3, illustrates the point that this is merely a derivative of Thrust #2.[33] Michigan's married women's property act read, *inter alia*:

> The real and personal estate of every female, acquired before marriage, and all property, real and personal, to which she may afterwards become entitled by gift, grant, inheritance, devise, or in any other manner, shall be and remain the estate and property of such female. * * * Actions may be brought by and against a married woman in relation to her sole property, in the same manner as if she were unmarried.[34]

Does this give a wife the right to "maintain suit against her husband for a personal tort, committed upon her while they were living together as husband and wife?"[35] Common law would not allow such a suit, and the Michigan supreme court said the statute did not change that.

Against the common law background, and social conventions as understood by the late nineteenth century judiciary, this is hardly surprising.[36] Chief Justice Grant explained that "The result of plaintiff's contention would be another step to destroy the sacred relation of man and wife, and to open the door to lawsuits between them for every real and fancied wrong, —suits which the common law has refused on the ground of public policy."[37] No property was involved. To the 1898 Michigan Supremes, allowing the plaintiff battered wife a cause of action would be purely judicial innovation. This is a reading "in the light of the common law" but the statute is hardly one "affirming a common law rule." It is not much of an illustration of Thrust #3, is it?

Llewellyn might have used the 1914 North Dakota case, *Reeves & Co. v. Russell*,[38] as an illustration of the second part of Thrust #3. Between a prior recorded chattel mortgagee and the blacksmith who repaired it and retained possession of it, who has priority in a threshing machine? In 1906, when the blacksmith first took possession and made the repairs, there was no statute on point; it came in 1907, and gave the blacksmith's possessory artisan's lien priority. Was this statutory priority good *ab initio*? Indeed it was, for it was merely a reiteration of the common law artisan's lien and its priority so long as possessory. The reasoning was transparent: absent the statute, the common law would have governed exactly as does the statute (for the obvious reason that without the repair the chattel mortgagee's lien would be of little value.) Thrust #3 says no more.

---

33 117 Mich. 80; 75 N.W. 287 (1898).

34 2 How. Stat. §§ 6295, 6297

35 117 Mich. at 81, 75 N.W. at 287.

36 It is thus an illustration of Thrust #2, *Canons* 401, or Thrust #20, *Expressio unius est exclusion alterius.*

37 117 Mich. at 82-83, 75 N.W. at 288.

38 28 N.D. 265; 148 N.W. 654 (1914).

***Parry* #3**: "The common law gives way to a statute which is inconsistent with it and when a statute is designed as a revision of a whole body of law applicable to a given subject it supersedes the common law."

The first part of this, "The common law gives way to a statute which is inconsistent with it," is merely a restatement of the democratic principle of legislative supremacy. In the context of Llewellyn's list, it is surplussage, having been dealt with in Pairs 1 and 2. The interesting, non-repetitive part is the rest, the second conjunct.

The "defect" in the common law at the time of enactment may not have been in substance so much as in organization, formulation, or publicity, or, in the United States, in uniformity across more than fifty jurisdictions. Suppose a set of statutes replaces a whole field of common law; it may be declaratory of the common law, in derogation of it, or include elements of both. When it comes to applying an uncertain statute in this codification, what should guide interpretation? Parry #3 answers that the statutory scheme or code should. An interpretive or interstitial decision should accord with the legislative scheme and not with the common law it displaces.

R.C.L., Llewellyn's cited secondary source, explains at §280:

> A great many of our statutes ... consist merely of codifications, sometimes general, but in most cases only partial, of some particular rule or principle of the common law; and should the courts hold that when any rule or principle of the common law is by the legislature partially incorporated into a statute, the remainder of the rule is thereby repealed or annulled, endless trouble and confusion would result ...

This contrasts with an express legislative intent to abrogate or modify the common law. *R.C.L*: "Where the statute laws on a particular subject, taken together as forming an entire system, are wholly repugnant to and inconsistent with the common law on that subject, it must be assumed that it was the intention of the legislature to supersede the common law on that subject altogether."[39] Legislative intent, a fundamental aspect of the democratic principle of legislative supremacy, dominates and directs interpretation in both circumstances.[40]

Llewellyn cites two cases in support of Parry #3: *Hamilton v. Rathbone*,[41] a District of Columbia Married Women's Property Act case in the 1899 United States Supreme Court, and *State v. Lewis*,[42] from the North Carolina supreme court of 1906. *Hamilton v. Rathbone*, although

---

39 25 R.C.L. *Statutes* §280, 1055, giving a single citation, *Rozelle v. Harmon*, 103 Mo. 339; 15 S.W. 432 (1890).

40 Llewellyn also cites 25 R.C.L. *Statutes* §289 in support of Parry #3. The section, however, is about the interpretation of a revised statute in light of its predecessor, and basically states a plain meaning rule: "...when a provision is plain and unambiguous the court cannot refer to the original statute for the purpose of ascertaining meaning." 25 R.C.L. *Statutes* §289, 1065. It thus has nothing to say about Parry #3.

41 175 U.S. 414; 20 S. Ct. 155; 44 L. Ed. 219 (1899)

42 142 N.C. 626; 55 S.E. 600 (1906).

a rich and fascinating resource on statutory interpretation, is not at all relevant to Parry #3.[43] *State v. Lewis* is scarcely better. Lewis was charged by a grand jury in Union County with breaking into a jail in adjacent Anson County to remove an inmate, John V. Johnson, charged with murder, to "unlawfully, wilfully, wickedly, and feloniously [] injure, lynch and kill" him.[44] At common law, a grand jury indictment would have to be in the county in which the offence occurred; however, "[o]wing to the prejudice or sympathy which in cases of lynching usually and naturally pervades the county where that offense is committed, the General Assembly, upon grounds of public policy, deemed it wise to transfer the investigation of the charge to the grand jury of an adjoining county."[45] The issue was whether the legislature had power under the United States' and North Carolina's constitutions thus to change the common law. It had.

Resolution:

There is no clash between Thrust #3 and Parry #3. Each applies in circumstances quite different from and unlikely to be confused with the domain of the other. Thrust #3 is an element of the reasoning supporting Pair 2. Justification for it is hardly worth spelling out: If the legislative intent expressed in the statute and the common law are the same, the former being declarative of the latter, there is no ground for disagreement, so why disagree? Why even formulate a canon? It's hardly surprising that examples are scarce.

Parry #3 is an ill-mixed conglomeration, one that does not lend itself to a single, canonical formulation. The first part is an expression of legislative supremacy, a basic precept of all statutory interpretation. The second part covers an interesting situation: Where a set of statutes is intended to cover a field hitherto governed by common law, how should a particular, under-determinate statute in that set be construed? This is not a circumstance within the contemplation of Thrust #3; one has to struggle to find an overlap. Yet it is interesting on its own account.

Early twentieth century writers were well aware of examples of statutes displacing whole domains of social intercourse previously governed by common law. The Negotiable Instruments Law,[46] and the Uniform Sales Act[47] both included formulaic statements of standard common law

---

43 Perhaps the mistake arose because of the condition in Parry #3, "when a statute is designed as a revision of a whole body of law applicable to a given subject": *Hamilton v. Rathbone* is on the interpretation of the 1874 revision of an 1869 statute; it bears no relation to anything else related to the canon in question here. It is, however, a fine illustration of the "plain meaning rule", Thrust #12.

44 142 N.C. at 626; 55 S.E. at 600.

45 142 N.C. at 630; 55 S.E. at 602. The North Carolina statute in question was also a revision --"Ch 461, Laws 1893 ... now Revisal, 3698." 142 N.C. at 628, 55 S.E. at 601 --but this was not at issue.

46 Generally *see* J. Crawford, THE NEGOTIABLE INSTRUMENTS LAW (1897). The Negotiable Instruments law was eventually enacted in all states. It was based on the English Bills of Exchange Act of 1882, 45 & 46 Vict. Ch.61, itself a compilation of English common law, Charles L. McKeehan, *The Negotiable Instruments Law*, 50 AM. L. REG. 437 (1902); Nathan M. Crystal, *Codification and the Rise of the Restatement Movement*, 54 WASH.L.REV. 239 (1979); generally, *see* Michel Sinclair, *The Case of the Air-Conditioned Allonge*, 9 ANNUAL REV. OF BANKING LAW 143, 149-150 (1990); *Codification of*

provisions and some revisions of common law positions thought substantively maladaptive. There were also the probate codes, such as that at issue before the 1890 Missouri supreme court in *Rozelle v. Harmon*,[48] the solitary cite at *R.C.L.* §280. Missouri's statutory probate law did not expressly provide for the point at issue: plaintiff creditor would prevail under the preceding common law, defendant debtor if the gap was filled in the spirit of the statute. The key question in such a situation is whether the legislature intended its statutory scheme to occupy the field.

> [T]he statute laws of this state on the subject of administration, taken together as forming one entire system, are wholly repugnant to, and inconsistent with, the common law in respect to administrators de son tort. We must, therefore, conclude that the intention of the legislature was to supersede the common law on that subject altogether.[49]

So defendant won.

In 1953 Llewellyn himself must have been acutely aware of the collection and organization of whole areas of common law as he was one of those principally responsible for the Uniform Commercial Code, at that time just coming on the market.[50] It contained both provisions following the common law and prior statutes, such as the Negotiable Instruments Law and Uniform Sales Act, and provisions changing them. Think, for example, of the contract formation rules of U.C.C.§§2-203--2-207. How should a court interpret §2-205, cautiously eliminating the requirement of consideration for a limited range of option contracts? or §2-207, forthrightly doing away with the mirror image rule for contracts formed by exchange of paper? Should they be construed liberally as part of a remedial scheme or narrowly as in derogation of the common law? Llewellyn's solution was to pre-empt argument by statute. For areas covered expressly (if less than determinately) by a provision, §1-102(1) tells us "This Act shall be liberally construed and applied to promote its underlying purposes and policies."[51] But if the subject was not

---

Negotiable Instruments Law: A Tale of Reiterated Anachronism, 21 U.TOLEDO L.REV. 625, 640-642 (1989-90).

47 The U.S.A. was eventually adopted by 37 states and was also based on a set of English statutes based on common law . Samuel Williston (famous for his treatise on contracts) drafted the Uniform Sales Act early in the 20th century. He copied much of it from the English Sale of Goods Act of 1894, but made significant advances in some key places, such as §15, governing warranty in the sale of goods. *See* Samuel Williston, THE LAW GOVERNING SALES OF GOODS AT COMMON LAW AND UNDER THE UNIFORM SALES ACT (1909). *See* Mooney, *Old Kontract Principles and Karl's New Kode,* 11 VILL. L. REV. 213, 235.

48 103 Mo. 339; 15 S.W. 432 (1890).

49 103 Mo. at 344, 15 S.W. at 432.

50 Llewellyn was Chief Reporter of the Uniform Commercial Code (U.C.C.). *See* Robert Braucher, *The Legislative History of the Uniform Commercial Code*, 58 COLUM.L.REV. 798 (1958); William A. Schnader, *Pennsylvania and the Uniform Commercial Code*, 37 TEMP.L.Q. 265 (1964); Soia Mentschikoff, *Highlights of the Uniform Commercial Code*, 27 MOD.L.REV. 167 (1964)(Soia Metschikoff was Llewellyn's principal assistant on the project.) The U.C.C. was first enacted in Pennsylvania in 1953. PA.STAT.ANN. tit. 12A §§1-1011 to 10-104 (Purdon 1954), *revised and re-enacted*, 1959 Pa.Laws 1023 (revised to conform with revisions developed in New York). Other states adopted the Code throughout the 1950s and 1960s.

51 Those purposes and policies are immediately stated in §1-102(2).

covered, §1-103 provides: "Unless displaced by the particular provisions of this Act, the principles of law and equity, including the law merchant and the law relative to the capacity to contract, principal and agent, estoppel, fraud, misrepresentation, duress, coercion, mistake, bankruptcy, or other validating or invalidating cause shall supplement its provisions." Llewellyn himself, and his fellow drafters, knew better than to rely on uncertain, scarcely known, canons of construction!

***Comment*:**

Neither Thrust #3 nor Parry #3 should be on a list of canons. One would think that for a verbal formula to be a canon it should at least be somewhat canonical! That would require it to be (a) familiar, at least to those professionally concerned with the law, and (b) significant. Thrust #3 and Parry #3 fail both counts.

Thrust #3 is not significant; it is so obvious it is not even sufficiently familiar to be a cliché. This, perhaps, is why its footnoted support is so thin: only one of the four treatises (25 R.C.L. *Statutes*) comes close to mentioning something like it, and that as a general observation, and the one case (*Bandfield v. Bandfield*[52]) only comes close in a quotation in *dicta*. One can come up with an illustrative case (*Reeves & Co. v. Russell*[53]) but it did not rest on Thrust #3.

That Parry #3 falls short of canonical stature can be seen from its conglomerate formulation. Canons tend to be quite focused; they are implements for particular problem situations, not hodge-podges like this. This again is illustrated by the failure of the footnoted support, and the extreme paucity of cases. (It is hard to find further cases like *Rozelle v. Harmon*,[54] exactly on one of the subjects of Parry #3.) The problem here, I think, is that where there is a possible problem that Llewellyn's formula would address, the codification itself or the legislative intent behind it make its solution clear. Thus Parry #3 fails to be significant, and the absence of historical use suggests obscurity, not familiarity or accessibility to legal decision makers, let alone authority.

---

52 117 Mich. 80; 75 N.W. 287 (1898)

53 28 N.D. 265; 148 N.W. 654 (1914).

54 103 Mo. 339; 15 S.W. 432 (1890).

Pair Four

> **THRUST**: "Where a foreign statute which has received construction has been adopted, previous construction is adopted too."
> **PARRY**: "It may be rejected where there is conflict with the obvious meaning of the statute or where the foreign decisions are unsatisfactory in reasoning or where the foreign interpretation is not in harmony with the spirit or policy of the laws of the adopting state"[1]

Thrust #4: ""Where a foreign statute which has received construction has been adopted, previous construction is adopted too."

This one deserves its place on a list of cannons. Sources abound and the verbal variation is minor. But although it is often recited, its exceptions are too, and in decisions they are usually investigated, so Thrust #4 seldom provides a canon's characteristic boost in authority. For example, "Subject to the qualifications hereinafter stated, a statute adopted from another state or from another country will be presumed to be adopted with the construction placed upon it by the courts of the state or country of its adoption."[2] The cases reciting a version of this formula are numerous, but so too are variations on the equivocation "...in the absence of an expression of legislative intent to the contrary."[3] *R.C.L.* gives a nice page of examples from England, including "for instance, ... the statute of frauds, or the statute of Elizabeth against fraudulent conveyances, or the statute of limitations."[4]

The reason is apparent, a straightforward example of basic interpretive procedure. We had it first from Aristotle:

> When the law speaks universally, then, and a case arises on it which is not covered by the universal statement, then it is right, where the legislator fails us and has erred by over-simplicity, to correct the omission --to say what the legislator himself would have said had he been present, and would have put into his law if he had known.[5]

---

1 *Canons* at 402.
2 59 C.J. Statutes §627, 1065-68; *sim.* 25 R.C.L. *Statutes* §294, 1069, Black, at §176, 597.
3 *For example*, 25 R.C.L. *Statutes* §294 gives one-and-a-half pages.
4 25 R.C.L. *Statutes* §294, 1072.
5 Aristotle, NICHOMACHEAN ETHICS, *supra* at Bk.V, Ch.10, 1137b; *see also* Aristotle's Rhetoric, Bk.1, Ch.13.

It is the method of *Heydon's Case,*[6] and of Plowden.[7] Nor has judicial thinking changed in the four centuries since. Second Circuit Judge Jerome Frank: "Most of the modern expositions of legislative construction are but restatements, with here and there a bit of embroidery, of what Aristotle said."[8] Here, we might focus on the fourth of the *Heydon's Case* questions, "The true reason of the remedy."[9]

Why did the legislature choose to copy legislation already in place elsewhere? We might presume it was because that legislation had proven effective at remedying exactly the societal ill being addressed. And surely we might presume that the relevant legislators knew this because, *inter alia*, the cases of that jurisdiction had demonstrated its effectiveness. That is, we may presume "the law was enacted in the light of the construction given it by the courts or country from which the statute was taken."[10] Of the English statute against monopolies, Justice Story wrote, that "[t]he words of our statute are not identical with those of the statute of James, but it can scarcely admit of doubt, that they must have been within the contemplation of those by whom it was framed, as well as the construction which had been put upon them by Lord Coke."[11]

Llewellyn illustrates with a picturesque case from the Illinois Supreme Court of 1873, *Freese v. Tripp.*[12] Freese, a saloon operator, may have sold liquor to William Tripp, a lush. Mary Ann, William Tripp's wife, won $100 exemplary damages at trial under a statute "entitled "An act to provide against the evils resulting from the sale of intoxicating liquors in this State," in force July 1, 1872." The statute provided a cause of action to "every husband, wife, child, parent, guardian, employee or other person who shall be injured in person or property or means of support" as a result of intoxicating liquor. The statute was both penal and in derogation of the common law and so "should, according to the well understood canon, receive a strict construction."[13]

Two of the questions involved concern us: First, did "the anguish or pain of mind, feelings the plaintiff suffered, if any, by reason of such intoxication of her husband" count as injury in person in the absence of a physical injury? No, because "[t]he Supreme Court of Ohio, from which State our statute is derived, substantially, hold it is not proper, in such a case, to charge the wife has suffered mental anguish, disgrace or loss of society or companionship--all

---

[6] 76 Eng. Rep. at 638, citations omitted.
[7] In commentary after his report of *Eyston v. Studd*, 2 Plow. 459, 75 Eng. Rep. 688 (1574).

[8] Jerome Frank, *Words and Music: Some Remarks on Statutory Interpretation*, 47 COLUM. L. REV. 1259, 1259 (1947).
[9] 76 Eng. Rep. at 638.
[10] 25 R.C.L. *Statutes* §294, 1071; *sim.* Black, at §176, 599 (adding that the presumption is stronger if the statute is ancient and its meaning well settled, in which case the presumption would be "of great weight and practically conclusive.")
[11] *Pennock v. Dialogue*, 27 U.S. 1, 20-21 (1829).
[12] 70 Ill. 496 (1873).
[13] Id at 497-99; see Pair #2, above.

that does not amount to injury of the person, within the meaning of the statute. Mulford v. Clewell, 21 Ohio St. 191." Second, in the absence of actual damages, was it proper to authorize the jury to award exemplary damages? Again the Illinois supreme court answered "No": "This is the construction placed upon the act by the highest court of the State of Ohio, and it is reasonable to suppose the legislature adopted the law with the construction put upon it, as generally held. Schreider v. Hosier, ib. 98."[14] It is a fine illustration of Thrust #4 in action, without thought to rationale, albeit with a little help from Thrust #2 and lenity.

Thrust #4 is fragile. Treatise writers introduce it with equivocation: "Subject to the qualifications hereinafter stated ...;" "...in the absence of an expression of legislative intent to the contrary;" it is not absolute, imperative, but "is subject to numerous exceptions," and should be followed only if the foreign interpretation is "sound and reasonable."[15] All this, of course, flows from basic principles of interpretation; no interpretive device should trump clear legislative intent to the contrary. But of Thrust #4, writers are more than usually equivocal; it is merely persuasive we are told, not binding, and not to be followed if there is "sound reason why it should not be followed."[16]

Parry #4: "It may be rejected where there is conflict with the obvious meaning of the statute or where the foreign decisions are unsatisfactory in reasoning or where the foreign interpretation is not in harmony with the spirit or policy of the laws of the state adopting it."

This is little more than the usual list of equivocations to Thrust #4. They make good sense: where there are reasons for doubting that the legislature, enacting the foreign statute, really did intend to adopt it as applied by the courts of the jurisdiction of the statute's origin, then that foreign court ought not be followed.[17] But in real-life interpretive decision-making, would a court ever need Thrust #4, as compared with actually exploring one or more of its elements and basing its decision on that?

What about those disjunctive elements of Parry #4? First, Thrust #4 "may be rejected where there is conflict with the obvious meaning of the statute..." If the meaning of the statute is plain, one does not need interpretive devices such as canons, nor, in case of Thrust #4, the foreign sources, even when those foreign sources do not consist with the plain language. The Washington supreme court explained: "We think that the presumption that the legislature knew the plain import of the language they used is much stronger than the presumption that they knew

---

[14] Id at 500-501. A three person "dissent" concurred in the judgment and concurred in this part of the majority decision for this reason. Id at 502-03.

[15] 25 R.C.L. *Statutes* §295,1070-71, 1073.

[16] 59 C.J. Statutes §628, 1068. 1069.

[17] 59 C.J. Statutes §628, 1070 (Thrust #4 does not apply "where it is plain that the legislature adopting it had a different intention.")

of one or two decisions of the supreme court of California."[18] It is basic interpretation lore: one only needs resort to exogenous sources "where the terms of the statute are of doubtful import, so as to require construction."[19]

Second, Thrust #4 "may be rejected ... where the foreign decisions are unsatisfactory in reasoning." Indeed; one might sufficiently trust the legislature not to have intentionally adopted poorly reasoned, ill-decided cases as illustrative of its intentions!

Third, Thrust #4 "may be rejected ...where the foreign interpretation is not in harmony with the spirit or policy of the laws of the adopting state." This is exactly as in Black, and very similar to other treatises.[20] The idea is plain: our legislature can be presumed not to be adopting a statute intending its meaning to be out of accord with prevailing values.

But on the other hand, to change the current values may sometimes be exactly what the legislature intended (the bifurcation in Pair #2.) In *Metropolitan Railroad Co. v. Moore*,[21] the District of Columbia had followed Maryland civil procedure prior to the legislation, setting, one would think, "the spirit and policy of the laws;" the legislation enacted, however, copied New York's. It was a general scheme, covering a field of behavior, so the Supreme Court held that prior New York decisions on point should be followed, and not Maryland decisions. The fulcrum is the intent of the legislature: to change the current legal spirit and policy or not? Parry #4 includes this debatable element, one would think, not to demand a decision contrary to the foreign precedents, but to alert the interpreter to the fragility of Thrust #4 and the need to look further.

Treatise writers add more equivocating exceptions. Was the decision from the highest court of the prior state? If not then following it is optional.[22] Did the adopting state follow the language of the original statute exactly, or make changes to it? If the latter, how significant were the changes? Thrust #4 should not apply if the changes were substantial.[23] If "radical and material changes were made in the statute," it is reasonable to assume the legislature intended a difference, an intent itself which would be motivated by judicial applications made of the original language of the statute.[24] This too, is hardly a compelling inference, merely one that should provoke further investigation. The Supreme Court in *Allen v. St. Louis Bank*: "If the legislature of Missouri had adopted the words of that provision of the New York Factors' Act, the meaning

---

18 *Spokane Manufacturing & Lumber Co. v. McChesney et al.*, 1 Wash. 609, 615; 21 P. 198, 200 (1889).

19 25 R.C.L. *Statutes* §295, 1073. Thrust #12.

20 Black, §176, 600, 602; 59 C.J. Statutes §627, 1068, §628, 1070 (Thrust #4 does not apply where the foreign case law is not "in harmony with justice and public policy" or is "contrary to the spirit and policy of its [the adopting state's] laws.")

21 121 U.S. 558, 570-72 (1887).

22 *Smith v. Baker*, 5 Okla. 326, 339; 49 P. 61, 65 (1897)(" The meaning of a statute cannot be considered as settled by judicial construction, so as to carry that construction with it to the jurisdiction where it is adopted, when it has not been so settled by the highest judicial authority which can pass upon the question.")

23 Black, §176, 601.

24 25 R.C.L. *Statutes* §295, 1073.

of which had been thus settled on full consideration by the highest courts of that state and by this court, there would be the strongest ground for holding, in accordance with a familiar canon of construction, that it had enacted those words with that meaning. ... But the statute of Missouri of March 4, 1869, differs widely in language and in purpose ... ."[25]

Llewellyn's example, *Bowers v. Smith*,[26] serves the purpose many times over, illustrates other canons, and more. It was an election law case: plaintiff, the Democratic candidate for sheriff, lost by a mere thirty-three votes; if he could have more than three thousand ballots from the city of Sedalia declared invalid because of defects in their printing, he should win. "Both parties rely on the recent statute concerning elections (Revised Statutes, 1889, secs. 4756-4794), commonly known as the "Australian Ballot Law," as first enacted in this state."[27] It had been enacted elsewhere in various forms and many interpretive decisions anteceded Missouri's adoption of it.

The court's analysis began with a statement of general policy in election cases, a very principled democratic policy, worthy perhaps of being called a canon.

> The suffrage is regarded with jealous solicitude by a free people, and should be so viewed by those intrusted with the mighty power of guarding and vindicating their sovereign rights. Such a construction of a law as would permit the disfranchisement of large bodies of voters, because of an error of a single official, should never be adopted where the language in question is fairly susceptible of any other.
>
> Or, as a very able judge once tersely said: "All statutes tending to limit the citizen in his exercise of this right [of suffrage] should be liberally construed in his favor."[28]

The intent of the ballot law was to improve voting procedures, for the benefit of the public. Accordingly it should be liberally construed to this end.

Parry #4 came into play in the rejection of a poorly reasoned case from Montana[29] and one from Connecticut because the language of their statutes differed too greatly from

---

25 120 U.S. 20, 34-35 (1887).

26 111 Mo. 45; 20 S.W. 101 (1892)(Note that Shepard's gave the case a negative notation.)

27 111 Mo. at 52; 20 S.W. at 102 ("Plaintiff's contention is that the entire returns from Sedalia should be thrown out of the final count, for several reasons.")

28 111 Mo. at 55-56; 20 S.W. at 103, citing Wells v. Stanforth (1885), 16 Q. B. Div. 245 and Owens v. State ex rel. (1885), 64 Tex. 500.

29 "...Price v. Lush (1890), 10 Mont. 61, 24 P. 749. "With all respect due to the court that decided it, we think it embodies a misapplication of the English precedents which it cites. It entirely omits to mention or consider the effect of section 19 of the Montana statute (General Laws Montana, 1889, p. 140, substantially the same as our section 4778), which should be given some significance to prevent such unjust consequences to voters as have been explained, and which are impossible under the English ballot act, which that case purports to follow and expound." 111 Mo. at 58; 20 S.W. at 104.

Missouri's.[30] Generally, Thrust #4 must give way to stronger considerations of policy and legislative intent:

> We mention these cases neither to approve nor to disapprove them; but to indicate how inapplicable they are to the case in hand, and to show that, even with language as positive as that they construe, how reluctant are the courts to adopt an interpretation, the effect of which is to deprive a large number of their fellow citizens of the electoral franchise.[31]

In general, then, it might be said that Parry #4, in some form, will supersede Thrust #4 "whenever it is plain that the legislature adopting it [the statute in question] had a different intention" from that found in the proposed precedent. Discoverable legislative intent takes judicial priority over rules of presumption.

Resolution:

Thrust #4 and Parry #4 do not clash, even superficially. On its face, Parry #4 announces that it is an exception and proceeds to list circumstances in which it applies. In those circumstances, Thrust #4 does not apply. No problem.

Comment:

Thrust #4 should not be confused with its first cousin once removed, "The statutes of a foreign state will be interpreted according to the decision of the courts of that state."[32] This applies to the judicial interpretation of another state's statute, not one adopted by this state. For example, in *Usatore v. The Victoria,*[33] Judge Frank had to interpret and apply Argentinean maritime law. He did so according to the intentions of the Argentinean legislature as interpreted by Argentinean authority, explaining the process in a remarkable series of footnotes, itself a treatise on statutory interpretation. Of course this makes sense for the very same reason that Thrust #4 and Parry #4 make sense, even where the foreign legislature in question was not democratically elected.

---

[30] "In Talcott v. Philbrick (1890), 59 Conn. 472, 20 A. 436, the supreme court of Connecticut had to deal with a statute so unlike the Missouri law that it does not even provide for printing the list of candidates at public expense ..." 111 Mo. at 58-59; 20 S.W. at 104.

[31] 111 Mo. at 59; 20 S.W. at 105; this part of the decision then concluded solidly: "Having regard to the spirit and purpose of the Missouri statute, and to the general principles governing the treatment of popular elections by the courts in this country, we think it should be held that where a candidate for public office causes no timely objection to be made before the election (as permitted by section 4778), he should be regarded as having waived all objections that may exist to the presence on the official ballot of any names of nominees not properly entitled to be there. Compare Reg. v. Bradburn (1876), 6 Ont. Pr. 308, and Allen v. Glynn (1892), 17 Colo. 338, 29 P. 670; S. C., 17 Colo. 338, 29 P. 670." Id.

[32] 59 C.J. Statutes §614, 1037, cited by Llewellyn in support of Thrust #4; *Canons* at 402, n9.

[33] 172 F.2d 434 (2d. Cir., 1949).

Pair Five

THRUST: "Where various states have already adopted the statute, the parent state is followed."
PARRY: "Where interpretations of other states are inharmonious, there is no such restraint."[34]

Thrust #5: "Where various states have already adopted the statute, the parent state is followed."

Thrust #5 is ambiguous. Does "parent" refer to the state from which this state's legislature actually copied the statute in question? Or, supposing more than one state has the statute in question or a substantially similar one, does it refer to the state of origin, the progenitor of the statute?[35]

Llewellyn seems to have in mind the former. He cites only a single case, *Burnside v. Wand*,[36] and no secondary sources, and that case, from the 1902 Missouri Supreme Court, illustrates the former. The statute under interpretation could have come from either of two ancestors, one England,[37] the other New York,[38] with England the originator. The court makes a totally convincing argument that the Missouri legislature was looking to New York's statute, based not only on language similarities and differences but also because "the mind is at once prompted to look to the statutes of the State of New York, principally because so large a part of our statute laws have been borrowed from that State."[39] It thus followed New York's interpretation. The closest the opinion comes to Thrust #5 is a recitation —as a "rule of law" —

---

[34] *Canons* at 402.
[35] Curiously, for this to be relevant the second state in its decisions would probably not have followed the progenitor state's interpretation, thus violating Thrust #4. (One says "probably" because it is possible that all decisions interpreting the statute in the progenitor state came after it had been adopted in the second state.) Might there have been a reason for not following the progenitor state (for not following Thrust #4), perhaps some of those exceptions listed in Parry #4, so common they make Thrust #4 tentative and instable?
[36] 170 Mo. 531, 71 S.W. 337 (1902)
[37] Statute of 8 and 9 William III., 170 Mo. at 575, 71 S.W. at 350.
[38] "sections 12 and 13 of title II of chapter VI, vol. 2, page 353, Revised Statutes of New York 1829." , 170 Mo. at 575, 71 S.W. at 350.
[39] 170 Mo. at 575, 71 S.W. at 350.

of Thrust #4.[40] If *Burnside v. Wand* is support for Thrust #5, it is by accident, not by the Missouri Supreme Court's interpretive design.

Although he cites no secondary source, Llewellyn could have found Thrust #5 in Black, in the section he cited in support of Thrust #4:

> Finally, if it appears (as is now frequently the case) that the statute under consideration is not peculiar to the state from which it is alleged to have been taken, but that another state or several states have identical or substantially similar statutes on their books, the endeavor should be made to ascertain which particular state was the parent of the statute as adopted by the state where it is in controversy. If this can be settled with certainty, the construction worked out in the parent state will ordinarily be followed in the adopting state.[41]

Citing *Burnside v. Wand, supra*, Black immediately launches into equivocations.

On this interpretation Thrust #5 is a rather trivial lemma to Thrust #4, scarcely worthy of inclusion on its own. No wonder Llewellyn could find no sources for it as stated. If it is justified, it is as for Thrust #4: it is reasonable to assume that a legislature copying another state's statute would be aware of its judicial interpretations.[42]

The other possibility is that "parent" refers to the original, the progenitor, even though it was not copied by the legislature. Unlike the above interpretation, this would at least not be a redundant corollary to Thrust #4. Indeed, it exactly contradicts Thrust #4 and its justification, and flies in the face of prima facie legislative intent. Not surprisingly, support for this position is almost as scarce as for the former interpretation. There is a line in R.C.L. (one of the secondary sources used by Llewellyn in support of Pair 4) supporting it: "Where a statute construed in the state where it was enacted is adopted by another state, where it receives a different construction, and is then borrowed from the latter by a third state, the original construction may be followed in preference to the different one."[43] And there is a case, *Coulam v. Doull*, from the 1904 Supreme Court.[44] In dicta the Court found that the difference between California's language —the immediate source of Utah's statute of wills —and that of the progenitor, Massachusetts, did not justify following an interpretation from the California supreme court, almost on point.[45] It may be thin, but it caught the notice of the R.C.L. editors.

---

[40] "It is a rule of law that when a statute is borrowed from another State, the decisions of the State from which the statute is borrowed, interpreting such statute, are borrowed also." 170 Mo. at 576, 71 S.W. at 350.

[41] Black, at §176, 603; in all the sources he cites for Pairs 4 and 5, only here does the word "parent" occur.

[42] *Burnside v. Wand*, 170 Mo. at 576, 71 S.W. at 350, immediately after reciting its version of Thrust #4.

[43] 25 R.C.L. *Statutes* §295, 1074.

[44] 133 U.S. 216 (1904) (affirming that the omission of the plaintiff pretermitted heirs from decedent's will was intentional.)

[45] 133 U.S. at 231-32 ("It is contended that the statutory provision in question was copied from that of California, and that we are bound by the construction previously put upon it by the courts of the latter State. ... But in the Matter of the Estate of Garraud, 35 California, 336, it was held that evidence aliunde the will

Parry #5: "Where interpretations of other states are inharmonious, there is no such restraint."

What if several states had adopted the statute and their courts had given it a variety of constructions? Corpus Juris (one of Llewellyn's sources for Pair 4) says Thrust #4, which encompasses Thrust #5, "does not apply where other jurisdictions having the identical or substantially the same provision had given the language a different construction prior to the adoption in question." Rather, a court "will in such case adopt that construction which it regards as the most reasonable."[46] Parry #5.

Llewellyn cited no secondaries in support of Parry #5, but provided a single case, *State v. Campbell.*

> It has been held that where the statute is not peculiar to the state from which it was adopted, but other states have substantially the same statute, which their courts have construed differently, and when the construction placed upon it by the courts of the state from which it was taken is contrary to the weight of authority, the decision is not binding.[47]

The Kansas supreme court then quotes from various treatises, and concludes that "A statute copied from a similar statute of another state is presumed to be adopted with the construction it had already received. The presumption, however, is not conclusive, and where the same provision exists in several states, there is no presumption that the construction of any particular state was in view."[48] It offers no reasoning, only conclusory quotes.[49]

How is a court to overcome the presumption that when the legislature copied another state's statute it adopted that state's interpretations? The 1901 Wyoming Supreme Court, in *Coad v. Cowhick,*[50] faced up to the task:

> We fully concede that the rule relied upon, that in adopting the statute of another State we also adopt the construction which it has received, is one of great

---

was not admissible to show that the omission to make provision for children was intentional, and, in respect to the Massachusetts decisions, the court was of opinion that the words "and not occasioned by any mistake or accident," found in the statute of Massachusetts but not in that of California, were very material, and furnished the real ground for the admission of extrinsic evidence. We do not think so. While those words may strengthen the argument in favor of the admissibility of the evidence, it by no means follows that the construction of the statute should be otherwise in their absence." Id) Note in passing that apparently the Supreme Court here disregards Thrust #4, called a "rule of law" by the Missouri supreme court in *Burnside v. Wand,* 170 Mo. at 576, 71 S.W. at 350. "Rule talk" when dealing with canons can be very misleading.

[46] 59 C.J. *Statutes* §628, 1071, citing ten cases.

[47] 73 Kan. 688, 704 (1906).

[48] Id, 73 Kan. at 704-05, quoting "volume 3 of Current Law, page 739."

[49] Nevertheless it is an oft-cited source of authority; for example *Sutton v. Heinzle*, 85 Kan. 332, 333 (1911)(" We prefer, however, to base our judgment upon another proposition. The rule as to the binding effect of a decision rendered prior to the adoption of a statute is not absolute. It does not apply "where other jurisdictions having the identical or substantially the same provision had given the language a different construction prior to the adoption in question." (36 Cyc. 1157; *The State v. Campbell*, 73 Kan. 688.)"

[50] 9 Wyo. 316 (1901).

> importance and very generally applied; but it is based upon a specific and sufficient reason, which is, that the Legislature are presumed to have known the construction which the words of the statute have received, and if they had intended any other construction, they would have used apt words to express the change. But this statute is not peculiar to the State of Ohio. Other States have the same provision, using either the identical words or language which is in substance the same. And they have, almost without exception, given to the language a different construction. Must it not also be presumed that the Legislature knew the construction given to it generally by the courts of this country and England?[51]

Ohio was the acknowledged source, but as it had followed other states with other interpretations, the presumption that the Ohio courts' interpretations were the only ones before the Wyoming legislature could not be made.[52] If there is enough noise in a system, the inference to legislative intent loses its security.

Llewellyn's illustration to Parry #4, *Bowers v. Smith*,[53] is on point: there were many prior enactments and interpretations of the "Australian Ballot Law," but the court didn't take the earliest, nor try to determine precisely which, if any, the legislature chose to copy; it sifted through interpretations and followed only those supporting its overarching criterion of enhancing the reality of the franchise, the legislative purpose. In the terms used by Llewellyn in Parry #5 the key is harmony: the court facing the question decides which "interpretations of other states are inharmonious" and which are harmonious. One would hope, and in the cases tends to find, as in *Bowers v. Smith*, that the criterion of harmony sought out and applied was also the legislature's intent in enacting the statute.

Resolution:

Pair #5 is a rarity in Llewellyn's list: a genuine clash. But it is a clash only because Thrust #5 seems to have been created on no authority whatsoever simply to contradict Parry #5.

Parry #5 is another in the list begun in Parry #4 of exceptions to Thrust #4. Where many states' legislatures have enacted and their courts interpreted a statute, even though our state's legislature may have adopted the particular wording of one of those state's statute, we cannot be confident that it did so in the light of that state's courts' interpretations alone. That seems reasonable. Its precise contrary would be Thrust #5.

---

[51] Id, 9 Wyo. at 323.

[52] The Wyoming Supremes went further: "The adoption of the identical words of the Ohio statute is not specially significant in view of the fact that they are but a part of our code of civil procedure, covering more than two hundred pages of our Revised Statutes, and adopted bodily, almost without change, from the code of Ohio." 9 Wyo. at 323. (Sound realism!)

[53] 111 Mo. 45 (1892).

Pair Six

THRUST: "Statutes *in pari materia* must be construed together."
PARRY: "A statute is not *in pari materia* if its scope and aim are distinct or where a legislative design to depart from the general purpose or policy of previous enactments may be apparent."[1]

Thrust #6: "Statutes *in pari materia* must be construed together."[2]

Statutes "*in pari materia*" "...relate to the same person or thing, or to the same class of persons or things, or which have a common purpose;" "...statutes which stand together though enacted at different dates, relating to the same subject."[3] It is natural that they should be construed together, at least so that conflicting constraints or demands not be placed on their subject matter.[4]

Should further justification for Thrust #6 be necessary, it is to be found in the standard procedure for determining legislative intent "What was the [] law before the making of the Act? ...What was the mischief and defect for which [that] law did not provide?"[5] It is not reasonable to think that a legislature would survey all law, or look to the entire fabric of the law when seeking to repair or reorient an aspect of it; but it is certainly to be expected that it will look to the aspect being addressed. After all, that is why it is taking action. Thus we might presume that in enacting this statute, and those related to it on the same subject matter, the legislature will be pursuing a coherent theme, "a uniform and consistent design ... to apply the original to changing conditions or circumstances."[6] Accordingly all the statutes in that plan of governance of the domain in question should be construed together.

---

[1] *Canons* at 402.
[2] "...statutes in pari materia should be construed together." 25 RCL *Statutes* §285, 1060.
[3] *See* Black at §104, 334; SUTHERLAND (1904), §443, 844; 25 R.C.L. *Statutes* §285, 1060.; *Mitchell v. Witt*, 98 Va. 459 (1900); *Milner v. Gibson*, 249 Ky. 594, 604 (1933); *The United Society v. The Eagle Bank of New-Haven*, 7 Conn. 456, 469-70 (1829).
[4] 25 R.C.L. *Statutes* §285, 1061-62 (Thrust #6 "proceeds upon the supposition that the several statutes relating to the one subject were governed by one spirit and policy, and were intended to be consistent and harmonious in their several parts and provisions."); *State ex rel Perry v. Clark*, 54 Mo. 216, 218 (1873) ("The two acts were passed at the same session of the legislature, they relate to the same subject matter -- they are *in pari materia*, and, to arrive at the true legislative intent, they must be construed together.")
[5] *Heydon's Case*, *supra*, 3 Co. at 7b, 76 Eng.Rep. at 638.
[6] Black at §104, 333.

In the same vein, we are entitled to presume that the legislature would not issue inconsistent control data, nor incoherent instructions, to the governed. It is sometimes stated more generally as a principle of construction that one ought to construe a statute "if possible, so as to avoid any repugnancy or inconsistency between different enactments of the same legislature."[7] One cannot expect perfect consistency across all the myriad legislation and rulemaking in the modern state, but one can within the same subject matter, that is within the bounds of the domain *in pari materia.* Especially would this be so if the statutes in question were enacted at the same time or by the same legislature.[8]

Sutherland gives no less than seven pages of examples, as if it would be difficult to convince readers of the sound common sense of this canon.[9] Black lists as examples "all the laws of the same state relating to the property rights and contracts of married women removing their common law disabilities," and "a statute relating to the segregation and confinement of dipsomaniacs is in pari materia with other laws providing for the detention, care, and discharge of insane patients."[10]

Llewellyn's illustration, *Milner v. Gibson,*[11] was really about the constitutionality of a statute governing the liquidation of a bank, but it did have a question about the application of two enactments, one in 1912 and its successor in 1932. Having quoted 25 R.C.L. *Statutes*, the opinion continued "The acts of 1912 and 1932 are statutes in pari materia and it should be conceded that the section of the former requiring and providing the manner of giving notice to, and providing for a hearing of, the depositors and creditors must be regarded as a part of the latter... ."[12] This illustrates the strength of the inference encapsulated in Thrust #6: it applies even to statutes one or more of which may have been repealed.

If there is uncertainty as to the meaning of a word in a particular statute, one might look to its use in another statute on the same subject matter for guidance. Words notoriously can serve different purposes in different contexts, so one cannot presume similar meanings of lexicographically similar words across a wide range of statutes. As we all love to quote, "A word is not a crystal, transparent and unchanged, it is the skin of a living thought and may vary greatly in color and content according to the circumstances and the time in which it is used."[13]

---

7 Black at §104, 333.

8 *Mitchell v. Witt, supra,* 98 Va. At 459 ("Especially should effect be given, if possible, to statutes in pari materia enacted at the same session of the Legislature." Id,); 25 R.C.L. *Statutes* §286, 1062 ("... it is not to be presumed that the same body of men would pass conflicting and incongruous acts.")

9 SUTHERLAND (1904) §§444-48, 848-54.

10 Black at §104, 335; *e.g., Ex parte Schwarting*, 76 Neb. 773 (1906).

11 249 Ky. 594 (1933).

12 Id, 249 Ky at 605.

13 *Towne v. Eisner*, 245 U.S. 418, 425 (1918) *per* Holmes, J.

But among statutes *in pari materia*, one can reasonably expect similar uses, especially if they are part of an intentionally coherent scheme.[14]

It should then be clear that, as with all canons, Thrust #6 applies only to the extent that a contrary interpretation is not clear on the face of the statute;[15] one refers to other statutes *in pari materia* to *resolve*, not to *create* an interpretive problem.

> Indeed, the cases are so numerous in this court to the effect that the province of construction lies wholly within the domain of ambiguity, that an extended review of them is quite unnecessary. The whole doctrine applicable to the subject may be summed up in the single observation that prior acts may be resorted to, to solve, but not to create an ambiguity. [16]

Of course clearly indicated legislative intent to the contrary should always defeat a mere rule of inference.

Parry #6: "A statute is not *in pari materia* if its scope and aim are distinct or where a legislative design to depart from the general purpose or policy of previous enactments may be apparent."

It looks like an extension of the definition, doesn't it? Definitions of "*in pari materia*" typically include "having a common purpose" and "related to the same person or thing, or to the same class of persons or things."[17] But we avoid, if we can, a definitional solution for two reasons. First, it turns Thrust #6 into mere semantics: if statutes to be *in pari materia* have to be, *inter alia*, consistent, then of course they should be interpreted as consistent.[18] Second, if Parry #6 is merely definitional of "*in pari materia*," then there is no chance of incompatibility between it and Thrust #6. In principle, we should look for interpretations optimizing Llewellyn's thesis, never simply defining it away.[19]

The idea should be that statutes *in pari materia* are about the same subject matter. But two statutes could be about one subject matter yet to utterly different purposes; then they would

---

[14] "Undoubtedly, there is a natural presumption that identical words used in different parts of the same act are intended to have the same meaning." *Atlantic Cleaners & Dyers, Inc. v. United States*, 286 U.S. 427, 433 (1932); *Helvering v. Stocholms Enskilda Bank*, 293 U.S. 84, 86-87 (1934); *Stillwell v. State Bar*, 29 Cal.2d 119, 123 (1946); *County- Seat of Linn County*, 15 Kan. 500, 527 (1875)(excellently quotable).

[15] 25 R.C.L. *Statutes* §285, 1062 (Thrust #6 "is, of course, applicable only where the terms of the statute to be construed are ambiguous or its significance doubtful."); *sim.* Black at §104, 341.

[16] *Hamilton v. Rathbone*, 175 U.S. 414, 421 (1899); Black at §104, 341.

[17] *Milner v. Gibson*, 249 Ky. 594, 604 (1933); Black at §104, 334.

[18] Unfortunately many sources do it. For example Llewellyn's illustration/authority for Parry #6 quotes Sutherland "Nor is an act in pari materia though it may incidentally refer to the same subject, if its scope and aim are distinct and unconnected." (Suth. Stat. Con. § 286.)"; *Wheelock v. Myers*, 64 Kan. 47, 54 (1902); *sim.* "Statutes which are not inconsistent with one another, and which relate to the same subject matter, are in pari materia, and should be construed together;" *Mitchell v. Witt*, 98 Va. 459 (1900); SUTHERLAND (1904) §449, 855; Black at §104, 337.

[19] The Principle of Charity: Always so construe the argument under scrutiny as to make its validity most probable, and thus to make it most difficult to knock down.

not need to be interpreted consistently. For example, consider a statute generally banning the use of vehicles on the highways while intoxicated. Is a bicycle a vehicle for that purpose? Probably it is; one would look to the harm the legislature sought to alleviate and decide accordingly. Another statute sets a price for all vehicles at the toll gate for the local state park. Is a bicycle a vehicle for its purpose? Most probably not.[20] If vehicles are the common subject matter then, on a restricted definition of "*in pari materia*," Thrust #6 would apply, demanding a common interpretation of "vehicle" as applied to bicycles. But we can construe Parry #6 to say, to the contrary, that because of the completely different purpose, the two statutes are not *in pari materia* so need not be construed together nor as consistent in the meaning of "vehicle."[21]

Llewellyn's chosen case, *Wheelock v. Myers*,[22] illustrates Parry #6 and Pair 6 with all their difficulties. Wheelock was the assignee of a note and mortgage made and granted by Myers to Rickert Investment Company in 1889, but had failed to record the assignment when made. In 1897 he sought to foreclose the mortgage. On the first round he failed. The law on point was new, "chapter 160 of the Laws of 1897": it gave a six month window to record, which Wheelock did not meet, and provided that unless recorded "no assignment of a mortgage should be received against the mortgagor." The choice of words mattered; it was a rule of evidence, precluding the admission of the mortgage. That law "was repealed by chapter 168 of the Laws of 1899 (Gen. Stat. 1901, §§ 4234-4239)", which gave a new four month window, and for unrecorded mortgages gave the mortgagor and successors "a complete defense to any action on such mortgage or note to the extent of payments made to the original mortgagee without knowledge on the part of the mortgagor of an assignment of the mortgage."[23] This time Wheelock had recorded in time, prior even to the new statute's coming into effect. This time he won.

There were many grounds of argument but the one that is relevant concerns another statute effective on the same date as chapter 168 of the Laws of 1899, "chapter 155 of the Laws of 1899 (Gen. Stat. 1901, § 4243)." Defendant mortgagor Myers argued that chapter 168 should be interpreted in conjunction with and take meaning from chapter 155 as the latter was also about mortgages and assignments of them. The Kansas Supremes wouldn't bight. Chapter 155's "purpose is to legalize defective assignments of mortgages theretofore made," whereas "Chapter 168 has relation to the effect of payments made by mortgagors to original mortgagees who have assigned their mortgages but who have not recorded the assignments. The two acts are not in pari materia."[24]

---

[20] As presently in Michigan.
[21] *Williams v. Ellis*, L.R. 5, Q.B.Div. 175 (1880); Black at §104, 337.
[22] 64 Kan. 47 (1902).
[23] Id., 64 Kan at 50.
[24] Id, 64 Kan at 53, quoting Sutherland: ""Nor is an act in pari materia though it may incidentally refer to the same subject, if its scope and aim are distinct and unconnected." (Suth. Stat. Con. § 286.)"

That was all. But the point is clear: because the purposes of the statutes were so different, the court said they were not in pari materia, Thrust #6 did not apply. It is an example of Parry #6 in definitional form. But it begs the question of what counts as similarity —as "*in pari*" —among purposes. The opinion didn't offer any help on that. Shifting the argument from the merely semantic, one might say the two statutes were about the same sort of thing, namely mortgages and their assignments; but that alone did not justify an inference that the legislature intended them to be construed together because the legislature plainly manifested such a different purpose for each.

Resolution:

Latin "pari" means "equal;" "materia" means "material," "substance," "matter," or, in a word, "stuff." But if Thrust #6 were to be confined to *materia* as in Latin it would fail too often to be useful as a ground of inference to legislative intent. Extending the definition to include the legislative intent —"scope and aim" in Llewellyn's Parry #6 —completely defangs the canon, making it simply that one should construe similarly two statutes of similar legislative intent. As a teenager might say: "Duh!" The converse is captured by the rest of Parry #6 (so far ignored): "where a legislative design to depart from the general purpose or policy of previous enactments may be apparent."

It takes a very restrictive definition for us to construe Pair 6 as a clash of maxims. One has to stipulate an interpretation of "*in pari materia*" as in the Latin. Then a statute about the same sort of stuff will be *in pari materia* and still, if the "scope and aim" or "legislative design" or "general purpose or policy" of the statutes is not the same, then they need not be construed together.

Clash? Yes, but also no canon: Thrust #6 would then require joint construction of the statutes in question despite legislative intent to the contrary. Llewellyn's chosen sources exclude this interpretation of Thrust #6: Even if the statutes "may incidentally refer to the same subject, if [their] scope and aim are distinct and not connected…" they need not be construed together.[25]

Comment:

One can see here the attraction of self-translating, easily remembered Latin. (We shall see it again.) It looks learned, authoritative even: pronounce it, and the argument is over. But to preserve its jurisprudential significance this one required either that the Latin be so broadly translated as to reduce the canon to a verbal platitude, or so narrowly and precisely translated as to make it inconsistent with fundamental principles, and denying its canonical status.

---

[25] Black at §104, 337; SUTHERLAND (1904) at §449, 855, uses almost identical words.

Like all canons, this one is no better than, no more useful than its justification.

Pair Seven

> **THRUST**: "A statute imposing a new penalty or forfeiture, or a new liability or disability, or creating a new right of action will not be construed as having a retroactive effect."
> **PARRY**: "Remedial statutes are to be liberally construed and if a retroactive interpretation will promote the ends of justice, they should receive such a construction."[1]

Thrust #7: "A statute imposing a new penalty or forfeiture, or a new liability or disability, or creating a new right of action will not be construed as having a retroactive effect."

Black:

> A statute imposing a new penalty or forfeiture, or a new liability or disability, or creating a new right of action, will not be construed as having a retroactive operation, if such consequences can fairly be avoided by interpretation.[2]

Except for a misplaced comma, changing only a single word ('effect' for 'operation'), Llewellyn has tracked Black's section caption up to its condition. He cites no other secondary source. This is not surprising: his other three favored secondaries have plenty about this sort of thing, but as parts of general discussions of retroactive legislation, to which there is a strong antipathy.[3]

Thrust #7 is a consequence of the fundamental principle of jurisprudence that a person cannot be bound by a law of which he or she has no notice.[4] Justice Marshall: "[B]ecause we assume that man is free to steer between lawful and unlawful conduct, we insist that laws give the person of ordinary intelligence a reasonable opportunity to know what is prohibited so that he may act accordingly … [and] must provide explicit standards for those who apply them."[5] One does not have an opportunity to know law yet to be made; one cannot plan or restrict one's conduct according to a law or social standard to be set only in the future. Hence the emphasis in Thrust #7 on newness, and on changing rights. If the standard codified is already part of the law, be it common law or a prior statute, or if it is not one governing conduct, then retroactivity may

---

1 *Canons* at 402.
2 Black at §119, 401, in bold print, the section's caption.
3 Sutherland (1904), §§641-651, 1157-75; 59 C.J. *Statutes* §§690-713, 1157-79; 25 R.C.L. *Statutes* §§34-40, 785-93.
4 *See* Introduction, above.
5 *Grayned v. City of Rockford*, *supra*, 408 U.S. 104, 108 (1972).

be acceptable. But a novel standard of behavior set by legislation cannot be known in advance of its promulgation. Therefore, one can see the abhorrence of retroactive legislation and/or interpretation as a corollary of Thrust #2, resting on the same foundation.

Many of the cases using Thrust #7 or variations on it involve railways as defendants. In the eighteenth century railway worker accidents were many and serious.[6] But the common law defenses of assumption of risk, fellow servant negligence, and contributory negligence protected the employer railroad from liability notwithstanding its own negligence's being the cause. When this inhumane state of the law was changed by statute, persons injured prior to the date of enactment claimed a cause of action: were they to be dismissed following Thrust #7 or was the statute remedial thus permissibly retroactive, as in Parry #7?

> The statute may be expedient, just, and salutary in its objects and purposes, and it shows a manifest legislative intent to remedy what was regarded as existing evils arising from extra state judicial decisions; but, as the statute contains no express provision for retrospective operation, I must conclude to observe the general and sound rule for the construction of statutes, and give this state statute only prospective operation. ... I will not consider such questions further than to say that, in my opinion, a retrospective operation of the statute in this case would clearly and injuriously affect vested rights acquired by contract, and impose new liabilities, which were not in existence, and were not contemplated by the parties, when they entered into the relation of master and servant for the operation of the railway.[7]

Usually defendants prevailed.

Llewellyn's example, *Keeley v. Great Northern Ry.*,[8] is a railway employee injury claim but with a twist. Keeley was killed by being crushed between two railroad cars which collided because of engineer and company negligence, but after the enactment of a statute removing the traditional common law defenses. However the original statute limited damages to $5,000. In 1907, the same year as Keeley's death, a replacement statute reset the damage limit at $10,000. The jury awarded Keeley's executrix $6,615 under an instruction that the latter statute controlled. Wrong:

> When this accident happened the plaintiff had a claim for the recovery of not exceeding $5,000. Beyond this amount she had no claim or cause of action. When the legislature afterward said that in such cases there might be a recovery up to the sum of $ 10,000, they in effect created a new cause of action for the second $5,000. It was not a mere change in remedy, but to all practical purposes

---

6 "Statistics furnished by the Interstate Commerce Commission show that during the year ending June 30, 1891, there were forty-seven different styles of car couplers reported to be in use, and that during the same period there were 2,660 employés killed and 26,140 injured. Nearly 16 percent of the deaths occurred in the coupling and uncoupling of cars, and over 36 percent of the injuries had the same origin." *Johnson v. Southern Pacific Co.*, 196 U.S. 1, 19 (1904), quoting President Harrison's annual message to congress of 1892.

7 *Wright v. Southern Ry. Co.*, 80 F. 260, 263 (C.C.W.D.N.C. 1897). Numerous cases are similar.

8 139 Wis. 448 (1909).

> it created a new right of action. If it created a new right and did not merely change the remedy, it is not applicable to prior transactions. This is familiar law.[9]

The usual justification for hostility to retroactive statutes doesn't apply here: the defendant railroad was on notice of its duty. Perhaps it was on notice that it need only take precautions or insure to $5,000, but that would be an exceedingly strained argument in these circumstances. (The engineer mistakenly backed a line of cars into those Keeley was working between.) So here the judge is woodenly and formalistically following a rule. Does it accurately reflect the intent of the legislature? In any event it very well illustrates, by misuse, the importance of Thrust #7.

***Parry** #7*: "Remedial statutes are to be liberally construed and if a retroactive interpretation will promote the ends of justice, they should receive such a construction."

It is easy to be confused over this; the Texas Appeals Court in Llewellyn's illustrative case, *Falls v. Key*,[10] certainly was. What is it for a statute to be remedial?

It could be about remedies, not about substantive behavior. One would not ordinarily think of this as a genuine possibility as such statutes are usually addressed as a separate, special exception to the "prohibition" on retrospective interpretations. But the Texas court in *Falls v. Key* discusses it as though relevant to the case, and with no differentiation from other possibilities.[11]

It could be about a glitch in the prior state of the law, as addressed by the first two *Heydon's Case* questions.[12] *Falls v. Key* offers Blackstone's definition, a rough equivalent: "A remedial statute is one which supplies defects, and abridges superfluities in the former law."[13] But that was the sense in which it was used in Parry #2, generalized to include statutory as well as common law. Alone it does not justify retroactivity, although it does justify a liberal reading to effect the legislature's purpose.

A third sense is the relevant one here. Something is awry between a statute and the law as understood by the governed; it needs to be fixed and in such a way as not to disturb the settled expectations of those who acted in reliance on their common misunderstanding. The problem with the impossibility of notice if a statute is given retrospective force thus does not arise. The classic explanatory example is in the opinion of Justice Willes in *Phillips v. Eyre*:

---

9 Id, 139 Wis. at 454.

10 278 S.W. 893 (Tex. App. 1925).

11 *Falls v. Key*, *supra*, 278 S.W. at 896 ("The presumption against the retrospective construction of statutes is founded on the principle that they should not be given such a construction as will make them unconstitutional or unjust, and therefore as a general rule does not apply to statutes that relate merely to remedies and modes of procedure.")

12 "1st. What was the common law before the making of the Act. 2nd. What was the mischief and defect for which the common law did not provide." *Heydon's Case*, *supra*, 30 Co. at 7a, 76 Eng. Rep. at 637.

13 *Falls v. Key*, *supra*, 278 S.W. at 896, citing Blackstone, I COMMENTARIES ON THE LAWS OF ENGLAND, 86 (1938).

> One instance of retrospective legislation obviously just, to render valid the acts of persons who had fallen honestly into error, and by which infinite actions were killed in embryo, may suffice. When the result of the judgment, finally affirmed by the House of Lords, in the Queen v. Millis, 10 Cl.& F. 534, was to declare null and void numerous marriages celebrated in Ireland by Presbyterian ministers and others not episcopally ordained, one effect of the decisions was to disclose, by the new light thrown upon the relations of families previously supposed to be legitimate, a prospect of vast and interminable litigation, springing from a host of vested rights of action of every description. This result was averted (in so far as it was possible without making persons liable to prosecution who were not so liable before) by the Acts 5 & 6 Vict. c.113, 6 & 7 Vict. c.39, and 7 & 8 Vict. c.81, s.83. By these beneficial and just statutes the past marriages were ratified and confirmed from the beginning, for it was in terms enacted that they should "that they be adjudged and taken to have been and to be" of the same force and effect as if canonically had and solemnized.[14]

Such remedial or curative legislation affirms as proper what everyone had taken to be the law anyway; it "restores a situation that was affirmatively anticipated and provided for."[15]

Contrast the situation in which there was no doubt as to the law prior to the enactment of the statute —and no doubt that it was not wise, not how it ought to be. Think, for example, of the workings of the "mirror image rule" in contract formation prior to Uniform Commercial Code §2-207. The statute cures the law, but in a quite different sense. Everyone had behaved under the prior law knowing what it required and knowing that was unwise but nevertheless still law; now the maladaptivity has been fixed. But it would be utterly inappropriate —in fact exactly contrary to principle —to make that new, *remedial* statute retroactive.

Parry #7 should be applied only in the third sense of 'remedial', the sense explained by Justice Willes in *Phillips v. Eyre*; only in this sense is it justified. The condition built into it, *viz*, "and if a retroactive interpretation will promote the ends of justice," should ensure its application's being limited to the proper situations, although propriety here, as always, is for judicial judgment.

As with Thrust #7, Llewellyn appears to have derived Parry #7 directly from Black, although this time more heavily editing the caption.[16] Black uses the following splendid quote to offer the basic justification of giving effect to legislative intent:

---

[14] 6 Q.B. 1, 24-25 (1870).

[15] W. David Slawson, *Constitutional and Legislative Considerations in Legislative Lawmaking*, 48 CAL.L.REV. 216, 239 (1960); Ballard, Frederick A., *Retroactive Federal Taxation*, 48 HARV.L.REV. 592, 596 (1935).

[16] Black at §120, 403-04: "Remedial statutes are to be liberally construed; and if a retrospective interpretation will promote the ends of justice and further the design of the legislature in enacting them, or make them applicable to cases which are within the reason and spirit of the enactment, though not within its direct words, they should receive such a construction, provided it is not inconsistent with the language employed." (some caption!)

> … the general proposition [is] that statutes are to be construed and applied prospectively, unless a contrary intent is manifested in clear and unambiguous terms. This is undoubtedly the general rule, and it is sometimes held that, to work an exception, the intent favoring retrospective application must affirmatively appear in the words of the statute. The better rule of construction, and the rule peculiarly applicable to remedial statutes, however, is, that a statute must be so construed as to make it effect the evident purpose for which it was enacted, and if the reason of the statute extends to past transactions, as well as to those in the future, then it will be so applied, although the statute does not in terms so direct, unless to do so would impair some vested right or violate some constitutional guaranty.[17]

Black's interest here may be more general, but the argument does support Parry #7.

Llewellyn illustrates with *Falls v. Key*.[18] But while it may include recitations in accord with Parry #7, it doesn't follow it. Ms. Falls, married to but estranged from Meguiar, had purchased real estate in 1916. At that time her ability to own and administer land independently of her husband was provided by a 1913 statute;[19] however it required her husband's signature in addition to her own in order to alienate real property, allowing her to avoid the requirement by judicial order only in case "the husband shall refuse to join in such incumbrance, or conveyance, or transfer of such property…".[20] In 1917 the statute was amended, allowing judicial permission to do without the husband's signature also in case "the husband shall have permanently abandoned his wife."[21] In 1920 Ms. Falls sold the land to Broad without Meguiar's signature, Broad having full knowledge of the situation; she retained a vendor's lien. After a series of mesne conveyances the property, still subject to the lien, came to Simon in 1924; he did not know of the problem with the signatures. Falls' and Meguiar's divorce had become final in 1923. When Simon learned of the cloud on the conveyance, he stopped paying. Falls said she'd get Meguiar's signature but instead she sued to foreclose the mortgage, naming Simon, all intermediate purchasers, and Meguiar as defendants. Was the initial conveyance valid? The trial court said "No" and denied the foreclosure.

Falls' first argument was that at common law courts permitted an exception to the requirement of the husband's signature when "the two are permanently separated," but to no avail: that, said the court, "rested entirely on the necessity of the situation, and the injustice of permitting an abandoned wife and her children to suffer for the necessaries of life, by reason of her statutory inability to incumber or sell her separate property." The opinion continued in hopeful style for Ms. Falls: "The amendment to article 4621, enacted in 1917, was merely remedial to the terms of the statute as it existed prior thereto, by adding the words "if the husband shall have permanently abandoned his wife, be insane," etc., to the act." As an illustration to

---

[17] *The Connecticut Mutual Life Insurance Co. v. Talbot*, 113 Ind. 373, 378 (1887).

[18] 278 S.W. 893 (Tex. App. 1925).

[19] Tex.Rev.Civ.Stat. art 4621 (1913).

[20] 278 S.W. at 895.

[21] Vernon's Ann. Civ. St. Supp. 1918, art. 4621. 278 S.W. at 895.

Parry #7, this should have allowed Ms. Falls to succeed, especially as her reliance (if indeed she did rely on the statute) came later, in 1920. But such was not to be. "We conclude that the plaintiff below, merely by the fact that she purchased the land in question prior to the amendment of article 4621, in 1917, did not acquire a vested right in the procedure necessary for her to dispose of said land without the signature of her husband some three years later, and believe that the trial court committed no error … ." It may have been remedial, but the 1917 statute still failed as to both Parry #2 and Parry #7. Perhaps the court thought 'remedial' applied only to remedies, or procedure; the language immediately prior to this quoted conclusion suggests as much. But, as decided, the case exemplifies Thrust #7, not Parry #7.[22]

Resolution:

If 'remedial' is used in the appropriate sense, the sense that accords with the underlying jurisprudential basis of judicial abhorrence of retroactive legislation and interpretation, there is no clash between Thrust #7 and Parry #7. Thrust #7 applies to statutes creating new rights, powers, liabilities or disabilities, thus encroaching on old or previously accepted legal standards and relations. The governed should have been justified in planning and acting on the law of the time; having that law changed retrospectively by judicial interpretation would be indeed unjust. Parry #7 applies only where the previous state of rights, duties, etc., *qua* legal standards and relations, was not known or accepted, but generally misunderstood or ignored. No reliance interests are disturbed by applying a curative statute retroactively in such a situation; to the contrary the generally accepted —rather than the misunderstood legal —rights will be ratified by the retrospective application of the statute. The condition "if a retroactive interpretation will promote the ends of justice" in Parry #7 limits its application to this situation.

The thrust and parry of Pair 7 are not especially antipathetic. They both fit their justifications and natural exceptions. Only if used mindlessly should they generate potential conflict. Llewellyn's illustrative cases exemplify such use.

---

[22] Id, 278 S.W. at 895-96.

Pairs Eight, Nine, and Ten

Thrust #8: "Where design has been distinctly stated no place is left for construction."
Parry #8: "Courts have the power to inquire into real –as distinct from ostensible –purpose."
Thrust #9: "Definitions and rules of construction contained in an interpretation clause are part of the law and binding."
Parry #9: "Definitions and rules of construction in a statute will not be extended beyond their necessary import nor allowed to defeat intention otherwise manifested."
Thrust #10: "A statutory provision requiring a liberal construction does not mean disregard of unequivocal requirements of the statute."
Parry #10: "Where a rule of construction is provided within the statute itself the rule should be applied."[23]

Communicating control data can be difficult, and communicating determinate controls for all possible situations in a finite number of words is impossible. Justice Frankfurter:

> Anything that is written may present a problem of meaning, and that is the essence of the business of judges in construing legislation. The problem derives from the very nature of words. ... The intrinsic difficulties of language and the emergence after enactment of situations not anticipated by the most gifted legislative imagination, reveal doubts and ambiguities in statutes that compel judicial construction."[24]

Legislatures, which surely should seek clarity and determinacy insofar as reasonably possible, sometimes help limit the range of "doubts and ambiguities" under their enactments by enacting interpretive instructions as part of the legislation.

Interpretive instruction clauses come in three general kinds. The most familiar are definitions of key words and phrases that occur in the act, but also familiar enough are statements of purpose and of interpretive strategy. The Uniform Commercial Code gives us examples in

---

[23] *Canons* at 402-03.
[24] Felix Frankfurter, *Some Reflections on the Reading of Statutes*, 47 COLUM. L. REV. 527, 528 (1947). Similarly, *see* James C. Carter, THE PROPOSED CODIFICATION OF OUR COMMON LAW, 83 (New York Evening Post Job Printing Office, 1884), H.L.A. Hart, THE CONCEPT OF LAW, 123-26 (Oxford University Press, 1961). Similarly, and more generally: "[W]e cannot speak without incurring some risk, at least in theory; the only way of being absolutely safe is to say absolutely nothing." Isaiah Berlin, *Logical Translation*, in Henry Hardy, ed., CONCEPTS AND CATEGORIES: PHILOSOPHICAL ESSAYS (London, 1978) at 78.

Article 1. In Section 1-102(1) it gives instructions as to interpretation: "This Act shall be liberally construed and applied to promote its underlying purposes and policies."[25] Then immediately, in sub-section (2), it tells us those purposes and policies:

> Underlying purposes and policies of this Act are
> (a) to simplify, clarify and modernize the law governing commercial transactions;
> (b) to permit the continued expansion of commercial practices through custom, usage and agreement of parties;
> (c) to make uniform the law among the various jurisdictions.

And in Section 1-201 it defines words and phrases from "Action" to "'Written' or 'writing'."

Does the legislature have the power to do this? Does it have dominion over such intrinsically judicial functions as interpretation and determining word meanings? In a word, yes.[26] Interpretive instructions are binding on users of the legislation, be they judges or lawyers or denizens, and are as subject to interpretive difficulties as any other statute. That is what Llewellyn's Pairs 8, 9, and 10 are about. Together they map the territory and its difficulties, describing the parameters of the process of implementing legislative intent under interpretive statutes and dealing with inconcinnities between interpretive provisions and other parts of the act.

Pair 8 is about statements of purpose, called "design" in Llewellyn's chosen formulation. Pair 9 is about both definitions and interpretive instructions, and Pair 10 is about interpretive instructions. Thus Pair 10 is but a limited case of the more general Pair 9. The conflation in Pair 9 of two kinds of interpretive rules —definitions and rules of construction —may be common enough in captions to treatise sections, but it does not work very well as a rule of construction. The differences in kind precludes coverage by a single rule. Nowhere but on this list will you find such a conflation called a canon.

None of Llewellyn's Pairs 8, 9 and 10 serves his purpose of showing canons of construction to be contradictory or inconsistent or a matter of judicial selective whim.

***Pair 8*:**

> **THRUST**: "Where design has been distinctly stated no place is left for construction."
> **PARRY**: "Courts have the power to inquire into real –as distinct from ostensible –purpose."[27]

---

[25] U.C.C. 1-102(1); other sections also give interpretive instructions, for example "§1-104. Construction Against Implicit Repeal.", "§1-106. Remedies to Be Liberally Administered.", and the prince of them all, "§1-109. Section Captions. Section captions are parts of this Act."

[26] *State v. Standard Oil Co.*, 61 Ore. 438, 445 (1912)("We find, as to the rule for the construction of interpretation clauses, that any provision in a statute which declares its meaning or purpose is authoritative."); R.C.L. §275, 1047, 1049; 59 C.J. *Statutes* §567, 948, Black at §89, 269; Michael Sinclair, TRADITIONAL TOOLS OF STATUTORY INTERPRETATION, 59-65 (Vandeplas Publishing, 2013).

[27] *Canons* at 402.

Thrust #8: "Where design has been distinctly stated no place is left for construction."

The wording of Thrust #8 appears to have come from Corpus Juris: "Ordinarily, where the law-making power distinctly states its design, no place is left for construction."[28] But this is copied from *Coulter v. Pool*,[29] the 1921 California case that Llewellyn cited for Parry #8, with a one word change ("place" instead of "room".)[30] What is meant here by 'design'? It does not mean "overall plan/pattern" or similar, but rather "intent" or "purpose" as in contrast with accident ("Whether by accident or design, her …".)

Llewellyn's cited case, *Federoff v. Birks Bros.*,[31] is not very helpful. It was a dispute over the mileage to be paid to a witness under a statute,[32] but the only statement of legislative purpose came from a prior case;[33] the opinion concludes with four quotes about legislative purpose —Thrust #8 is third, copied from and citing *Coulter v. Pool* —but none of the four has determinative relevance. After that the opinion announces a decision without further ado. In Sutherland, the other source Llewellyn cited for Thrust #8, only a general, introductory paragraph about statements of legislative intent or purpose comes close.[34]

A better illustration is *Smith v. State*,[35] the case Llewellyn chose to cite for Thrust #9. Indiana had passed a statute defining embezzlement; prior to it, Smith's crime would have looked like larceny, but with a defense; he was convicted of embezzlement. The key point came up in the Indiana Supremes' rehearing of his appeal. Chief Justice Frazer made it clear:

> the second section contains precisely as clear an indication of the legislative intent, when, in assigning a reason for the emergency clause, putting the act into

---

[28] 59 C.J. *Statutes* §570, 960.

[29] 187 Cal. 181 (1921).

[30] "…when the law-making power distinctly states its design in the enactment of a particular statute, no room is left for construction …" 187 Cal. at 185. Both sources immediately back off: "but a legislative declaration that a law was intended to promote a certain purpose is not binding on the courts…", 59 C.J. *Statutes* §570, 960; "…legislative declaration, whether contained in the title or in the body of a statute, that the statute was intended to promote a certain purpose is not conclusive on the courts…", 187 Cal. at 185.

[31] 75 Cal. App. 345 (1925).

[32] Cal.Pol.Code §208.

[33] 75 Cal. App. at 347.

[34] Sutherland (1904), §358, 684:

> Where the law-maker declares its own intention in the enactment of a particular law, or defines the sense of the words it employs in a statute, it not only exercises its legislative power, but exercises it with a plausible aim; for it professes to furnish aid to correct understanding of its intention, and thus to facilitate the primary judicial inquiry in the exposition of the law after it is finished, promulgated, and has gone into practical operation.

So we may properly take the occurrence of "design" in Thrust #8 as a rhetorical accident, and not significantly different from other sources on the same subject. That certainly fits with the idea that this is plausibly a candidate canon; for example R.C.L., which puts it in the negative: "An interpretation which defeats any of the manifest purposes of the statute cannot be accepted." 25 R.C.L. *Statutes* §253, 1014 (with numerous cites.) An esoteric formulation such as used in Thrust #8 does not specially fix the meaning of an interpretive canon. We shall see this reinforced in *Coulter v. Pool*, below.

[35] 28 Ind. 321 (1867).

> immediate effect, it is declared that "there is no law punishing the offense" defined. If it had been intended to embrace offenses already punishable, this would have been simply a falsehood. The legislature certainly knew its own intent, and to the majority of the court, this language is conclusive that it was meant by the act to provide for cases not previously punishable.[36]

Despite —or perhaps *because of*—the simplicity of Thrust #8, one does not find many good examples. Many cases —like Llewellyn's chosen illustration, *Federoff v. Birks Bros.* —are cited only for their clear statements, even if merely part of a list of interpretive principles. For example, in *S.S.White Dental Manufacturing Co. v. Commonwealth*[37] the constitutionality of a tax hinged on whether it was an excise tax or a property tax. The court tells us "It is expressly declared by the terms of the statute to be an excise. The declared purpose of the act is to be accepted as true, unless incompatible with its meaning and effect."[38] But then it gives us pages of differentia and historical tradition to establish that this was, indeed, an excise tax.

Parry #8 is more interesting and fertile.

Parry #8: "Courts have the power to inquire into real –as distinct from ostensible –purpose."

The secondary sources are much more sympathetic to Parry #8 than Thrust #8. Corpus Juris, the only one cited by Llewellyn, begins a section captioned "Other Guides to Intent" with an approximation of Thrust #8,[39] then continues:

> ...but a legislative declaration that a law was intended to promote a certain purpose is not binding on the courts, and they have the power to inquire as to its real, as distinct from its ostensible purpose.[40]

Black includes a similar qualification in his approximation of Thrust #8: "The declared purpose of the act is to be accepted as true, unless incompatible with its meaning and effect."[41]

The reasoning here is transparent. The express language of a statute particularly applicable to a situation in dispute should not be revised to suit a general, overarching purpose even if stated in the act of which the statute is a part. When the legislature chose the words of the statute in question, it was focusing on their particular application, not on a general purpose; thus giving them their clear effect should further legislative intent more accurately. "[T]he words of a statute cannot be stretched beyond their reasonable import to accomplish a result not expressed."[42]

---

[36] Id at 325-26.
[37] 212 Mass. 35; 98 N.E. 1056 (1912).
[38] Id, 212 Mass. at 40; 98 N.E. at 1059.
[39] 59 C.J.*Statutes* §570, 958 ("Ordinarily, where the law-making power distinctly states its design, no place is left for construction … .)
[40] Id.
[41] Black at §253, 1014.
[42] Black at §253, 1015.

Coulter v. Pool, Llewellyn's chosen illustration, is the originator of the language of Thrust #8; but it too follows the pattern of the secondary sources in immediately stepping back.

> [L]egislative declaration, whether contained in the title or in the body of a statute, that the statute was intended to promote a certain purpose is not conclusive on the courts, and they may and must inquire into the real, as distinguished from the ostensible, purpose of the statute...[43]

And in stepping back it appears also to be the origin of Parry #8. The case was about the constitutionality of California's "County Engineer Act."[44] Under the act if the county engineer was a county officer then the act was unconstitutional, if an employee then not.[45] The act expressly deemed the county engineer an employee,[46] but then all the remaining provisions fit the role of a county officer as contemplated in the relevant section of the California constitution.[47] Accordingly "we are satisfied that the act in question contemplates the creation of a county office and does, in fact, provide for something more than a mere employment by the board of supervisors of a person to be known as the county engineer."[48]

This is not especially helpful as an illustration of Parry #8, even if it is the source of the language. Rather than a decision between a general statement of design and an incompatible particular statement, it is between a particular classificatory statement and a whole set of general provisions, the requirements of the role.[49] The court decided that "The label placed by the legislature upon its work cannot be permitted to give it a meaning not fairly contemplated within its terms."[50] This is hardly characterizing the "labeling" provision as a governing expression of legislative intent.

In passing, we should note that despite its work at establishing the "real" as opposed to ostensible legislative intent as to the nature of the job, the decision still is contrary to another canon, sometimes called "the *Ashwander* principle": "The Court will not pass upon a constitutional question although properly presented by the record, if there is also present some

---

43 187 Cal. at 185.

44 Id. 187 Cal. at 183-85 ("An act providing for a county engineer for each county in the state, . . . his appointment, manner of removal, qualifications, compensation and duties; transferring to such engineer certain powers, functions and duties heretofore vested in and performed by the county surveyor and members of the board of supervisors; . . . to provide for abolishing the office of county surveyor and for the fixing and levying of taxes for road purposes." (Stats. 1919, p. 1290.) Section 13 of this act provides that it shall be known and designated as "the County Engineer Act,"... We shall concern ourselves only with the constitutionality of the act, for if it be held, as we think it must, to be unconstitutional, then it does not invalidate the plaintiff's claim...")

45 Under Cal. Const., art. XI, sec.4; Id, 187 Cal. at 185.

46 Id, 187 Cal. at 185 ("the verbiage of the act, industriously employed, which, among other things, declares that the county engineer appointed by the board of supervisors "shall be deemed an employee and not a county officer . . . subject to the control and supervision of the board of supervisors."")

47 Id, 187 Cal. at 186-90.

48 Id, 187 Cal. at 185.

49 The opinion provides some five pages of review of provisions of the act requiring the job be classified as a county office. Id, 187 Cal. at 185-190.

50 Id, 187 Cal. at 185 (quoting the district court.)

other ground upon which the case may be disposed of."[51] It makes sense. It is reasonable to presume that our legislature would never intentionally make an unconstitutional law; therefore an interpretation without constitutional problems must have been intended. In *Coulter v. Pool* one might guess that the court thought the only reason the legislature sought to classify county engineers as employees rather than officers was to avoid making otherwise unconstitutional law; thus the intended effect was unconstitutional, the classification provision a mere ruse. The *Ashwander* principle also enhances the legal system's resilience, its methods of damage control. A constitutional decision is terribly difficult to correct; outside the Court only an amendment will turn the trick. So finding another ground —e.g., an interpretation of a statute or a common law decision —that can be over-ruled through the legislative process preserves flexibility and adaptability in the system.

Pairs Nine and Ten

> ***Thrust #9***: "Definitions and rules of construction contained in an interpretation clause are part of the law and binding."
>
> ***Parry #9***: "Definitions and rules of construction in a statute will not be extended beyond their necessary import nor allowed to defeat intention otherwise manifested."
>
> ***Thrust #10***: "A statutory provision requiring a liberal construction does not mean disregard of unequivocal requirements of the statute."
>
> ***Parry #10***: "Where a rule of construction is provided within the statute itself the rule should be applied."[52]

What a mix up! Pair 9 and Pair 10 are paraphrases of each other in converse order: Parry #10 is a sub-part of Thrust #9, and Parry #9 includes Thrust #10. They are about the other two categories of legislated interpretive instructions, definitions and interpretive strategy. Treatises tend to conflate them in their captions,[53] and, after the first generalization, to have little or nothing further to say about definitions.

Definitions and instructions on interpretive strategy ("rules of construction," as they are called in Thrust #9) should be taken separately; the levels of control that can be exercised by each, and thus their effectiveness for communication and determinacy in interpretation are different. Definitions of words made part of an act should be more difficult to avoid than general, overarching statements of interpretive policy.

---

[51] *Ashwander v. TVA*, 297 U.S. 288, 347 (Brandeis, J., concurring). *See* Michael Sinclair, TRADITIONAL TOOLS OF STATUTORY INTERPRETATION, 82-88 (Vandeplas Publishing, 2013).

[52] *Canons* at 402-03.

[53] *E.g.* "Legislative Construction Generally; Statutory Definitions and Interpretation Clauses." R.C.L. *Statutes*, §275, 1047.

I shall treat definitions and rules of interpretation separately, conflating Pairs 9 and 10 to maximize the contrasts.

Thrust #9: "Definitions and rules of construction contained in an interpretation clause are part of the law and binding."

Parry #10: "Where a rule of construction is provided within the statute itself the rule should be applied."

Parry #10 is contained in Thrust #9, so they can be treated together. Llewellyn took Thrust #9 from Black: "The definitions and rules of construction contained *in an interpretation clause* are a part of the law and binding on the courts."[54] Parry #10 is quoted from Llewellyn's illustrative case, *State ex rel. Triay v. Burr*,[55] "Where a rule of construction is contained *in the statute itself*, that rule should be applied if it is necessary to use any rules of construction in determining the meaning of effect of the law."[56]

Definitions:

Only symbols or signs, such as words, can be defined; you cannot define a thing, even though you can talk about it. We cannot even define words except for extremely limited purposes. I can with authority define a term as I use it within a particular text that I write; but I do not have power or authority to do more.[57] Language is public; to communicate with others I have to use public language with its public meanings. A dictionary is a report of public usages, an empirical compendium of a linguistic culture.[58]

Even legislatures do not have the power to dictate the meanings of words to speakers of the language.[59] But just as a writer or speaker may define a term for a limited text and purpose, legislatures also have the power to define the terms to be used in their statutes. When they do so, it is imperative to pay attention; that special definition controls for that legislation.[60]

---

[54] Black at 269, §89 (captioned "INTERPRETATION CLAUSE"), emphasis added.

[55] 79 Fla. 290 (1920), emphasis added.

[56] Id, 79 Fla. at 332.

[57] Of course you will often hear people ask speakers to define their terms. And you will sometimes hear speakers —or read writers —defining their terms. When that happens, one should be on the alert for the rhetorical sleight of hand that will almost always follow.

[58] *See* Michael Sinclair, TRADITIONAL TOOLS OF STATUTORY INTERPRETATION 59-62 (2013).

[59] This is not new. Sutherland (1904) at §360, 687: "Such definitions [in statutes] can, in the nature of things, have no effect except in the construction of the statutes themselves. The meaning of language depends on popular usage, and cannot unless in very slight degree, be effected by legislation."

[60] For example, the Nebraska Supremes: "This definition is furnished by the act itself, and the definition is as much a part of the act as any other portion. The right of the legislature to prescribe the legal definitions of its own language must be conceded." *Herold v. State*, 21 Neb. 50, 52-53; 31 N.W. 258, 259-60 (1887); or New York's Court of Appeals: "[T]he right of the legislature enacting a law to say in the body of the act what the language used shall, as there used, mean, and what shall be the legal effect and operation of the

Definitions do not inspire much attention from the treatise writers; perhaps their validity and effect are too obvious, the challenges to them too few. The New Hampshire supreme court in *Jones v. Surprise*[61] made a very clear statement and became a favored cite. Plaintiffs were trying to enforce an illegal contract for the purchase and delivery of "spirituous liquor" arguing, *inter alia*, that wine, the subject of the contract, was not a spirituous liquor.

> One question in this case is, whether intoxicating wines are included within the terms of this statute. The legislature has defined intoxicating liquor as follows: "By the words spirit,' spirituous,' or intoxicating liquor,' shall be intended all spirituous or intoxicating liquor, and all mixed liquor, any part of which is spirituous or intoxicating, unless otherwise expressly declared." G. L., c. 1, ss. 1, 31. As intoxicating wines and other intoxicating fermented liquors are not expressly excluded from the operation of ss. 13, 18, 19, c. 109, of the Gen. Laws, the only conclusion is that they come within the prohibition of its terms.[62]

Plaintiffs thus lost this point and generally. Courts may often provide quotable language, but seldom, as in this case, where there is a genuine issue over definition.

Parry #9: "*Definitions* and rules of construction in a statute will not be extended beyond their necessary import nor allowed to defeat intention otherwise manifested."

This too comes straight from Black, separated from Thrust #9 only by a semi-colon.[63] But Black, like Llewellyn's other cited secondary source, Corpus Juris, pays little further attention to definitions.

Treatises find one quote doubting a legislated definition to their liking. "[T]he rule applicable to defining clauses is that they should be used only for the purpose of interpreting words that are ambiguous or equivocal and not so as to disturb the meaning of such that are plain."[64] However the case tells us little about problematic applications of definitions in substantive statutory clauses as it dealt with a clash of definitions, one of which had to give way. Following the standard procedure for such problems, the Alabama Supremes used the more particular.[65]

---

law, is undoubted. If they have mistaken the meaning of the words they have used, when read in their ordinary and popular sense, or as legally and technically understood, still they may, in terms, declare what the law shall be for the future, under and by virtue of the terms employed." *The Farmers' Bank of Fayetteville v. Hale*, 59 N.Y. 53, 62-63 (1874); Black at §89, 269-70; 59 C.J. *Statutes* §567, 948.

[61] 64 N.H. 243 (1886).

[62] 64 N.H. at 245.

[63] Black at §89 ,269 (captioned "INTERPRETATION CLAUSE"). ("but they [definitions and rules of construction contained in an interpretation clause] will not be extended beyond their necessary import, nor will they be allowed to defeat the intention of the legislature otherwise clearly manifested.")

[64] *Ivey v. Railway Fuel Co.*, 218 Ala. 407, 409 (1928), quoted at 59 CJ *Statutes* §567, 948.

[65] Id. ("[W]here there is a conflict in sections or provisions in pari materia, one dealing specially with a subject and the other doing so generally, the special section must prevail. "Generalibus specialia derogant."")

A definition applies generally throughout the act of which it is part, while a particular substantive provision of the act constrains particular behavior. On this ground Sutherland makes an argument for the possibility of negating a statutory definition.

> Where positive provisions are at variance with the definitions which it [the act in question] contains, the latter, it seems, must be modified by the clear intent of the former on the principle that the special controls the general.[66]

The case cited in support, *Egerton v. Third Municipality*,[67] shows a remarkable, but perhaps in the circumstances understandable hostility to definitions.[68] Egerton was a creditor of the defendant municipality and wanted to garnish the tax obligations of residents, apparently arguing that by the statutory definitions his debtor was not a civil or political corporation, so lacked sovereign immunity.[69] He failed.

Other than isolated forays such as these, legislated definitions have commanded their fields. With respect to definitions, then, support for Llewellyn's Parry #9 is scant at best, and examples are too few to qualify it as a rule or canon of construction. For the limited extent of the act of which it is part, a definition rules.

Rules of Construction:

"Where in an act it is declared that it shall receive a certain construction, the courts are bound by that construction, though otherwise the language would have been held to mean a different thing."[70] This is categorical as to the authority of rules of construction, but in application it may not be so clear.

Sutherland, in a useful passage quoted in full by Black, distinguishes definition and interpretation clauses in application by relative generality:

> There is a manifest difference between definitive or interpretation clauses which are special and those which are general; the former always have the most

---

[66] Sutherland (1904) §360, 687. The same argument also occurs at Black at §89, 272-73.

[67] 1 La. Ann. 435 (1846). The only other cited case, *Farmers' Bank v. Hale*, 59 N.Y. 53 (1874), does not support the argument; it deals with resolving the relationship between state and national banking limitations when they are required to treat state and national banks equally.

[68] Much of the Louisiana Code of the time had been translated from French, generating peculiar jurisprudential problems:

> The definition relied on from the English side of one of the articles of the Code, proves nothing but the ignorance of the person who translated it from the French. Definitions are, at best, unsafe guides in the administration of justice; and their frequent recurrence in the Louisiana Code, is the greatest defect in that body of laws. ... [T]he former Supreme Court said that, the statutory provisions of the Code were often at variance with the definitions it contains, and that, in those cases, it was a sound rule of interpretation to consider the definitions as limited or modified by the clear intent of the positive enactments.

Egerton v. Third Municipality, 1 La. Ann. at 437.

[69] Id, 1 La. Ann. at 437. ("It has been argued that the defendants are not a civil or political corporation, under the definition given by the Civil Code.")

[70] *Smith v. State*, 28 Ind. 321, 325 (1867).

> controlling effect where it is obvious that the legislature, without misconception of the effect of other legislation, have precisely in view the particular words or provisions to which the clause in question ostensibly applies.[71]

A definition has a particularity in point that is unlikely in an interpretation clause. Not surprisingly, therefore, interpretation clauses have met with more equivocation —and in England, with outright hostility[72] —than have definitions. Especially is this so where the scope of the construction rule is general.

> The terms of a general construction act should be read into every statute subsequently enacted, but it is not intended to dispense with the usual rules of interpretation.[73]

Parry #9 and Thrust #10 thus have some grip here.

Parry #9: "Definitions and *rules of construction* in a statute will not be extended beyond their necessary import nor allowed to defeat intention otherwise manifested."

Thrust #10: "A statutory provision requiring a liberal construction does not mean disregard of unequivocal requirements of the statute."

Thrust #10 is a subcategory of Parry #9; it appears to paraphrase Corpus Juris.[74]

Llewellyn's illustrative case for Thrust #10, *County of Los Angeles v. Payne*,[75] is the only case Corpus Juris cites. Payne claimed, *inter alia*, that notice of a proposed municipal waterworks project was improper.[76] Wrong, said the court, albeit that "We proceed to the inquiry with the mandate of the statute in mind that it shall be liberally construed to effect the purposes thereof." The words of the statute were clear and had clearly been complied with, if only just.[77]

Llewellyn's illustrative case for Parry #9, *In re Bissell*, [78] is not especially illustrative. Milton Bissell wanted to be a candidate in the Jamestown mayoral election but failed to file the required petition. He argued that sound jurisprudence and the statute itself required a liberal interpretation of election law, allowing him onto the ballot. But this general interpretive policy could not defeat the clearly expressed requirements of the statute: "While it is provided in the law that the law itself is to receive a liberal construction, this does not authorize us to disregard

---

[71] Sutherland (1904) §360, 686; Black at §89, 274.

[72] *State v. Standard Oil Co.*, 61 Ore. 438, 445-46 (1912); Black at §89, 270-72.

[73] 59 CJ *Statutes* §566, 947.

[74] 59 C.J.*Statutes* §567, 948: "Where the language of the statute is clear, it must be complied with, even though the statute contains a provision for liberal construction."

[75] 82 Cal. App. 210; 255 P. 281 (1927)

[76] "The County Water Works District Act (Deering's Gen. Laws of 1923, p. 3784) requires that "The said clerk shall also cause a notice . . . to be published at least once a week for two consecutive weeks in a newspaper of general circulation..."; Id, 82 Cal. App. at 212.

[77] Id, 82 Cal. App. at 212; 255 P. at 282 ("notice thereof was given by the clerk by posting in three public places and also by publication in the "Compton News-Tribune" on January 19, 1926, and January 26, 1926."

[78] *In re Bissell*, 245 A.D. 395, 282 N.Y.S. 983 (1935)

any of its provisions. Here we have no reason offered as to why the law was not complied with and we feel that the terms of the law are conclusive against the contention of the appellant."[79] Of course.

The more frequent examples are of criminal statutes, usually construed narrowly under the rule of lenity,[80] but specifically required by statute to be broadly construed. Then the specifically legislated interpretation prevails.

> But this rule [lenity] has been abolished in this State by the Penal Code, the fourth section of which provides that "the rule of the common law, that Penal Statutes are to be strictly construed, has no application to this code. All its provisions are to be construed according to the fair import of their terms, with a view to effect its objects and to promote justice."
>
> Tested by this rule of construction, it is evident, we think, that in making it a felony to steal a cow, the Legislature intended to include under that designation a heifer also, which is but a young cow.[81]

It makes sense. Lenity is a standard inference from accepted societal presumptions to legislative intent. Obviously the legislature itself can expressly negate that inference.

A good example is *People v. Dobbins* from the California supreme court. Two sections of the California Penal Code gave conflicting rules for how much district attorney Dobbins could keep of the fines he collected; the earlier Penal Code said one half, the more recently enacted "fish commission fund" gave the state only a quarter.[82] The California Political Code had an interpretive provision making "the section[] last in numerical order" prevail,[83] contrary to the general interpretative resolution that the more recently enacted better indicated prevailing legislative intent. The court found a way out, narrowly construing the interpretive section of the California Political Code to apply only where the clash is between statutes enacted together, as part of the same act;[84] thus it saved the old maxim of priority to the temporally later, and for the district attorney a quarter of the fines for the state.[85] Legislative intent, even though not so clearly manifested, prevailed over an enacted interpretive rule.

As the interpretive goal is to determine legislative intent and apply it to the case at hand, it makes sense to construe general interpretive edicts from the legislature in such a way as not to

---

[79] *In re Bissell*, 245 A.D. at 396, 282 N.Y.S. at 984. *Sim. People v. Zito*, 237 Ill. 434, 439 (1908).

[80] "The doctrine of strict construction in cases of penalties has been long and uniformly established in this court. ... The doctrine is so elementary and well recognized that it does not need other authorities for its support." *Hankins v. State*, 106 Ill. 628, 632(1883)(citations omitted.)

[81] *People v. Soto*, 49 Cal. 67, 70 (1874).

[82] 73 Cal. 257, 258-59 (1887).

[83] 73 Cal. at 259 ("section 4484 of the Political Code ... provides as follows: "If conflicting provisions are found in different sections of the same chapter or article, the provisions of the sections last in numerical order must prevail, unless such construction is inconsistent with the meaning of such chapter or article."")

[84] Id. ("So it has always been the rule that when different provisions of a statute, all passed at the same time, could not be reconciled, the one that came last in point of position must prevail.")

[85] Id. 73 Cal. at 259-60.

disrupt that process or negate that goal. Parry #9, even though not a formulation of canonical stature, encapsulates exactly that sense; Thrust #10 is continuous with Parry #9 and rests on the same rational, as the better examples make clear.

Resolution

Statements of Purpose

Thrust #8, "Where design has been distinctly stated no place is left for construction," claims much too much. The legislature may state its design or purpose as distinctly as you wish, but that does not mean the application of following substantive provisions will be free from interpretive difficulties. The illustrative cases, *Smith v. State* and *S.S.White Dental Manufacturing Co. v. Commonwealth*, amply demonstrate the point: how to serve the clear legislative purpose in the circumstances at issue still required interpretation and reasoning. Cases decided with reference to a legislated statement of purpose show that while it constrains interpretive choices, eliminating those contrary to it, it does not determine which among the remaining interpretive possibilities must be applied. Thus the accurate contrary of Thrust #8 would be: "Where design has been distinctly stated there may still be room left for construction."

Parry #8, "Courts have the power to inquire into real —as distinct from ostensible — purpose," does not state the contrary of Thrust #8; it doesn't even intersect with Thrust #8. Literally, it is about legislative duplicity: the "real —as distinct from ostensible —purpose"? Enacting a provision without intending what it says? One would hope that instances, and subsequent cases, should be exceedingly rare.

Coulter v. Pool, Llewellyn's chosen illustration and source of the language of both Thrust #8 and Parry #8, may be such a case: the legislature seems to have deemed the county engineer an employee solely for the purpose of avoiding constitutional constraints. But the case is not about a general statement of purpose or design at all; it is about the clash of one provision of an act —deeming the county engineer an employee —with all the other sources on the topic making him or her a county officer. I have not seen another illustration of similar legislative sleight of hand.

Even if we were to reformulate Pair 8 into something more plausible (for example "A distinct statement of legislative purpose constrains interpretation of substantive provisions" and "The purpose of a particular provision determines its application") there is no serious problem of incompatibility here. The court must use the language of the legislation and ordinary interpretive procedures to resolve the issue.

The generally applicable argument is summarized in another canon: "The general gives way to the particular," or "If one provision is more particular, focuses more precisely on the subject matter at hand, it has to be followed rather than the more general one."[86] Strikingly, *Coulter v. Pool*, Llewellyn's chosen illustration of Parry #8 is a counter example, giving the general provisions legal effect against the particular![87]

Definitions

If we confine Pair 9 to definitions, there is no problem. Thrust #9$^{def.}$, "Definitions contained in an interpretation clause are part of the law and binding," would simply state the power of the legislature to define the terms used within an act. Parry #9$^{def.}$, "Definitions in a statute will not be extended beyond their necessary import nor allowed to defeat intention otherwise manifested," would be a compatible truism, literally a corollary of Thrust #9$^{def.}$. If the legislature chooses to define a term, a court has no mandate to expand the term's meaning beyond that definition.

Sutherland's argument that a substantive provision inconsistent with a definition should take priority "on the principle that the special controls the general"[88] is fallacious. A definition takes as its domain of application the act of which it is part; as to that it is general. A substantive provision within the act governs a particular aspect of behavior, and thus may be called particular. But the domains of governance are utterly different: the definition governs meanings within the statute, a part of law; the substantive provision governs behavior in the world, exogenous to the law. To compare particularity and generality of the two is to compare incommensurables, a category mistake.[89] In Llewellyn's secondary sources, the only other quotable language hostile to definitions rested on a case of incompatible definitions; of course a choice —preferably a reasoned preference —of one over the other would be necessary.

So you might dredge up the odd quibble, but the only generality on statutory definitions worth mention is that they control meanings within their prescribed domain. Of course that doesn't mean they are always clear or themselves require no construction. Nor does it mean that they control meanings outside the act of which they are part. But within their limited sphere of control, definitions command.

Interpretation clauses

Thrust #9$^{stat.}$, "Rules of construction contained in an interpretation clause are part of the law and binding," and its equivalent, Parry #10, "Where a rule of construction is provided within the statute itself the rule should be applied," are also underlyingly compatible with their supposedly contrary pairs, Parry #9$^{stat.}$, "Rules of construction in a statute will not be extended

---

86 *See* Michael Sinclair, TRADITIONAL TOOLS OF STATUTORY INTERPRETATION 129-30 (Vandeplas Publishing, 2013).

87 Perhaps kinder would be to construe it as an interpretation of the California constitutional provision in question —Cal. Const., art. XI, sec.4 —saying it applied to substance not merely to labels.

88 Sutherland (1904) §360, 687.

89 Gilbert Ryle, THE CONCEPT OF MIND, 16-17 (1949).

beyond their necessary import nor allowed to defeat intention otherwise manifested," and its corollary, Thrust #10, "A statutory provision requiring a liberal construction does not mean disregard of unequivocal requirements of the statute."

That an act includes an interpretation clause does not mean that the legislature does not intend what the words of the substantive provisions say. A rule requiring a liberal construction does not grant license to ignore or go beyond the language of a substantive statute within its scope, as Parry #9 and Thrust #10 suggest. That would make the intent of the legislature in enacting that substantive provision irrelevant, contrary to the fundamental precept of interpretation, to implement legislative intent. Worse, it would make the legislative effort in formulating the language and enacting and promulgating the substantive provision irrelevant, ineffective, contrary to Thrust #16, "Every word and clause must be given effect."

However, if in a particular statute within an act the legislature intends an interpretation other than according to the general interpretation clause, why should it not have the power to implement that intent? Parry #9$^{stat.}$, "Rules of construction in a statute will not be extended beyond their necessary import nor allowed to defeat intention otherwise manifested," says no more than that. Suppose the legislature tells us, for example, "generally interpret this act liberally" but in this particular section, "interpret strictly"? This would simply make an exception in the statute to a more general requirement.[90]

Pairs 8, 9, and 10: Conclusion

It would have been better for Llewellyn's list of dueling canons had Pairs 8, 9 and 10 not been included. There is no dueling going on among their thrusts and parries (although one can find inconcinnities with other canons.) Indeed, there is nothing canonical about any of the selected formulae, nor much in the way of cases to illustrate or support them.

The premises of these pairs are that implementing legislative intent is the goal of statutory interpretation and a legislature has power over that intent. Should it choose to tell us its purposes, or how to interpret its statutes, or what key words are to mean, it has the power to do so and interpreters are as bound as the governed are by substantive provisions. Of course such interpretive clauses do not solve all problems of interpretation. But one ought not to claim canonical status for corollaries or examples or intentional exceptions (especially when they lack judicial support.)

---

[90] In 1953, Llewellyn must have been well aware of this in his work on the Uniform Commercial Code. Generally it is to be interpreted liberally (§1-102(1)), but some sections are clearly to be interpreted strictly, for example §2-205 "Firm Offers" and the contractual delivery risk allocation sections, §§2-319 to 2-322, and demonstrate that intent by their choice of language.

Pair Eleven

THRUST: "Titles do not control meaning; preambles do not expand scope; section headings do not change language."
PARRY: "The title may be consulted as a guide when there is doubt or obscurity in the body; preambles may be consulted to determine rationale, and thus the true construction of terms; section headings may be looked upon as part of the statute itself.."[1]

There are three separate pairs here, the first to do with the use of titles of acts, the second to do with preambles and the third to do with section captions. It would have been sensible to have separated them into three, as I shall do. Different considerations apply to the use of titles and captions, and preambles are functionally quite different; the idea that a single canon should cover all three is obviously implausible. And if demonstrating inconsistency was the aim, Llewellyn might have found formulations that create at least a chance of potential clash. The mismatches of their verbs —'control,' 'expand' and 'change'; 'consult,' 'consult' and 'look up' respectively —preclude contrariety.

Thrust #11a: "Titles do not control meaning."

Parry #11a: "The title may be consulted as a guide when there is doubt or obscurity in the body."

The words appear to be adapted from Black at §83, "The title cannot control or vary the meaning of the enacting part, if the latter is plain and unambiguous. But if there is doubt or obscurity in the body of the act, the title may be consulted as a guide to the probable meaning of the legislature, and should be accorded some weight in the interpretation."[2] In ordinary usage there is no clash, nor incompatibility nor inconsistency in Pair #11a.

Worse: Thrust #11a is mostly false in those states that have constitutional "one subject" provisions, where titles do control the scope of their subject statutes.[3] For example, New Jersey:

---

[1] *Canons* at 403.
[2] Black §83, 244, in the section captioned "TITLE."
[3] For more on titles see Michael Sinclair, TRADITIONAL TOOLS OF STATUTORY INTERPRETATION, 53 (Vandeplas Publishing, 2013).

> To avoid improper influence which may result from intermixing in one and the same act such things as have no proper relation to each other, every law shall embrace but one object, and that shall be expressed in the title.[4]

The point is to give notice of what's to come, not just to the governed but also to legislators voting on a bill.[5]

Llewellyn cites in support of Thrust#11a only the relatively recent *Westbrook v. McDonald*,[6] a dispute about the procedure for a referendum to amend Arkansas divorce law. Petitioners had collected the necessary signatures, but had made minor errors on the forms for which their referendum had been denied by the elections official. They sought a writ of mandamus. Among the errors was a slight inaccuracy in the number and date of the statute to be amended. The Arkansas Supreme Court said:

> The purpose of stating the number of the act and the date of its approval was to aid in its identification, but these errors could not have been misleading when an exact copy of the act otherwise appeared on the petition. It is settled law that even the title of an act is not controlling in its construction, although it is considered in determining its meaning when such meaning is otherwise in doubt.[7]

The last sentence does support Thrust #11a on titles, but it is plainly dictum —a comparison — and is immediately undermined, giving equal support to Parry #11a. So the case scarcely supports Thrust#11a, let alone a clash with Parry#11a.

The reason titles deserve weight in interpretation is the role they play in communicating to one searching for the right statute to guide their behavior. A title suggesting a scope narrower than the statute would be deceptive, perhaps turning away the researcher;[8] but a title of breadth more encompassing than the statutory text would deceive only the lazy.[9] It would not, however, contain the substantive constraint provided in the body of the statute. Thus one might reasonably argue that a title cannot change the scope of a statute.

Nevertheless, the question may not be about scope so much as the meaning of the statute itself and the intent of the legislature. Then the title could provide an interpretive clue, although

---

4 New Jersey constitution, Art.4, §7, ¶4.

5 *See e.g. Stockton v. The Central Railroad Co. of New Jersey*, 50 N.J. Eq. 52, 70 (1892); *People v. Tibbitts*, 56 ILL. 2d 56, (1973).

6 184 Ark. 740 (1931).

7 Id, 184 Ark. at 746.

8 "The title of the act is unquestionably limited to "receivers of public money;" a term which undoubtedly excludes the defendants in the present case." *United States v. Fisher*, 6 U.S. (2 Cranch) 358, 387(1805); *contra United States v. Briggs*, 50 U.S. (9 How.) 351, 355 (1850)(The title restricted the subject timber to that used for naval purposes, the text of the statute had no such limitation. The latter controlled.)

9 *Eastman v. McAlpin*, 1 Ga. 157, 171 (1846).

it should still be treated with caution as a title is "not always or necessarily subject to the same scrutiny" as the statute itself (often called "the enacting clause.")[10]

Llewellyn cites just such a case, *Brown v. Robinson*,[11] in support of Parry#11a ; it is also one of those rare cases in which the title seems to have made an interpretive difference, not merely lending support to an otherwise established interpretation. The plaintiff driver clearly had right of way; the defendant would have been defenseless except that the plaintiff's car had a new motor, not recorded in its registration: was it registered according to the required formalities? The statute allowed "A motor vehicle ... shall be deemed to be registered ... notwithstanding any mistake in so much of the description thereof contained in the application for registration as relates to the engine, serial or maker's number thereof." But the owner of the car may not have been mistaken: he understood little English —"his wife attended to most of the details concerning the automobile" —thus was simply ignorant of the requirements. The title of the act read "An Act relative to the effect of certain misstatements in applications for registration of motor vehicles ... ." Thus:

> Resort may be had to the title of a statute as an aid in its interpretation. ... "Misstatements" in the title is a word of broader signification than "mistake" in the body of §1 and has a tendency to indicate that the latter was not designed to be used in a narrow or technical sense.[12]

Judgment for plaintiff was affirmed.

Resolution:

There is not even a superficial inconsistency between Thrust and Parry #11a; when they occur in cases, with nearly canonical regularity they occur together. Even Llewellyn's exemplar for Thrust #11a, *Westbrook v. McDonald*, illustrates. The particular enacting clause is the primary control, but if it is under-determinate for some reason —ambiguity, fuzziness, indeterminate scope ... —then naturally resort may be had to its title , just as it may be had to other indicators of the intent of the enacting legislature.[13] This is simply a version of the Plain Meaning Rule, Pair #12, plus the fundamental democratic premise of statutory interpretation, legislative supremacy.

---

10 Black at §83, 251. *But see Caminetti, supra*: the title, "The White-slave Traffic Act," probably got more attention than the very detailed wording of the operative clauses of the statute. [242 U.S. 482] Certainly the Court's construction of the act was of broader scope than this title would lead one to believe; no slavery, nor anything mistakable for slavery, was involved.

11 275 Mass. 55 (1931).

12 Id, 275 Mass. at 57-58.

13 See, for example, *Bradford v. Jones*, 1 Md. 351, 369 (1851), *People v. O'Brien*, 111 N.Y. 1, 60 (1888).

Thus the general position is that the title may be used as an interpretive aid if the relevant statutory text is under-determinate, but that it cannot contradict or change the statute.[14] Splitting this sensible and justified position into two creates neither a pair of canons nor a legitimate clash.

Thrust #11b: "[P]reambles do not expand scope;"

Parry #11b: "[P]reambles may be consulted to determine the rationale, and thus the true construction of terms."

A preamble should contain the reason motivating the statute's enactment —facts about society showing the need for legislative control —and the ends or goals of the legislation, winding up with "… wherefore be it enacted that:". A good preamble will effectively answer the first three *Heydon's Case* questions:

> 1st. What was the common law before the making of the Act.
> 2nd. What was the mischief and defect for which the common law did not provide.
> 3rd. What remedy the Parliament hath resolved and appointed to cure the disease of the commonwealth.[15]

Thus they can be a great help to a judge if the statute itself is under-determinate. It cannot be repeated too often that if the language of the statute itself is clear and determinate and not absurd or monstrous in application, then resort to other interpretive resources is not justified. Courts say it about preambles; for example: "A preamble … is not to be entirely rejected where the statute is ambiguous, although it will not be resorted to to create a doubt or misunderstanding which otherwise does not exist."[16] By being published along with the statute, and having been in the contemplation of the enacting legislature, preambles have the appearance of authority; they look more authoritative than, say, a committee report. Many writers like to quote that "The preamble is the key to open the understanding of the statute."[17]

The problem with using a preamble is that it is not enacted, it is not a part of the statute, and thus is not law.[18] It couldn't be law: A legislature cannot legislate facts. For example, when

---

[14] Black at §83, 246; *State ex rel. City of Mobile v. Board of Revenue*, 202 Ala. 303, 304 (1918); *Hadden v. The Collector*, 72 U.S. 107, 110 (1866); *Church of the Holy Trinity v. United States*, 143 U.S. 457, 462 (1892).

[15] *Heydon's Case*, 30 Co. 7a, 76 Eng.Rep. 637 (Exch. 1584).

[16] *Huntworth v. Tanner*, 87 Wash. 670, 676-77 (1915)(Llewellyn's chosen illustration for Thrust #11b).

[17] *E.g.*, *Coosaw Mining Co. v. South Carolina,* 144 U.S. 550, 562 (1892), *Price v. Forrest*, 173 U.S. 410, 427 (1899), attributing it variously to Lord Coke (*Huntworth v. Tanner*, 87 Wash. 670, 677 (1915)) or Francis Bacon (*Montesquieu v. Heil*, 4 La. 51, 54 (1832)) or both, (*White v. Levy*, 91 Ala. 175, 177 (1890)), or to other sources, such as Sedgwick on the Const. of Statutes and Const. Law (2d Ed.), p. 43, (Id) or Bouvier, Law Dictionary, tit. Preamble., and (*Huntworth v. Tanner*, 87 Wash. 670, 677 (1915).

[18] "[T]he preamble is no part of the act" *Yazoo and MississippiValley RR Co. v. Thomas*, 132 U.S. 174, 188 (1889); "The preamble to an act neither confers nor restricts powers, rights, privileges or duties, and, strictly speaking, is no part of the act itself." *White v. Levy*, 91 Ala. 175, 176 (1890).

in 2007 astronomers officially demoted Pluto from planetary status, New Mexico enacted a statute saying that nevertheless, when it passed over New Mexico, Pluto was indeed a planet.[19] Did that statute, make any difference to Pluto, or to the astronomers' (even New Mexico astronomers) classification?

Thrust #11b, "[P]reambles do not expand scope," is, then, a truism; it follows from the nature of the preamble and the powers of the legislature. To expand the scope would be to legislate over a domain greater than the statute; to narrow the scope would be to take away from the domain of the statute; either would be to legislate. It is repeated by the writers of treatises and judicial opinions: "The preamble to a statute can neither expand nor control the scope of application of the enacting clause … ."[20]

If the statute itself is clear, interpretation is at an end, no resort to preambles (or titles, captions, interpretation clauses or legislative history) is necessary. But if it is not clear, if its application to the problem at hand is not obvious, then the preamble is often going to be a valuable source of indicia of legislative intent. Thus Parry #11b, "[P]reambles may be consulted to determine the rationale, and thus the true construction of terms," is also generally accepted.[21] The difficulty, and the potential for a genuine clash between Thrust and Parry #11b, is that the unclarity that makes resort to "the rationale, and thus the true construction of terms" of a statute necessary very commonly comes from under-determinacy of a common noun phrase or predicate: to whom or what does it apply? That looks like a question of scope.[22]

Llewellyn's case in support of Thrust #11b, *Huntworth v. Tanner*,[23] illustrates. Huntworth ran a school teacher employment agency, placing school teachers in positions throughout the Pacific Northwest for an application fee of $2 plus a placement fee of 5% of the teacher's first year's salary. Washington State adopted by ballot initiative a prohibition on employment agencies' charging employees, "Initiative Measure No.8, being popularly known as the Employment Agency Law." The language of the operative prohibition was:

---

[19] HOUSE JOINT MEMORIAL 54, 48TH LEGISLATURE - STATE OF NEW MEXICO - FIRST SESSION, 2007: " …NOW, THEREFORE, BE IT RESOLVED BY THE LEGISLATURE OF THE STATE OF NEW MEXICO that, as Pluto passes overhead through New Mexico's excellent night skies, it be declared a planet and that March 13, 2007 be declared "Pluto Planet Day" at the legislature."

[20] Black at §84, 253, quoted *Huntworth v. Tanner*, 87 Wash. 670, 676 (1915); *sim*. Sutherland ('04) §341, 652 ; 25 R.C.L. *Statutes* §266, 1030.

[21] *Price v. Forrest*, 173 U.S. 410, 427 (1899), *United States v. Fisher*, 2 Cranch, 358, 386; *United States v. Palmer*, 3 Wheat. 610, 631; *Beard v. Rowan*, 9 Pet. 301, 317; *Holy Trinity Church v. United States*, 143 U.S. 457, 462; *Coosaw Mining Co. v. South Carolina*, 144 U.S. 550."); similar language is commonplace in states; *see, e.g.*, *White v. Levy*, 91 Ala. 175, 177 (1890); *Gemmer et al. v. State, ex rel. Stephens*, 163 Ind. 150, 159 (1904); *Huntworth v. Tanner*, 87 Wash. 670, 677 (1915); *City of Mobile v. Revenue and road Commissioners*, 202 Ala. 303, 304-05 (1918); and secondary resources: 25 R.C.L. *Statutes* §266, 1030; Sutherland ('04) §341, 654; Black at §84, 253; 59 CORPUS JURIS §598, 1004-05.

[22] Of course this is to conflate meaning and scope.

[23] 87 Wash. 670 (1915).

> Sec. 2. It shall be unlawful for any employment agent, his representative, or any other person to demand or receive either directly or indirectly from any person seeking employment, or from any person on his or her behalf, any remuneration or fee whatsoever for furnishing him or her with employment or with information leading thereto.[24]

Did "any person seeking employment" include school teachers? The preamble, by using the word "worker" rather than "any person," gave reason for doubt:

> Section 1. The welfare of the state of Washington depends on the welfare of its workers and demands that they be protected from conditions that result in their being liable to imposition and extortion.
>
> The state of Washington therefore exercising herein its police and sovereign power declares that the system of collecting fees from the workers for furnishing them with employment, or with information leading thereto, results frequently in their becoming the victims of imposition and extortion and is therefore detrimental to the welfare of the state.[25]

Thus the dispute: plaintiff Huntworth, seeking to enjoin his prosecution, argued that section 2 did not reach school teachers; the attorney general argued that "any person" was completely general and school teaching was employment. The trial court agreed with the attorney general and upheld the defendant attorney general's demurrer. The Washington Supreme Court disagreed; it gave Huntworth his injunction.

But to disagree it had to allow the preamble's "worker" to restrain section 2's "any person," contrary to Thrust #11a. One way out was available: despite its placement and its fitting the general definition of a preamble, section 1 was not a preamble.

> While it may be true that the ballot title and section 1 are in a sense preambulary [*sic*], they nevertheless go further than to declare merely an evil and a purpose to correct it by legislation. ... Under these rules section 1 is as much a part of the act as sections 2 and 3.[26]

In addition section 1, the preamble manque, was voted on in the referendum and, significantly, was within the scope of the performative matrix "Be it enacted by the people of the state of Washington:".[27]

---

[24] Id, 87 Wash. at 672,

[25] Id.

[26] Id, 87 Wash. at 676-77; Further: "A 'preamble' is, strictly speaking, matter that is descriptive of the purpose of the law, making general reference to its objects. ... A clause at the beginning of a Constitution or statute explanatory of the reasons for its enactment and the objects sought to be accomplished. ... It not only defines an evil and a purpose to correct it, but also recognizes and defines a certain class, 'workers,' as being the object of the law's solicitude, and, as a class, entitled to the protection of the police power. The preamble is not wholly descriptive. It is a declaration of a policy that is intended to advance the police power into a new field, and to bring within its protection a certain class of men ... ." and more, a veritable text book! Id, 87 Wash. at 676-78.

[27] Id, 87 Wash. at 672. Perhaps the best definition of 'preamble' may be the functional "Language published along with the statute immediately preceding "Be it enacted that"."

The decision's support for either Thrust or Parry #11b is *dictum* at best. One less devoted to the thaumaturgical power of words might have acknowledged that section 1 was a preamble and gave meaning to the enacting clause, section 2, thus better reflecting legislative intent. One hostile to judicial interpretation might well say, as the dissent did, that this was using the preamble as a key, a key to unlocking and greatly reducing the clear intent expressed in section 2.

Resolution:

If the statute is less than clear in application to the problem at hand, then the preamble, like the title, is a reliable and easily accessible aid in determining the intent of the legislature. Coming as it does along with the printed text of the statute actually enacted, and like the title presumably read by those legislators who actually read the statute (perhaps by more), it carries with it a presumptive reliability. The key problem is not the use of a preamble to solve a problem of statutory under-determinacy, but to create it. Using exogenous resources to create an indeterminacy in an otherwise clear statute is exactly what the Plain Meaning Rule, Thrust #12, prohibits. The Washington Supremes' opinion in *Huntworth v. Tanner* did precisely that, but having first finessed the issue by deciding the preamble was not a preamble.

Thrust #11c: "[S]ection headings do not change language."

Parry #11c: "[S]ection headings may be looked upon as part of the statute itself.."

Both primary and secondary sources with which Llewellyn worked provide little on section captions. There was certainly not enough reported litigation or commentator interest or consistency to produce a canon, let alone two. Llewellyn would have done better to have left captions out of Pair 11.

As it is, his Thrust #11c is trivially true: only revisionary legislation can change a statute's language. Presumably he meant something like "Its section heading does not change the meaning of a statute." I shall assume so, although there is nothing in Llewellyn's cited sources suggesting anything like canonical status for this or anything similar.

Section captions are distinguishable from the titles. Although the title of an act may be required by law and also be a part of the act itself, section captions commonly are not. Often you will find at the beginning of a compilation a disclaimer to the effect that section captions have been inserted by the editors and are for convenience only and not part of the statute. For example, in Michigan, "The Section and subsection headings have been editorially supplied."[28] It

---

[28] Michigan Compiled Laws Annotated, Preface to each volume at iii. *Sim.* "The section headings for Massachusetts General Laws Annotated have been editorially supplied." 13 Mass.Gen.Laws Ann. p.2 (1996).

is also important that captions not be titles so that they not come under constitutional "one subject" rules, giving them the power to limit —in a sense to change —meaning.

In *Gully v. Jackson International Co.*,[29] Llewellyn found a case that supported Parry #11c, although not perhaps directly. Plaintiff was a tax collector seeking a $200 tax from the defendant, which sold tractors for agricultural purposes only. The tax statute read: "Sec. 171. Road Machinery Dealers.—Upon each person engaged in the business of selling tractors and/or road machinery, a state wide tax of two hundred dollars." Was "Road Machinery Dealers" a title, restricting the scope of the statute under Mississippi's "one subject" law? Or was it merely a caption, for convenience of reference only? The Mississippi Supremes finessed the problem by re-characterizing such sub-headings as "lead lines," thus "part of the statute itself."[30] That way it could find that the legislature intended to tax only sales of road machinery, not agricultural tractors, and the defendant did not have to pay the tax.[31] It's thin support for Parry #11c, but as I said, the pickings are slim.

Yet Llewellyn might have found the California Supreme Court's straightforward statement that section captions are part of the statute itself in *Keyes v. Cyrus*,[32] and New York's Court of Appeals: "These headings or inscriptions … are rather parts of the statute itself limiting and defining its effect."[33] The Missouri Supreme Court found the exact contrary in *State v. Maurer*:[34]

> The headings of chapters, articles or sections are not to be considered in construing our statutes; these *indicia* are mere arbitrary designations inserted for convenience of reference by clerks or revisers, who have no legislative authority, and are, therefore, powerless to lessen or expand the letter or meaning of the law.[35]

Llewellyn's cited secondary source[36] and the United States Supreme Court take a middle road, treating captions not as part of the statute, but as a resource, potentially useful in curing

---

[29] 165 Miss. 103 (1933).

[30] 165 Miss. at 112-13 ("… We hold that these headings to the various sections of the privilege tax statute are not titles, nor subtitles in a strict sense; they are lead lines, and these lead lines are a part of the statute itself.")

[31] How did it deal with the "and/or"? The court held that "this symbol "and/or" was not a part of the English language. Laws are to be strictly construed against the taxing power. The power cannot be implied. All doubts must be resolved in favor of the taxpayer." [!] 165 Miss. at 113.

[32] 100 Cal. 322, 325 (1893).

[33] *People ex rel. Watson v. Lamphier*, 104 Misc. 622, 625, 172 N.Y.S. 247, 248 (1918).

[34] 255 Mo. 152 (1914).

[35] 255 Mo. at 160.

[36] 59 CORPUS JURIS: §599, p1007 "For the purpose of clearing up ambiguities in the enacting clauses of statutes, reference may also be had to the headings of portions of statutes, such as titles, articles, chapters, and sections."

ambiguities and other uncertainties in their statutes. In *Knowlton v. Moore*,[37] the 1899 Supreme Court used a caption to rebut one of the defendant taxpayer's arguments:

> On the very threshold, the theory that the tax is not on particular legacies or distributive shares passing upon a death, but is on the whole amount of the personal property of the deceased, is rebutted by the heading, which describes what is taxed, not as the estates of deceased persons, but as "legacies and distributive shares of personal property." This, whilst not conclusive, is proper to be considered in interpreting the statute, when ambiguity exists and a literal interpretation will work out wrong or injury.[38]

Resolution:

Not surprisingly then there is no uniformity of opinion or expression, nor even regularity of usage sufficient to support a canon on the interpretive role of section captions. Llewellyn must have been well aware of this as he made sure to eliminate uncertainty in the Uniform Commercial Code by including:

> **Section 1-109. Section Captions**
>
> Section Captions are part of this Act.

But even were either Thrust or Parry #11c an accurate reflection of general judicial views, the pair would not be inconsistent. Of course a caption cannot change the meaning of a statute, even in those states in which it is held to be a part of the statute or a lead line to it. At most it would be an interpretive resource; at least it would be of no relevance at all, and appropriately so where captions have been inserted by a publisher's clerk.

The pragmatic answer to the legitimacy and value of titles, captions, and preambles must be Chief Justice Marshall's dictum in *United States v. Fisher*: "Where the mind labors to discover the design of the legislature, it seizes everything from which aid can be derived … ."[39]

---

[37] 178 U.S. 41 (1899)

[38] 178 U.S. at 65.

[39] *United States v. Fisher*, 2 Cranch 358, 386 (U.S. 1805).

Pair Twelve

THRUST: "If language is plain and unambiguous it must be given effect."
PARRY: "Not when literal interpretation would lead to absurd or mischievous consequences or thwart manifest purpose."[1]

Pair 12 is Llewellyn's formulation of the Plain Meaning Rule: if the statute is clear, unambiguous and determinate, and not absurd or manifestly unjust as applied to the facts at hand, then interpretation is out of place, the court may look no further. It is not so much a canon of construction as a condition on construction: unless one or both of its conditions obtains, no interpretive questions arise. Llewellyn should have placed it first on his list.

Justice Day, in *Caminetti v. United States*,the most famous of all plain meaning rule cases:

> It is elementary that the meaning of a statute must, in the first instance, be sought in the language in which the act is framed, and if that is plain, and if the law is within the constitutional authority of the law-making body which passed it, the sole function of the courts is to enforce it according to its terms.
>
> There is no safer or better settled canon of interpretation than that when language is clear and unambiguous it must be held to mean what it plainly expresses, and no room is left for construction.[2]

The Plain Meaning Rule effects both legislative supremacy and the value of notice: where there is no obscurity, ambiguity, or under-determinacy, the legislature has succeeded and the denizen will have unequivocal notice from the statute alone. There is no need for interpretation. It is when these two foundational principles part company, when they pull in different directions, that interpretation becomes necessary, and canons may come into play.

That seems plain enough. But how exactly the Plain Meaning Rule conditions interpretation is subject to variation. Some —"literalists," "textualists" —would make under-determinacy (being "doubtful of meaning and susceptible upon its face of two constructions"[3]) the *only* ground for a court's looking further to determine a statute's meaning; others would allow

---

1 *Canons* at 403.

2 242 U.S. 470, 485-86 (1917).

3 *Hamilton v. Rathbone*, 175 U.S. 414, 421 (1899)(*per* Brown, J.)

interpretation also where the statute applied to the facts generates "absurdity or injustice."[4] Our courts have fluctuated between the two since they began interpreting statutes.[5] To this day, differences in judicial view persist.

Thrust #12: "If language is plain and unambiguous it must be given effect."

It is a fixture in the secondary sources. "Where the language of a statute is plain and unambiguous, there is no occasion for construction, ..."[6]

The most fundamental principle of statutory law is that the intent of the legislature controls. Thus Thrust #12 needs to be linked to legislative intent by the equally fundamental need to communicate that intention in the statute, in its words: "The intention of the legislature is to be obtained primarily from the language used in the statute."[7] Thus, says Chief Justice Marshall, eliding intent and words: "Where the intent is plain, nothing is left to construction."[8] To decide otherwise would be to subvert the basic principles of legislative supremacy and the necessity of notice.

Why Llewellyn should have chosen to cite *Newhall v. Sanger*[9] to support Thrust #12 eludes me. It was about complicated facts under a potential clash of statutes, and the decision rested on an implication from one of those statutes. In short, not much in the way of plain meaning is apparent. Fine illustrative cases abound, perhaps the most suited to Llewellyn's purposes —*i.e.* to illustrate a clash with Parry #12 —being *Caminetti v. United States*.[10]

The facts of *Caminetti* are well known: Caminetti took a young woman on a trip from California to Reno, Nevada, no doubt intending to "... induce, entice, or compel such woman or girl ... to give herself up to debauchery, or to engage in any other immoral practice," or, as Justice Day put it "that the aforesaid woman should be and become his mistress and concubine."[11] The Court's majority found the language of the White Slave Traffic Act clear and unambiguous,

---

4 *Sturgis v. Crowninshield*, 17 U.S. (4 Wheat.) 122, 202-03 (1819)(*per* Marshall, C.J.).

5 The infamous *Church of the Holy Trinity v. United States*, 143 U.S. 457 (1892)(to count a preacher as "perform[ing] labor or service of any kind" was too absurd or unjust.); half a century later, *United States v. American Trucking Associations, Inc.*, 310 U.S. 534 (1939)(" When aid to construction of the meaning of words, as used in the statute, is available, there certainly can be no "rule of law" which forbids its use, however clear the words may appear on "superficial examination.""); in between came *Caminetti v. United States*v242 U.S. 470, 485-86 (1917) with its determinedly strict, unrealistic, prudish interpretation.

6 59 C.J. *Statutes* §569, 953 with maybe a thousand cases cited. It's the same in 25 R.C.L. *Statutes* §213, (Llewellyn cites Sutherland §363 only for Parry #12, for which it offers no support.) and Black at §51, 141.

7 59 C.J. *Statutes* §569 , 952, under the caption "Ascertainment of Intention --(1)Language" and with a page of cites. 25 R.C.L. *Statutes* §217, 961-62 under the caption "Determination of Intention from Language Employed" is similar.

8 *United States v. Fisher*, 6 U.S. (Cranch) 358, 386 (1805) *per* Marshall, C.J.

9 92 U.S. 761 (1875).

10 242 U.S. 470 (1917).

11 242 U.S. at 483.

refused to look further into legislative intent, and affirmed Caminetti's sentence of eighteen months imprisonment and a $1,500 fine.[12]

In his dissent Justice McKenna did not dispute the strict version of the Plain Meaning Rule pronounced by the majority; nor did he exploit the absurdity or manifest injustice. Rather, he worked on the text of the statute itself, and the meanings of its terms in context.

> For the context I must refer to the statute; of the purpose of the statute Congress itself has given us illumination. It devotes a section to the declaration that the "Act shall be known and referred to as the "White-slave traffic Act." And its prominence gives it prevalence in the construction of the statute.[13]

Having demonstrated that the statute gave less than clear notice to the governed regarding its application to actions such as these, Justice McKenna was able to justify the use of legislative history, which demonstrated that legislative intent did not reach acts such as Caminetti's.

Caminetti thus illustrates Thrust #12, both the majority as a prohibition on further interpretation, and the dissent as a failure of its condition "If the language be plain and unambiguous." And in ignoring the absurdity and injustice of its application, indeed in ignoring independently manifest legislative intent, *Caminetti*'s application of the Plain Meaning Rule contrasts well with Parry #12.

Parry #12: "Not when literal interpretation would lead to absurd or mischievous consequences or thwart manifest purpose."

This too is a fixture of treatises, variously formulated, although usually incorporated with "under-determinacy" and its variants as a conjoint condition.

Why? Isn't this usurping the legislative function, defying legislative supremacy? It isn't if the language of the statute does not appear accurately to reflect legislative intent, at least as applied to the situation at hand. If the application of the statute would be so absurd or unjust as to shock the conscience, then presumably this instance must be an inadvertent oversight, not intended by the legislature.[14] The device to achieve the end is the implied exception: "It will always, therefore, be presumed that the legislature intended exceptions to its language, which

---

[12] Id at 496 ("Undoubtedly in the investigation of the meaning of a statute we resort first to its words, and when clear they are decisive.")

[13] Id at 497; *cf* Pair 11a, above.

[14] The Supreme Court explained:

> It is true there are cases in which the letter of the statute is not deemed controlling, but the cases are few and exceptional, and only arise when there are cogent reasons for believing that the letter does not fully and accurately disclose the intent. No mere omission, no mere failure to provide for contingencies, which it may seem wise to have specifically provided for, justify any judicial addition to the language of the statute.

United States v. Goldenberg, 168 U.S. 95, 103 (1897).

would avoid results of this character. The reason of the law in such cases should prevail over its letter."[15]

The threshold question is the criterion of absurdity or injustice or oppression. Chief Justice Marshall set it very high: " ...it must be one in which the absurdity and injustice of applying the provision to the case, would be so monstrous, that all mankind would, without hesitation, unite in rejecting the application."[16] Incarcerating Caminetti for his amicable vacation was not sufficiently absurd or unjust for the 1917 Supreme Court majority; to count a preacher as "perform[ing] labor or service of any kind" was sufficiently absurd and/or unjust for the 1892 Supreme Court.[17] This problem looks intractable: just as one can, if determined, find fuzziness in the scope of any (non-scientific) noun phrase, so too one can find monstrous injustice and oppression in pretty much any decision with which one disagrees.

A solution might be found in the principle of the necessity of notice: What would the ordinary person looking to the statute think? If she would find the statute plain on its face, she would have no reason to look further and should be able to rely on her reading. But if, on looking at the statute, she would say "What does that mean?" "This is unjust, it can't be right" or "I'd better find out more about this," then, and only then, should the court look to the tools of statutory interpretation, such as canons of construction and legislative history. *Plainness* for the purposes of the Plain Meaning Rule should be determined from the viewpoint of the ordinary reader governed by the statute. This, however, is not an approach that one finds in judicial opinions or the academic literature.

Examples may then cast more light. In *Clark v. Murray*[18] Llewellyn has chosen a singularly *un*-illustrative illustration. It was a problem of a clash between two statutes, both *in pari materia*.[19] In the course of the opinion the court says "The books are full of rules for statutory construction, but they were all enunciated with the idea of determining what the legislature had in mind in enacting the acts under consideration", and proceeds to recite a page or so of them, including a version of Parry #12, quoting from Black! [20] Only thus does the case illustrate Parry #12.

United States v. Kirby, from the 1868 United States Supreme Court, offers a perfect and authoritative illustration. [21] Sheriff Kirby of Gallatin County, Kentucky, and his posse stopped the steamboat General Buell in its passage up the Ohio River to arrest Farriss, who had been indicted by a Gallatin County grand jury for murder. But Farriss was a mail carrier, so Kirby

---

15 *United States v. Kirby*, 74 U.S. 482, 486-87 (1868).
16 *Sturgis v. Crowninshield*, 17 U.S. (4 Wheat.) 122, 202-03 (1819).
17 *Church of the Holy Trinity v. United States*,, 143 U.S. 457 (1892).
18 141 Kan. 533 (1935).
19 *See* Pairs ##1 and 6.
20 141 Kan. at 536, quoting Black at § 29, 66.
21 74 U.S. 482 (1868).

"was indicted for knowingly and willfully obstructing and retarding the passage of the mail and of a mail carrier," in violation of a federal statute prohibiting "knowingly and willfully obstruct[ing] or retard[ing] the passage of the mail, or of its carrier." But to convict and fine Sheriff Kirby and the members of his posse a hundred dollars each for this would be beyond both justice and reason. "All laws should receive a sensible construction. General terms should be so limited in their application as not to lead to injustice, oppression, or an absurd consequence."[22] And thus all laws have exceptions, intended by the legislature, for extraordinary situations such as this. It makes sense, doesn't it?

Resolution:

In Pair 12, Llewellyn has taken the Plain Meaning Rule and simply split the usual two conditions on interpretation: He has kept the general determinacy condition —that the meaning be plain and unambiguous —in the "thrust", and taken the sensibility and justice condition —that it be not absurd, oppressive, or patently unjust —and turned it into a "parry." But the history and variability of judicial use of the Plain Meaning Rule cannot be changed by such a device nor can the rule be made either more or less canonical than it always has been in judicial thinking.

There is some justification for treating the two conditions separately. In cases of ambiguity, obscurity or other under-determinacy of expression in the statute, a court cannot avoid interpretation; it must make a decision. Even though under-determinacy is not a perfectly non-judgmental statutory trait,[23] where it is found judges and commentators alike allow interpretation, whether based on canons or legislative history or both. Cases like *American Trucking*,[24] relying on legislative history even in the absence of significant under-determinacy in the statute, reduce the Plain Meaning Rule and Thrust #12 to irrelevance.

Nevertheless there is an inevitability to the determinacy condition that there is not with the sensibility and justice condition. In a case of absurdity or manifest injustice a court can plead legislative supremacy —"Congress ... may yield to sentiment and be capricious, subject only to due process."[25] —or righteously leave it to the legislature to amend the statute —"The remedy for a harsh law is not in interpretation, but in amendment or repeal."[26] —and make an absurd or

---

[22] Id at 485-86.

[23] *See e.g., Food and Drug Administration v. Brown & Williamson Tobacco Corp.*, 529 U.S. 120 (2000)(the U.S. Supremes split 5-4 on whether the statute was ambiguous.)

[24] *United States v. American Trucking Associations, Inc.*, 310 U.S. 534 (1939)(" When aid to construction of the meaning of words, as used in the statute, is available, there certainly can be no "rule of law" which forbids its use, however clear the words may appear on "superficial examination."")

[25] *United States v. International Boxing Club of New York, Inc.*, 348 U.S. 236, 249 (1955) (Frankfurter, J., dissenting).

[26] *State v. Catherine Duggan*, 15 R.I. 403, 409 (1886). *Similarly United States v. Missouri Pacific Railroad Co.*, 278 U.S. 269, 277-78 (1929)("Inconvenience or hardships, if any, that result from following the statute as written must be relieved by legislation.")

unjust decision. The judgmental quality of the sensibility and justice condition is also more interpersonally variable. Today's prevalent attitude to the White Slave Traffic Act's application to a commonplace weekend's vacation, as in *Caminetti*, would send all but the most anachronistically prudish judge to legislative history and acquittal. Thus the two conditions are different in application, but that hardly justifies omitting the more judgmental from a statement of the Plain Meaning Rule. Llewellyn's positing Thrust #12 and Parry #12 as separate canonical forms to create the appearance of conflict is artificial.

Pair 12, the Plain Meaning Rule, is a gatekeeper: unless one finds uncertainty, or absurdity etc., there is no need for interpretation; the statute provides the requisite guidance or the sought resolution of the problem. An overwhelming preponderance of occasions of resort to statute law must be like this. Issues of interpretation arise only in those few cases where the statute applies to the problem but is unclear or absurd.

Pair Thirteen

THRUST: "Words and phrases which have received judicial construction before enactment are to be understood according to that construction."
PARRY: "Not if the statute clearly requires them to have a different meaning."[1]

Some version of Pair 13 should be on most lists of canons. The source for the idiosyncratic expression Llewellyn uses is the black letter heading of Black section 65:

> WORDS JUDICIALLY DEFINED
> 65. Words and phrases in a statute which have received a settled judicial construction before enactment are to be understood according to that construction, unless the statute clearly requires them to bear a different meaning.[2]

Apart from omitting "in a statute" and "settled," Llewellyn's Thrust #13 tracks Black section 65 down to the comma. Parry #13 copies the "unless" clause of the heading, substituting "have" for "bear." In the text, Black emphasizes the importance of communicating the different meanings being used: "unless an intent of the legislature to have them understood in a different sense is unmistakably indicated." [3]

Llewellyn also cites Sutherland section 363, but this must be a mistake. Sutherland section 363 is about the centrality of legislative intent to statutory interpretation, with nothing on the subject of Thrust #13.[4] But he might easily have cited his other secondary sources, for example C.J.*Statutes* §613 or R.C.L. §236 which have similar content.

Thrust #13: "Words and phrases which have received judicial construction before enactment are to be understood according to that construction."

Justice Holmes: "The law uses familiar legal expressions in their familiar legal sense."[5] Justice Frankfurter: "Words of art bring their art with them."[6]

---

1 *Canons* 403.
2 Black § 65, at 186.
3 Black §65, at 187.
4 Sutherland at 693-96 ("§363. **The intent of a statute is the law.** –If a statute is valid it is to have effect according to the purpose and intent of the law-maker." followed by quotes from illustrative cases.)
5 *Henry v. United States*, 251 U.S. 393, 395 (1920) *per* Holmes, J.
6 Felix Frankfurter, *Some Reflections on the Reading of Statutes*, 47 COLUM.L.REV. 527,537 (1947).

The reason for the principle is not hard to see. Statutes give notice of legal constraints; those who consult statutes to guide their own or their clients' behavior either understand a statute's words in their accustomed legal usage or consult settled judicial usage. Their legitimate expectations should not be upset by a random shift in judicial interpretation. Legislatures know this just as well as judges and counselors, and accordingly "it must be presumed that a legislative body, using such terms in its enactment, is aware of the construction already placed upon them and expects that that construction will be adhered to."[7]

Llewellyn's cited case, *Scholze v. Scholze*,[8] from the Tennessee Appeals of 1925, is a fine illustration. In essence the dispute was over seven promissory notes made to "E. W. and Sue Scholze jointly."[9] The late E.W. Scholze bequeathed widow, Sue Fonda Scholze, a half interest in the notes; Sue Fonda claimed to hold a 100% interest by tenancy by the entireties or right of survivorship, concepts resting on common law judicial definition. Tennessee had enacted its Married Women's Property Acts in 1874, emancipating women's property ownership, but the key statutes came in 1913 and 1919, the first abolishing tenancy by the entireties and the right of survivorship, and its successor reinstating tenancy by the entireties. Tenancy by the entireties thus became a newly enacted, statutory concept. With ownership by survivorship eliminated by statute, Sue Fonda's case rested on the scope of tenancy by the entireties. The court, after a very thorough and scholarly research essay, found that at common law there was no tenancy by the entireties in personalty. Accordingly, on language similar to Thrust #13, it followed that the legislature must not have intended to create such an interest by the 1919 legislation.[10] And so Sue Fonda kept only a half share in the notes.

But surely a legislature has command of the words it chooses to enact; surely it can use words in whatever sense it chooses, provided only that it makes its choice clear to the governed.

Parry #13: "Not if the statute clearly requires them to have a different meaning."

Of course! If by the democratic principle of legislative supremacy the legislature can overrule the substantive decision of its jurisdiction's supreme court, then it can use words differently from the prior usage settled in that court. Like anyone else it can, to the extent of its statutory speech, give its words the meanings it chooses. The only limitation is that we, the governed, and our advisors and judges must be told about it, either expressly as in a definition or

---

7 Black at §65, 186; *sim. Case of Sewing Mach. Cos.*, 85 U.S. 553, 584 (1873)("... the well-established rule applies in construing the later act, that words and phrases, the meaning of which in a statute have been ascertained by judicial interpretation, are, when used in a subsequent statute, to be understood in the same sense. Such a construction in the case supposed becomes a part of the law, as it is presumed that the legislature in passing the later law knew what the judicial construction was which had been given to the words of the prior enactment." (citation omitted); 25 R.C.L at §236, 993.

8 2 Tenn. App. 80 (M.S. 1925).

9 Id at 87.

10 Id at 90-92.

by inescapable implication. This is simply a variation on the necessity of notice, the requirement that the legislature communicate its laws to those governed.

Llewellyn's cited case, *Dixon v. Robbins*, from the renowned New York Court of Appeals of 1927, is a fine illustration of Thrust #13, but fails even in dicta to support Parry #13.[11] Recitations of the exception are common, but good illustrative cases are not easy to find; nevertheless, Llewellyn's research assistant, even without the aid of an electronic search engine, should have found the Supreme Court's *Plummer v. United States* in the footnotes of his favored four secondary sources.[12] Plummer was an assistant surgeon in the United States Navy, and thus entitled to what they called "longevity pay," a 10% bonus for serving five-year periods. The dispute was over the meaning of "his current yearly pay," specifically as to the base year on which that 10% was calculated. The same language in the predecessor statute had been

> construed in *United States v. Tyler*, 105 U.S. 244 (1881) to require that the calculation of the longevity pay should be made, not upon the sum of the base pay, but on the base pay and previous increases thereof, that the same rule must be applied to the words as used in the provision of the statute above quoted. But, subsequent to the Tyler Case, by the act of June 30, 1882, 22 Stat. 118, c. 254, Congress expressly directed that the ten per cent longevity increase provided for in section 1262, Rev. Stat., should be "computed on the yearly pay of the grade. . . . That this act was passed for the express purpose of commanding a method of computation which would render inapplicable the construction adopted in the Tyler Case is not open to controversy.[13]

The argument to the contrary is that for the legislature to include an interpretation would be (unconstitutionally) to usurp an exclusively judicial function.[14] It is a transparently weak argument —in essence it denies the legislature the power to correct judicial decisions with which it disagrees —and is easily dismissed.[15]

Resolution:

Thrust #13 is transparently good sense, summarizing the reasons on which it rests. But those reasons are completely negated if the legislature itself in the legislation announces a different meaning for the words in the context of that legislation. Accordingly Parry #13 encapsulates not so much an exception to Thrust #13 as the appropriate canon of construction in case of authoritative and public negation of the reasons for Thrust #13. It is an instance of

---

[11] 246 N.Y. 169, 158 N.E. 63 (1927).

[12] 224 U.S. 137 (1912), cited at 25 R.C.L., 994 n17.

[13] Id at 144.

[14] *State Board of Assessors v. Plainfield Water Supply Co* , 67 N.J.L. 357, 358, 52 A. 230 (N.J. Sup. Ct. 1902); *Getz v. Brubaker*, 25 Pa. Super. 303, 305 (1904).

[15] *State Board of Assessors v. Plainfield Water Supply Co.*, 67 N.J.L. at 358: "We do not consider this to be the import of the words, ' "This act shall not be construed to apply to,'" when used in the connection in which they appear in this provision. Their purpose is not to curtail to any extent the judicial power of interpretation, but to limit the scope of the act itself; being equivalent to "This act shall not apply to.""

legislative supremacy of a kind with which we are now familiar as legislatures increasingly resort to a compendia of definitions at the beginning of an enactment. And it does not compromise the principle of notice.

Pair Fourteen

> **THRUST**: "After enactment, judicial decision upon interpretation of particular terms and phrases controls."
> **PARRY**: "Practical construction by executive officers is strong evidence of true meaning."[1]

Thrust 14 follows naturally from the judicial prerogative to interpret in order to apply legislation to particular situations and *stare decisis*. It is Thrust #13 without subsequent legislation, thus without the possibility of the "unless..." of Parry #13. Parry #14 simply, minimally, says interpretations by the third branch of government, the administration and its agencies, are "strong evidence of true meaning," not even claiming authority over meanings not defined in the statute. It's an odd match-up in a list of supposed contraries, not even nearly intersecting.

Black section 93 is Llewellyn's only secondary source cited for Thrust #14:

> JUDICIAL CONSTRUCTION
>
> 93. Judicial decisions previously made upon the interpretation of particular terms, and phrases used in a statute, and decisions subsequently rendered upon its effect, purpose, or scope, are strong evidence of its meaning, and are generally of controlling force in establishing its correct construction.[2]

Stare decisis applied to statutory law. Variations on Black's cautious and qualified version are common enough.

Llewellyn cites Black section 94 and R.C.L. section 274 for Parry #14; Black appears to be the source of the actual wording:

> EXECUTIVE CONSTRUCTION
>
> 94. A practical construction put upon a doubtful or ambiguous statute by the officers of the executive department, who are charged with its execution, if long acted upon and generally acquiesced in, is regarded as strong evidence of the true meaning of the law; and though it is not binding upon the courts, they will not interpret the law differently unless there are weighty reasons for doing so.[3]

---

[1] *Canons* at 404.
[2] Black at §93, 298.
[3] Black at §94, 300.

As in Thrust #14, in Parry #14 Llewellyn's loose paraphrase of Black reduces the heading to suitable "canon size," even though the omission of Black's qualifiers ("put upon a doubtful or ambiguous statute," "if long acted upon and generally acquiesced in," and "though it is not binding upon the courts, they will not interpret the law differently unless there are weighty reasons for dong so") lends Parry #14 a generality and dogmatism that undermine both its accuracy and its suitability to canonization.

Thrust #14: "After enactment, judicial decision upon interpretation of particular terms and phrases controls."

Black offers two justifications. First, an established judicial meaning of an expression will be presumed adopted in new legislation unless the legislature says otherwise (Pair 13.) Second, a judicial construction of a statute, "especially where [it is] supported by a line of uniform decisions, and where it has been acquiesced in by the legislature, . . . becomes as much a part of the statute as if it had been written into it originally."[4] That is, Thrust #14 enunciates foundational judicial method: *stare decisis*, the doctrine of precedent, applies to the interpretation of statutes. Justice Cardozo: "*Stare decisis* is at least the everyday working rule of our law."[5] It is basic to our system of legal governance, dating at least since 1803 and Chief Justice Marshall's "[I]t is emphatically the province and duty of the judicial department to say what the law is."[6]

The doctrine arguably applies more strictly to the judicial application of statutes than to either common law or constitutional decisions because if the legislature disagrees it can readily amend the statute.[7] Contrast constitutional interpretation for which, because legislative cure is unavailable, *stare decisis* should be relatively weak.[8]

---

[4] Id.

[5] Benjamin N. Cardozo, THE NATURE OF THE JUDICIAL PROCESS, 20 (1921).

[6] *Marbury v. Madison*, 5 U.S. (1 Cranch) 137, 177 (1803). *see also* F.F.Alexander Hamilton: "To avoid an arbitrary discretion in the courts, it is indispensable that they should be bound by strict rules and precedents, which serve to define and point out their duty in every particular case that comes before them … ." The Federalist No.78 at 510; also No.78, at 507-08, and No.81, at 531; William Blackstone, 1 COMMENTARIES ON THE LAWS OF ENGLAND *69 (1765); Sir Matthew Hale, THE HISTORY OF THE COMMON LAW OF ENGLAND 44 et seq. (1713)(Charles M. Gray, ed., U. Chicago Press, 1971).

[7] Neal v. United States, 516 U.S. 284, 295 (1996) (Kennedy, J.) ("One reason that we give great weight to *stare decisis* in the area of statutory construction is that 'Congress is free to change this Court's interpretation of its legislation.'" (quoting Illinois Brick Co. v. Illinois, 431 U.S. 720, 736 (1977))). *See also* William N. Eskridge, Jr., Correspondence, *The Case of the Amorous Defendant: Criticizing Absolute Stare Decisis for Statutory Cases*, 88 MICH. L. REV. 2450 (1990); Lawrence C. Marshall, Correspondence, *Contempt of Congress: A Reply to the Critics of an Absolute Rule of Statutory Stare Decisis*, 88 MICH. L. REV. 2467 (1990); Lawrence C. Marshall, *"Let Congress Do It": The Case for an Absolute Rule of Statutory Stare Decisis*, 88 MICH. L. REV. 177 (1989).

[8] Justice Brandeis: "[I]n cases involving the Federal Constitution, where correction through legislative action is practically impossible, th[e] court has often overruled its earlier decisions. The court bows to the

Llewellyn's cited case is *Eau Claire National Bank v. Benson.*[9] A disappointed creditor of a corporation sued to recover from one of the corporation's stockholders. At this the Wisconsin Supreme Court was not happy:

> No new question is presented for consideration on this appeal. Most of the questions discussed in the brief filed by counsel for appellant have been presented to this court over and over again and with the same result as when first presented some forty years ago. There must come a time when the presentation of a question to a court of last resort, and the consumption of its time in going over ground that has been repeatedly explored before, will be a mere waste of judicial labor.[10]

This is the efficiency justification for *stare decisis*. Following that, Wisconsin's Justice Marshall gave us the language followed by Black and encapsulated in Thrust #14:

> Courts are not responsible for the law. It is their province to declare and apply it and to construe statutes and constitutions in accordance with the will of the lawmaking power, where construction becomes necessary. When such construction has once been given to a law and finally established as a part thereof, it is as much a part of it as if embodied therein in plain and unmistakable language. When that situation exists it is the province of the legislature alone to change the law.[11]

The plaintiff lost.

Parry #14: "Practical construction by executive officers is strong evidence of true meaning."

There are many qualifications to Parry #14 in Black's heading from which it is derived. R.C.L., Llewellyn's other secondary source for Parry #14, is as qualified as Black on the interpretive authority of the administrative branch:

> 274. Executive or Departmental Construction
>
> It is a well settled rule that the contemporaneous construction of a statute by those charged with its execution and application, especially when it has long prevailed, while not controlling, is entitled to great weight, and should not be disregarded or overturned except for cogent reasons, and unless it is clear that such construction is erroneous.[12]

---

lessons of experience and the force of better reasoning, recognizing that the process of trial and error, so fruitful in the physical sciences, is appropriate also in the judicial function." *Burnet v. Coronado Oil & Gas Co.*, 285 U.S. 393, 406-08 (1932) (Brandeis, J., dissenting) (footnotes omitted).

9 106 Wis. 624 (1900).

10 Id, 106 Wis. at 627.

11 Id, 106 Wis. at 627-28.

12 25 R.C.L., at 1043. Corpus Juris 1025-28 is even more qualified.

Reliance is a powerful principle in statutory interpretation. If there has been no judicial interpretation, but the executive branch has adopted and acted on an interpretation not clearly erroneous, then surely a person or a legal advisor would be well advised to follow that interpretation. Such an interpretative practice, says Black, "for a long period of time, and generally acquiesced in, and not questioned by any suit brought, or any public or private action instituted, to test and settle the construction in the courts, is entitled to great respect . . . ."[13] In contrast, if the administration's interpretation is recent and there has been little action taken in reliance upon it, it "will have no weight or influence with the courts in their search for the true meaning of the law."[14] By eliding this contrast, Llewellyn's sweeping and unequivocal Parry #14 greatly diminishes the efficacy of this justification.

Llewellyn cites *State ex rel. Bashford v. Frear* from the Wisconsin Supreme Court as judicial support.[15] Bashford was appointed to finish the final six months of the term of a deceased Wisconsin Supreme Court justice and took office on the very day the state legislature approved a twenty percent salary increase for such justices. As the Wisconsin constitution "creates an absolute disability of the lawmaking body to change, in any way, either by increasing or decreasing, any public officer's compensation 'during his term of office'"[16] the defendant Secretary of State refused to pay Bashford the incremental $500 and Bashford brought this writ of mandamus, successfully. The interpretive question was about "his term of office": did it mean "term of office created," or "during the term for which they are respectively elected"? After a long and confusing opinion and conceding that "[i]f those who had early to do with the matter had had the benefit of the judicial reasoning on like provisions, which was postponed for some twenty years, a different conclusion might have been reached," Justice Marshall finally reached and rested upon a form of Parry #14:

> It requires a very clear case to justify changing the construction of a law, conceded to be somewhat involved, which has been uninterruptedly acquiesced in for so long a period as fifty years. . . . So the conclusion is . . . that "his term of office," as used in sec. 26, art. IV, of the constitution, has regard, primarily, to the personal element, the incumbent of the office; contemplates the period of incumbency, whether of a whole term, or a part of the entirety, under art. VII. As to the particular incumbent's term of service, during its pendency, the legislature is under complete disability to change the salary incident in any manner or to any extent; but as to any period, within a whole term, filled by appointment or election, the legislature has power, before the commencement thereof, to fix the compensation, different from that incident to the office during the preceding period.[17]

---

[13] Black at §94, 301-02. *Sim.* 25 R.C.L.*Statutes*, at 1043-44.
[14] Black at §94, 301.
[15] 138 Wis. 536 (1909)(*Per* Justice Marshall, as in *Eau Claire National Bank v. Benson, supra.*)
[16] *State* ex rel *Bashford v. Frear*, 138 Wis. at 542.
[17] Id, 138 Wis. at 556-57.

Many cases also reiterate that the interpretation relied upon must have been long established and that administrative acquiescence in a usage cannot outweigh clear legislative intent.

The unequivocal, assertive form of Llewellyn's Parry #14 lacks support from either primary or secondary sources, or in the reasoning underlying this Pair and Pair 13, but then it only claims administrative usage as "strong evidence of true meaning," not as authoritative.

Resolution:

For there to be a conflict here would require first that Parry #14 as stated be a canon, and second that it require administrative determinations of meaning to be given great weight as against a prior judicial interpretation. Neither condition obtains.

Thrust #14, in some form, has a place on any list of canons. It is simply the doctrine of precedent applied to the interpretation and application of statutes. As written, Parry #14 would have us believe that an administrative interpretation could be given great weight as against a prior judicial construction which has "become as much a part of the statute as if it had been written into it originally."[18] As of 1950, when *Canons* was published, this was not the case. Black, Llewellyn's primary source, expressly denies it: "When the courts shall have interpreted the laws, these officers are of course bound to accept and abide by their decisions."[19] No "great weight" or even "respect" is owed administrative usage; judicial interpretation governs. Secondary commentators heavily lace their formulations of the authority of the administrative branch over statutory meanings with conditions and equivocations; without those conditions and equivocations, Parry #14 is too general, and even as only "strong evidence" too absolute, too contrary to judicial practice to be valid, let alone a commonplace of interpretation.

Not until 2005 and the Supreme Court's decision in *National Cable & Telecommunications Assoc. v. Brand X Internet Services*[20] did Llewellyn's Parry #14 achieve a semblance of validity. (This was a major step in administrative law jurisprudence, way beyond the *Chevron* analysis we have come to know and love since 1984.[21]) The Ninth Circuit had previously resolved exactly the ambiguity at issue.[22] Justice Thomas wrote:

> A court's prior judicial construction trumps an agency's construction otherwise entitled to *Chevron* deference *only if* the prior court decision holds that its construction follows from the unambiguous terms of the statute and leaves no room for agency discretion. . . . [A]llowing judicial precedent to foreclose an agency from interpreting an ambiguous statute, ... would allow a court's

---

[18] Black at §93, 298.
[19] Black at §94, 301, shortly below the caption which Llewellyn reduced into Parry #13.
[20] 545 U.S. 967 (2005).
[21] *Chevron v. Natural Resources Defense Council*, 467 U.S. 837 (1984).
[22] *A.T.& T. v. Portland*, 216 F.3d 871 (9th Cir. 2000)

> interpretation to override an agency's. *Chevron*'s premise is that it is for agencies, not courts, to fill statutory gap.[23]

Justice Scalia's dissent (joined by Justices Souter, and Ginsburg) was fuming: the decision creates "a breathtaking novelty: judicial decisions subject to reversal by Executive officers ... even when the agency itself is party to the case in which the Court construes the statute."[24]

Later that same year, in *IBP, Inc. v. Alvarez*, the Court perhaps took a step back, suggesting that its own interpretations of ambiguous statutes did govern an agency and allowing that "considerations of *stare decisis* are particularly forceful in the area of statutory construction, especially when a unanimous interpretation of a statute has been accepted as settled for several decades."[25] We might expect this matter to be revisited, but until then, Llewellyn's Parry #14 has at last achieved a measure of validity, and with it the conflict in Pair 14 might approach genuine.

---

[23] 545 U.S. 982 at 2700.

[24] 545 U.S. at 1018 at 2719-20.

[25] 546 U.S. 21, 32 (2005).

Half Time: Interim Assessment

Although we are only half way through Llewellyn's list, it is not too early to make some general observations, especially as the principle conclusion so far is so obvious: there is no genuine contrariety between the thrusts and parries of the first fourteen pairs. There may be another fourteen pairs of canons yet to examine, and among them some of the better known and more controversial, but the first fourteen so uniformly failed to support Llewellyn's thesis that "there are two opposing canons on almost every point" [1] that one might consider the burden of persuasion shifted. The search should be not for canons that stand unequivocally alone but for a genuinely contrary pair.

Superficially, there is some inconsistency between Thrust and Parry #5, but that is only because Thrust #5 seems to have been created on neither reason nor authority simply to contradict Parry #5. In most cases the difference in conditions of application, sometimes stated in the formulation, meant no serious clash was possible. Looking to the reasons underlying the pair, reasons which also function as conditions for proper use of a canon, resolved what superficial contrariety remained. Of course if the applicable conditions do not obtain, then the canon will not apply and no conclusion will follow. It is a mistake to apply a canon without paying attention to its required conditions of application; it is this mistake that often produces a superficial appearance of antipathy between otherwise compatible canons.

The first half of the list included more than a fair proportion of thrusts and parries that one has difficulty calling canonical. A canon gets its status from the regularity of its occurrence, the relative stability of its formulation, the strength of its underlying reasoning, and its prolonged acceptance by the judiciary. Too many of the supposed canons among the first fourteen pairs did not come close to these criteria.

In some cases, such as Pair #13, duels failed to appear because the thrusts and parries quoted were merely parts of more complex, less superficial generalities from treatises. Section headings from a treatise or rough generalities about problems do not satisfy any reasonable criteria for canonization. And there was the implausible hodge-podge of Pair 11, throwing together titles, preambles, and captions, all subject to different considerations and differing in usefulness as interpretive aids. We have also seen a surprising number of pairs that are not well supported by the material cited.

---

[1] *Canons* at 400, Karl N. Llewellyn, *The Common Law Tradition-Deciding Appeals*, 521 (1960).

The Provenances of Llewellyn's Formulae

It was at about this stage in the initial project that it became inescapably clear what a shoddy, unscholarly job Llewellyn made in this list. I remember the sinking feeling, the disappointment, a real sadness. Llewellyn was, after all, a hero, *my* hero, the genius behind Article 2 (the best adapted code of modern America), in my jurisprudential pantheon up there with Francis Bacon and Lord Mansfield —how could he have done this? How could he let it go public over his name and, worse, repeat it in a book?

At Pair 14 one could no longer avoid the impression that Llewellyn's formulation of the pairs of canons too often bore a close resemblance to the captions of the sections cited from Black. Accordingly I checked the pairs in the whole list which offered Black as a secondary source, looking for signs of copying or paraphrase. Here are a couple of examples.

Pair 7

THRUST #7: "A statute imposing a new penalty or forfeiture, or a new liability or disability, or creating a new right of action will not be construed as having a retroactive effect."

PARRY #7: "Remedial statutes are to be liberally construed and if a retroactive interpretation will promote the ends of justice, they should receive such a construction."

Llewellyn's only secondary cite for Thrust #7 is Black section 119: "A statute imposing a new penalty or forfeiture, or a new liability or disability, or creating a new right of action, will not be construed as having a retroactive operation, if such consequences can fairly be avoided by interpretation."[2] Except for a misplaced comma, Llewellyn has tracked Black down to the latter's condition, changing only a single word, "operation" to "effect."

He cites only Black section 120 as a secondary source for Parry #7:

> REMEDIAL STATUTES
> 120. Remedial statutes are to be liberally construed; and if a retroactive interpretation will promote the ends of justice and further the design of the legislature in enacting them, or make them applicable to cases which are within the reason and spirit of the enactment, though not within its direct words, they should receive such construction, provided it is not inconsistent with the language employed.[3]

Parry #7 changes only punctuation and deletes the qualifications "and further the design of the legislature in enacting them, or make them applicable to cases which are within the reason and spirit of the enactment, though not within its direct words, . . . provided it is not inconsistent with the language employed."

---

[2] Black, at 401.
[3] Black, at 403.

Pair 17

THRUST #17: "The same language used repeatedly in the same connection is presumed to bear the same meaning throughout the statute."

PARRY #17: "This presumption will be disregarded where it is necessary to assign different meanings to make the statute consistent."[4]

Black section 53 is the only secondary source Llewellyn cites for both Thrust and Parry #17:

> USE OF SAME LANGUAGE AND CHANGE OF LANGUAGE
> 53. Where the same language is used repeatedly in a statute in the same connection, it is presumed to bear the same meaning throughout the act; but this presumption will be disregarded where it is necessary to assign different meanings to the same terms in order to make the statute sensible, consistent, and operative.

The paraphrase is too obvious; nor is the language so commonplace that its close repetition could be excused as a stock recitation of the familiar. Were that the case, Black, section 53, would not be the only secondary cite.

It would not matter if the words followed standard formulae —as for example in Thrust #20, "Expression of one thing excludes another," the commonplace Latin favorite "*Expressio unius est exclusio alterius*." —but where the words are idiosyncratic or the point not at all common, and especially with a sophomoric disguise such as substituting "statute" for "act," one cannot avoid the disillusion and its infection of the whole enterprise. In the following analysis of pairs 15 through 28 I shall note further examples of the same pattern. In particular, Pairs 18, 21, 25, 26, 27, and 28 are especially egregious.

… unless legislative intent is clearly otherwise

Canons are not and do not pretend to be universal rules. Perhaps more than most generalities about communication, they come with exceptions, some more clear than others, but always grounds for rebuttal. After all, because of legislative supremacy, "unless legislative intent indicates otherwise," where not express is implied in any statement of a canon. But Llewellyn's most frequent technique in creating the list was to take a familiar and acceptable statement about interpretation and split the exception from the main statement, making one the thrust and the other, usually the exception, the parry. So far we have seen it in pairs 2, 4, 5, 7, 12, 13, and shall see it again in pairs 15, 16, 17, 18, 21, 23, 27, and 28, in all fully half the pairs on Llewellyn's list.

---

4 *Canons* at 404.

Take for example Pair 13: Thrust #13, "Words and phrases which have received judicial construction before enactment are to be understood according to that construction," and Parry #13, "Not if the statute clearly requires them to have a different meaning." were derived from a general statement connected by an "unless," in particular Black §65:

> Words and phrases in a statute which have received a settled judicial construction before enactment are to be understood according to that construction, unless the statute clearly requires them to bear a different meaning.

This exemplifies a general form of canon, "Interpret such-&-such thus-&-so *unless/except where/but not if* … legislative intent is clearly otherwise." But the method itself is misconceived, incapable of producing genuine contradictions.

A canon applies where the reasons for it apply. An "unless …" clause says expressly that if those reasons do not apply, then nor does that canon, or principal clause of the whole canon. Pair 13, above, for example: Both main and "unless …" clauses depend on the circumstance, applying in mutually exclusive conditions. So the contrariety of the Thrust and Parry #13 depends on a logical sleight of hand that is illegitimate. Yet it is the most pervasive method in the production of Llewellyn's list

The method also has a curious reflexive consequence, namely, where the parry is of the form "*... unless legislative intent is clearly otherwise*," it negates the possibility of a contrary pair, in application if not, perhaps, in theory. If such an "unless…" clause is true then legislative intent is clear, and then the Plain Meaning Rule (Pair 12) tells us that interpretation is unnecessary, that there is no justification for looking at the thrust supposedly being parried. Clear legislative intent negates the possibility of contrary canons in actual application.

Again: a canon of construction does not purport to be a universal mandate of interpretation with something like constitutional inviolability. A canon offers prima facie wisdom in capsule form, binding neither court nor legislature even though, as prima facie *wisdom*, it should shift a burden of persuasion. Even so, most versions of Pair 13 include both Thrust #13 and Parry #13 connected by 'unless' in the same sentence, lest anyone be deceived by a bald statement of the underlying reason (as in Thrust #13). Simply splitting the two parts creates only the most superficial appearance of contrariety.

Pair Fifteen

> **THRUST**: "Words are to be taken in their ordinary meaning unless they are technical terms or words of art."
> **PARRY**: "Popular words may bear a technical meaning and technical words may have a popular signification and they should be so construed as to agree with the evident intention or to make the statute operative."[1]

Llewellyn might have followed his common pattern of separating the "unless" clause as the parry, but here he has chosen a more complicated parry, with exceptions to both the main thesis *and* the "unless" clause of Thrust #15. In this he appears once more to be following Black, in the caption of his cited section 63:

> TECHNICAL MEANING AND POPULAR MEANING OF WORDS.
> The words of a statute are to be taken in their ordinary popular meanings, unless they are technical terms or words of art, in which case they are to be understood in their technical sense.[2]

He also cites Sutherland section 390 and C.J.*Statutes* sections 577 and 578 for both Thrust and Parry #15. Both say much the same as Black section 63 but in somewhat different, more complicated words. Llewellyn's continued preference for Black as a base text to paraphrase is evident as he might equally well have chosen either of Sutherland's or C.J.*Statutes*'s rather more careful formulations.

Black section 63 also appears to be the source of Parry #15; the caption of the section, the first sentence of which (quoted above) is the source of Thrust #15, continues: "But popular words may bear a technical meaning, and technical words may have a popular signification, and they should be so construed when that is the evident intention of the legislature, or when it is necessary in order to make the statute operative."[3] Parry #15 replicates most this, even down to the stylistic choice of "signification" over the more accurate repetition of "meaning," varying only its last words.

Pair 15 continues the theme of Pairs 13 and 14, namely, the determinates of the meanings of words and phrases within statutes. Pairs 13 and 14 are about prior judicial or otherwise

---

1 *Canons*, at 404.
2 Black §63 at 175.
3 Black §63 at 404.

established legal meaning. What if there has been no judicial interpretation of the statute and no established legal meaning?

Thrust #15: "Words are to be taken in their ordinary meaning unless they are technical terms or words of art."

Pair 15 continues the interplay of the principle of legislative supremacy and the requirement of notice. Thrust #15, the most commonplace of rules of interpretation, follows naturally: In the absence of indicia of legislative intent to the contrary, meanings are those of common usage —ordinary meanings.[4] Justice Frankfurter: "[W]e assume that Congress uses common words in their popular meaning, as used in the common speech of men. The cases speak of the 'meaning of common understanding,' 'the normal and spontaneous meaning of language,' 'the common appropriate use,' 'the natural straightforward and literal sense,' and similar variants."[5] That is Thrust #15's primary thesis.

On the other hand, a technical word would ordinarily be understood by the ordinary reader in its technical sense, and a term of art as such. And if a statute is directed at a specific community with its own jargon, we should presume the legislature was aware of and spoke in that jargon. In section 393, which Llewellyn also cites for Thrust #15, Sutherland makes this a thesis with Parry #15 as its exception:

> **§ 393 Technical Words**. Technical words relating to an art, science or trade, when used in a statute dealing with the subject-matter of such art, science or trade, are ordinarily to be taken in their technical sense and will be so construed, unless the context or other considerations plainly show a contrary intent.[6]

Sutherland follows with a good example from the 1897 Missouri Supreme Court. In a statute governing mine work, the phrase "shooting coal off the solid" was to be understood as miners and mine operators would understand it. "The phrase is and has for many years been in common use and well understood among those owning and operating coal mines and their miners."[7] A legislature should be presumed to have in mind the audience addressed in an enactment, and verbal usages peculiar to it. In 1950 Llewellyn was following this presumption in Article 2 of the inchoate Uniform Commercial Code with his emphasis on usage of trade as determining meanings of contract terms.

Llewellyn's cited case, *Hawley Coal Co. v. Bruce*,[8] is not a very good illustration. Walter E. Price died in bankruptcy, and a judgment debtor for room and board from Eliza Bruce. Walter

---

4 *See* Michael Sinclair, TRADITIONAL TOOLS OF STATUTORY INTERPRETATION, 96 -97 (Vandeplas Publishing, 2013)
5 Felix Frankfurter, *Some Reflections on the Reading of Statutes*, 47 COLUM. L. REV. 527, 535 (1947).
6 Sutherland at 750.
7 *State v. Murlin*, 137 Mo. 297, 305-306 (1897).
8 252 Ky. 455 (1934).

once owned the Hawley Coal Company, but he transferred all stock in it to his wife, Mary E. Price, for consideration although failed to record the assignment. Mrs. Bruce wanted to get her legal hooks in the assets of the Hawley Coal Company, two parcels of real estate; to do that she needed first to get the company's stock certificates, now in the hands of Walter's widow, Mary Price. Under Missouri's Married Women's Property Act, a wife could purchase, own and transfer property, but to avoid deception of creditors section "2128, Kentucky Statutes" required that

> A gift, transfer or assignment of personal property between husband and wife shall not be valid as to third persons, unless the same be in writing, and acknowledged and recorded as chattel mortgages are required by law to be acknowledged and recorded; but the recording of any such writing shall not make valid any such gift, transfer or assignment which is fraudulent or voidable as to creditors or purchasers.[9]

Did "personal property" in that language mean all personal property, including stock certificates, or only tangible personal property, which would not include stock certificates? The latter interpretation was Mary Price's first line of defense.

There is quotable language along the lines of Thrust #15 ("Words and phrases are used in their technical meaning, if they have acquired one, and in their popular meaning if they have not."[10]), but the court found the language of the statute unambiguous, and only debated whether it could or should imply an exception. They wouldn't, so widow Mary lost this argument.

Over one hundred and seventy years ago, Justice Story laid out the reasoning of Thrust #15 in *United States v. Breed.*[11] How is a court to distinguish the varieties of sugar specified in a statute: 'brown sugar,' 'white, clayed, or powdered sugar,' 'lump-sugar,' 'loaf-sugar,' and 'sugar-candy'?[12]

> The question then is, whether, in the sense of the act, the sugar is, or is not loaf-sugar. . . .What, then, is meant by "loaf-sugar," in a commercial sense, by which I mean, not merely among merchants, but among buyers and sellers generally in the domestic trade? Has it any generally received, uniform meaning? If it has, then, that must be presumed to be the meaning adopted by the legislature in the act of 1816. I agree to the law laid down in the case of Two Hundred Chests of Tea. That case was as fully considered, and as deliberately weighed, as any which ever came before the court. It was there laid down, that, in construing revenue laws, we were to consider the words, not as used in their scientific or technical sense, where things were classified according to their scientific

---

[9] Id, 252 Ky. at 456-57.

[10] Id, 252 Ky. at 458.

[11] 24 F. Cas. 1222, 1 Sumn. 159 (Circuit Court, D. Massachusetts, 1832).

[12] Id, 24 F. Cas. at 1222 ("The words of the act of 1816, c. 107, as to duties on the article (sugar) now in controversy, are as follows: "On brown sugar, three cents per pound; white, clayed, or powdered sugar, four cents per pound; on lump-sugar, ten cents per pound; on loafsugar and sugar-candy, twelve cents per pound.")

> characters and properties, but as used in their known and common commercial sense, in the foreign and domestic trade.[13]

On this basis the question was easily decided by reference to trade usage: "All the witnesses, whether merchants, or refiners, or grocers, or confectioners, have spoken pointedly to this fact" that the "crushed sugar" at issue was not "loaf-sugar."[14]

Usually the principles of legislative supremacy and the necessity of notice work in sympathy, but when they do not, the democratic ideal behind legislative supremacy requires that legislative intent should prevail. Hence

Parry #15: "Popular words may bear a technical meaning and technical words may have a popular signification and they should be so construed as to agree with the evident intention or to make the statute operative."

There are two justifications built into this formulation. The first is legislative intent: following the evident intention of the legislature is, as Sutherland says, "the cardinal rule," a concomitant of the democratic principle of legislative supremacy. The second is the corollary that we should construe words so as "to make the statute operative." We are entitled to believe the legislature was intending its enactment to have some effect, that it was not merely wasting time and publication space.[15] What other presumption could we make? It follows that if one alternative interpretation is necessary for the statute to make sense, to be operative, then that is the only proper choice.

Llewellyn's cited case, *Robinson v. Varnell*, may have historically shameful facts, but illustrates the thesis well.[16] To a breach of contract action, defendant lessee pleaded the statute of limitations, not as to the claim for his failure to pay the price, which would be an action for debt, but as to his failure to return the property. Texas at the time distinguished between "actions of debt, grounded on any contract in writing," with a four year time bar, and "parol or verbal . . . contracts," with a two year time bar. The argument, it seems, is that not being of the specific kind designated for four years, (an "action for debt,") this aspect of the suit must be time barred under the remainder, a parol contract.

The court had to concede the premise, *viz*, that this was "not an action of debt, nor an action to recover a debt, technically so called." However:

---

[13] Id, 24 F. Cas. at 1222–23 (citation omitted).

[14] Id, 24 F. Cas. at 1224.

[15] *See* Thrust #16, *Canons* at 404 and below.

[16] 16 Tex. 382 (1856). Defendant had rented a slave from plaintiff, but had so "cruelly treated and abused the slave" that he ran away and was never recovered (perhaps the only redeeming feature of the story); defendant didn't pay, so plaintiff brought action for breach of contract, first for failing to pay, second for not returning the rented "property." *Id.* at 382–8.

> [W]e have no such action as an action of debt. If we were to construe the statute literally, according to the technical signification of its terms, it is plain, the present case would not come within any of its provisions. It is not technically an action of debt, or an action to recover a debt; but it is an action to recover a sum of money, technically damages, founded on the breach of a contract in writing for the delivery of specific property.

Accordingly,

> We have seen that the expression in the statute, "actions of debt," cannot receive a strict literal interpretation, without defeating the provision altogether: for we have no actions which come strictly and technically within that denomination. It must, then, receive such a reasonable and liberal interpretation as will give it effect according to the spirit and intention of the statute. To do this, we must disregard the technical distinctions of forms and terms, and look to the substance and manifest object of the statute.

Ergo, the plaintiff had the full four years in which to bring both aspects of the action.[17]

***Resolution*:**

As with Pairs 13 and 14, any inconsistency between the thrust and the parry of Pair 15 is superficial at best. Together Pairs 13 to 15 map some of the contours of meanings in legal governance by statute. Those contours are generated by the interaction of the fundamental principles, legislative supremacy and the necessity of notice.

A legislature must communicate with the denizens it governs, so it must be presumed to use words in accord with ordinary, popular usage, that is, with meanings familiar to the governed. And when the legislature is addressing a subgroup of the governed with its own "technical terms or words of art" it may be presumed to be aware of that fact and to use that jargon. This is simply an instance of the Wittgensteinian dictum that words take their meanings in the language-game which is their home.[18]

Yet a legislature may use a word or phrase in an odd or irregular sense, compromising communication with the governed. Legislative supremacy may dominate,[19] but the legislature will fail in its legislative purpose if it does not tell the governed of the special sense in which it intends the words in question. Given the ubiquity of "usage of trade" in Article 2 of the Uniform Commercial Code, this reasoning must have been quite familiar to Karl Llewellyn in 1950.

---

[17] *Robinson v. Varnell, supra*, 16 Tex. at 388-90.
[18] Ludwig Wittgenstein, PHILOSOPHICAL INVESTIGATIONS, e.g. at §116 (1953).
[19] Black §63 at 180 ("[T]he rule is subordinate to the great fundamental rule that the real intention of the legislature must in all cases prevail."); 59 *C.J.* Statutes §577 at 978 ("The meaning of doubtful words must be determined by the sense in which they are used by the legislature without regard to their primary meaning.").

Pair Sixteen

THRUST: "Every word and clause must be given effect."
PARRY: "If inadvertently inserted or if repugnant to the rest of the statute, they may be rejected as surplusage."[1]

Llewellyn's formulations of both Thrust and Parry appear to paraphrase Black's caption in the cited section 60:

> REJECTION OF SURPLUSAGE
> It is the duty of courts to give effect, if possible, to every word of the written law. But if a word or clause be found in a statute which appears to have been inserted through inadvertence or mistake, or which is repugnant to the rest of the act and tends to nullify it, and if the statute is complete and sensible without it, such word or clause may be rejected as surplusage.[2]

The omission of "if possible" in Thrust #16 is significant in light of the aim of finding a contrary in Parry #16. Parry #16 cuts the qualifiers from Black's rather more cautious continuation of section 60, and substitutes "statute" for "act."

Pair 16 breaks from the three previous pairs' theme of determining semantic meanings, but develops one of the exceptional circumstances justifying Parry #15, *viz* the need to give some meaning to a statute. We are entitled to presume that when the legislature enacts a string of words, the chief administrator signs off on them, and they are duly promulgated, some meaning was intended; it was not merely huffing and puffing.

Thrust #16: "Every word and clause must be given effect."

This is a familiar canon of construction, although it is usually expressed in less absolute, universal terms.[3] It is not just an exhortation not to ignore inconvenient statutory language. Rather, between alternative interpretations a court should take one which gives all the statute's language some effect, not one which leaves any part of the statute with no effect.

Sutherland offers a clear example, *State of Nebraska, ex rel. First Nat'l Bank of Crete v. Bartley*.[4] Nebraska law at the time required the state treasurer, Joseph S. Bartley, "to keep on

---

1 *Canons* at 404.
2 Black §60 at 165.
3 *See, e.g.*, Sutherland §380 at 731-32, also cited for Thrust #16.
4 39 Neb. 353 (1894).

deposit in the several banks designated as depositories all money received by him belonging to the state." Only three banks qualified, and of those Bartley snubbed plaintiff First National Bank of Crete, which sought a writ of mandamus. Bartley demurred; the statute, he said, required him only to deposit monies in the general fund in the qualified banks, and it had all been deposited in the other two, leaving nothing for the plaintiff. But the statute's actual words were "the amounts of money in his hands belonging to the several current funds in the state treasury" so the question hinged on the meaning of "the several current funds in the state treasury": Did it refer only to the general fund —"created for the purpose of paying the salaries of the state officers and defraying the general expenses of the state government" —or to all government funds?[5]

If "the several current funds" was intended to refer only to the general fund, why the plural "funds," and why "several"? "It is an elementary rule of construction that effect must be given, if possible, to every word, clause, and sentence of a statute" (Thrust #16 —"if possible"). If the plural "funds" and the adjective "several" were to have any effect, the whole phrase "the several current funds" must refer to other funds, such as the "sinking fund, permanent school fund, and others which it is unnecessary to stop now to enumerate." Accordingly, under Thrust #16 "it is not a difficult task to ascertain the legislature's intent." Of course the ultimate question of the writ of mandamus was not decided by this argument, but the state treasurer's demurrer was disposed of.[6]

Llewellyn's chosen case, *In re Terry's Estate*, is not especially illustrative.[7] The decedent had made gifts to charities, automatically leaving a right of reverter to the residuary beneficiary, perhaps a donee charity. Was that right of reverter subject to New York's transfer tax? Of course the state said it was, and not only that, at the full present value of the gift, and the Appellate Division agreed. The late Tootie McG, Terry's personal representative appealed; after all, what would you pay for that right of reverter?

In reversing, the Court of Appeals gave us one line supporting Thrust #16: "The Tax Law must be given a meaning whereby, if possible, all its provisions are read together and made effective." But this was not the ground on which the decision rested.

> Such construction presents no insurmountable difficulties when we consider the further rule of construction that the Transfer Tax Law is to be construed favorably to the persons *taxed* ..., and that the transfer tax is imposed on the right of succession and not on the property transferred. ...The question is wholly one of *valuation for taxation* first and taxation afterwards.[8]

There was a potential inconsistency between sections 222 and 230, but this was completely resolved by determining that only section 230 pertained to the charitable gift in question.

---

[5] Id, 39 Neb. at 358.

[6] Id.

[7] *In re Terry's Estate*, 218 N.Y. 218 (1916).

[8] Id, 218 N.Y. at 222-23 (citations omitted).

But as the number of statutes increases and our society becomes ever more complex, the presumption that a legislature would never enact two inconsistent provisions, or provisions with inconsistent applications, becomes ever less plausible. Statutes enacted at different times, by different legislatures, perhaps even about prima facie different subjects, may come to clash on unforeseen subject matter. With applicable but irreconcilably inconsistent statutes, courts have sometimes resorted to one of the most simplistic of canons: "[A]n old statute gives place to a new one."[9] The presumption is that the more recent legislature intended to rescind inconsistent prior statutes.

And sometimes a legislature may simply botch the job.

Parry #16: "If inadvertently inserted or if repugnant to the rest of the statute, they may be rejected as surplusage."

In the cited section 60, Black was more cautious than Parry #16, including the qualification that the words "tend to nullify [the act], and if the statute is complete and sensible without … such word or clause … ."[10] Llewellyn also cites Sutherland: "Where a word or phrase in a statute would make the clause in which it occurs unintelligible, the word may be eliminated and the clause read without it."[11] These are descriptions of circumstances in which satisfying Thrust #16 is not possible.[12]

Llewellyn's cited case, *United States v. York*, provides a very pretty illustration, although one that turned out to be irrelevant to the outcome of the case.[13] York was charged under U.S. Revenue Statute section 5424 and section 5427 for aiding another to utter a false statement as true. Although the details are not explicit, it seems that he was the forger who provided a certificate of naturalization to Bunoro to help Caggiano become a citizen. Section 5424 describes the primary offense and section 5427 adds aiding and abetting. These sections were part of the 1874 revision of the original 1870 statute.[14]

---

[9] William Blackstone, 1 COMMENTARIES ON THE LAW OF ENGLAND 89 (1765).

[10] Black §60 at 165.

[11] Sutherland §384 at 739.

[12] C.J.*Statutes* makes this problem the focus, with Thrust #16 merely a background presumption. 59 *C.J.*Statutes §592 at 992. R.C.L. has a more discursive account, generally taking a much more sympathetic attitude towards legislative text and its problems. 25 R.C.L. §§221 and 222, p.966-67, which, along with §227, p.978 (captioned "Correction of Mistakes, Errors, or Omissions.") have an excellent discussion.

[13] 131 F. 323 (S.D.N.Y., 1904). The case was decided on a very pretty scope ambiguity in section 5424, boosted by the rule of lenity and a plain language argument. *See United States v. York*, 131 F. at 326-31.

[14] *United States v. York*, *supra*, 131 F. at 324-27 ("The first question presented arises out of the revision of the statutes in 1874. Sections 5424, 5425, 5426, and 5427 of the Revised Statutes [U.S. Comp. St. 1901, pp. 3668-3670] are a revision of part of section 2 of chapter 254 of the act of Congress of July 13, 1870 (16 Stat. 254), with certain changes of phraseology to be hereafter noted.")

In making the revisions, the legislators contemplated defining "felony" as "a crime, punishable with death, or by imprisonment at hard labor," thus enabling the omission of serial statutory declarations that doing such-and-such is a felony in addition to prescribing the punishment. Accordingly sections 5424 to 5426 did not say their listed offenses were felonies. Sections 5427 followed the previous 1870 version in referring to "every person who knowingly and intentionally aids or abets any person in the commission of any felony denounced in the three preceding sections . . . " But then, in the final enacted version, they neglected to include the definition of "felony."[15]

York (and Bunoro) demurred. To allow a charge of aiding and abetting under section 5427 would make the words "any felony" inoperative, mere surplusage, as there were no felonies named in sections 5424 to 5426; Thrust #16. On this argument they lost. Legislative intent is simply too clear, the history of the section showing unequivocally how this oversight in drafting arose. It was a clear case of inadvertent use of language, "repugnant to the rest of the statute." "It does not seem the better judgment to hold that this inaccurate use of a term should be regarded as showing the intention of Congress, when the section otherwise, and the history of the revision, point clearly to a different intention."[16] Parry #16.

Resolution:

United States v. York illustrates one way in which some resolution between Thrust and Parry #16 is inescapable. Dogmatically to follow defendants' Thrust #16 on "any felony," pumped up by pronouncements of plain meaning,[17] would pretty much make all the rest of section 5427 surplusage. The obvious intent to make aiding and abetting also an offense would completely fail. A court must make a decision: enforce legislative intent or pedanticism.

When the presumption underlying Thrust #16 fails demonstrably, so too must the canon itself fail. As with all canons, it is no more than the reasoning on which it rests. Superficially one could say that Thrust and Parry #16 are opposed, but surely not often, let alone "on almost every point."[18]

---

[15] *United States v. York, supra*, 131 F. at 325-26.
[16] Id, 131 F. at 326.
[17] For example: "The primary and general rule of statutory construction is that the intent of the lawmaker is to be found in the language that he used. He is presumed to know the meaning of words and the rules of grammar. The courts have no function of legislation, and simply seek to ascertain the will of the legislator." *United States v. Goldenberg*, 168 U.S. 95, 102 (1897)
[18] *Canons* at 401.

Pair Seventeen

> **THRUST:** "The same language used repeatedly in the same connection is presumed to bear the same meaning throughout the statute."
> **PARRY:** "This presumption will be disregarded where it is necessary to assign different meanings to make the statute consistent."[1]

This pair comes from Black's §53, Llewellyn's only cited secondary source, by simplifying to canon size and, as we've seen before, substituting 'statute' for 'act', with the usual exception becoming the parry.

> USE OF SAME LANGUAGE AND CHANGE OF LANGUAGE
> 53. Where the same language is used repeatedly in a statute in the same connection, it is presumed to bear the same meaning throughout the act; but this presumption will be disregarded where it is necessary to assign different meanings to the same terms in order to make the statute sensible, consistent, and operative.[2]

Thrust #17: "The same language used repeatedly in the same connection is presumed to bear the same meaning throughout the statute."

The idea is straightforward, as is the prima facie justification: a legislature engaged in speaking to and controlling a domain of social intercourse may be presumed to use words in a stable, uniform manner. Instances of the converse should be rare, or flagged explicitly, for example in a definition, or by context. Thus one is entitled to use Thrust #17 as a presumption, but only "in the same act in relation to the same subject-matter."[3] What other presumption could one make?

The canon is useful if the meaning of a word in one instance is clear and in another under-determined. One can presume that both were used by the legislature in the same sense and thus use the clear instance to resolve the under-determinacy of the other. R.C.L. says it clearly in a brief section on the canon: "Where a word susceptible of more than one meaning is repeated in

---

1 *Cannons* at 404.
2 Black §53 at 145. Llewellyn appears to have ignored §54, a useful rule, if to drafters an exhortation to be boring: "§54Converesly, where different language is used in the same connection, in different parts of the statute, it is presumed that the legislature intended it to have a different meaning and effect."
3 Black §53 at 145.

the same section of an act ... a presumption arises, more or less forcible according to the circumstances, that it is used throughout in the same sense."[4]

Llewellyn's illustrative case, *Spring Canyon Coal Co. v. Industrial Commission of Utah*,[5] recites Thrust 17 but does not use it. After reciting the plain meaning rule and *expressio unius*, the opinion continues

> Among the other well-recognized rules applied in the construction of a statute are these: The language used must be read in a sense which harmonized with the general purposes and objects of the statute, 25 R. C. L. § 253, p. 1013; 2 Lewis' Sutherland Statutory Construction (2d Ed.) §§ 368-390,, pp. 706-714. Prima facie, the same meaning will be given to a word or phrase used in different parts of a statute. Beal, Cardinal Rules of Legal Interpretation (2d Ed.) p. 316; 25 R. C. L. § 238, p. 994; 2 Lewis' Sutherland Statutory Construction (2d Ed.) § 399, p. 758.[6]

A mining accident deprived Jesus Aspatia of the use of his legs useless, forcing him onto crutches. The Industrial Commission had determined that this was equivalent to losing his legs and awarded him compensation accordingly. Spring Canyon, his employer, appealed, contending that despite his losing the use of his legs, Aspatia still had them so should be compensated at a lower rate.[7] The decision was based on the plain meaning rule. "The loss of both hands or ... both legs..." means only that: "It cannot well be said that Aspatia has lost both legs when, in fact, he has both legs. The fact that he has both legs belies the statement that he has lost both legs."[8] The case merely provides a recitation of Thrust #17 not an example or illustration.

Llewellyn might have used the first case cited by Black, *Rhodes v. Welty*,[9] a challenge to a will by an after-born daughter, for whom no provision had been made; it depended critically on what it is to *provide* for such a child under the statute.[10]

> It would not be a sound proposition to say that the same word occurring in different places in the same statute always means the same thing. It may sometimes call for a radically different construction. But where the same word or phrase is used more than once in the same act, especially in the same section and in the same sentence, in relation to the same subject-matter and looking to the same general purpose, it is a fundamental rule of statutory construction that if in

---

[4] 25 R.C.L. at §238, pp.994-95.
[5] 74 Utah 103 (1929).
[6] Id, 74 Utah at 115.
[7] Id, 74 Utah at 110.
[8] Id, 74 Utah at 113-14.
[9] 46 Ohio St. 234 (1889).
[10] Id, 46 Ohio St. at 234 ("The solution of this case depends upon the construction of section 38 of an act relating to wills, passed May 3, 1852, S. & C. Stat. 1622, which provides: "If the testator had no children at the time of executing his will, but shall afterwards have a child living, or born alive after his death, such will shall be deemed revoked, unless provisions shall have been made for such child by some settlement, or unless such child shall have been provided for in the will, or in such way mentioned therein, as to show an intention not to make such provisions, and no other evidence to rebut the presumption or revocation, shall be received." (Sec. 5959, Rev. Stats.)")

> one connection the meaning is clear and in the other it is otherwise doubtful or obscure, it is in the latter case to be construed the same as in the former.[11]

One could scarcely wish for a more clear statement, and it was not mere recitation: the decision depended its application: "Giving to the word "provision" in the one phrase substantially the same construction which the word "provisions" is clearly entitled to in the other, and the conclusion is that Elizabeth was not "provided for in the will" by the devise … ."[12]

The idea of Thrust #17 is not without its critics. For example:

> The tendency to assume that a word which appears in two or more rules, and so in connection with more than one purpose, has and should have precisely the same scope in all of them runs all through legal discussions. It has all the tenacity of original sin and must constantly be guarded against.[13]

Hence:

Parry #17: "This presumption will be disregarded where it is necessary to assign different meanings to make the statute consistent."

Black was more fulsome in the conditions under which Parry #17 rather than Thrust #17 would apply: "where it is necessary to assign different meanings to the same terms in order to make the statute sensible, consistent, and operative."[14]

Llewellyn's cited case is a fine illustration. In 1900 the defendant William H. Knowles argued successfully in the Criminal Court of Baltimore City that the governing statute,

> Any person twenty-one years of age, who has graduated at, and holds a diploma from, a university or college authorized to grant diplomas in dental surgery by the laws of any one of the United States, and who is desirous of practicing dentistry in this State, may be examined by said board with reference to qualifications, and after passing an examination satisfactory to the board, his or her name, residence or place of business, shall be registered in a book kept for that purpose, and a certificate shall be issued to such person. Any graduate of a regular college of dentistry, may, at the discretion of the examining board, be registered without being subjected to an examination.[15]

was unconstitutionally void for creating a "purely personal and arbitrary power."[16] The argument under Thrust #17 worked on the word "may" in each sentence: in the second sentence, coupled

---

11 Id, 46 Ohio St. at 242.

12 Id, 46 Ohio St. at 243.

13 Walter W. Cook, LOGICAL AND LEGAL BASES OF THE CONFLICT OF LAWS 159 (1942).

14 Black §53 at 145.

15 Act of 1896, ch. 378, which repealed and re-enacted with amendments Art. 32 of the Code of Public General Laws of Maryland, entitled "Dentistry.", Section 5, quoted and cited, *State v. Knowles*, 90 Md. 646, 653, 45 A. 877, 877 (1900).

16 Citing *Yick Wo* v. *Hopkins,* 118 U.S. 356, 369, 6 S. Ct. 1064, 1071 (1886), ("[W]hen we consider the nature and theory of our institutions of government, the principles upon which they are supposed to rest,

with "at the discretion", it clearly indicates a free choice for the board, so it must be the same in the first sentence; thus it is a matter of whim whether the board would require an applicant for a dentistry license to take an examination or not. The court of appeals wasn't buying it.

First it looked at the first sentence alone, as if there were no second sentence:

> Would it not necessarily be construed "shall," or "must," in conformity with the established rule of law that where the duty to be performed, is for the benefit of the public or third persons, it shall be so construed? The duty of examination upon application (where there is no express discretion to waive examination) is for the benefit of both the public and the applicant. For the benefit of the public, because it protects the public against ignorant and incompetent practitioners, and for the benefit of the qualified applicant, because it puts him before the public with the seal of approbation from a competent and disinterested tribunal.

Now put back the second sentence and ask whether it makes a difference. The meaning of the "may" in the second sentence is inescapable, thus (even though "The law does not permit itself to be frightened out of its propriety by the hobgoblin of inconsistency") there must be a difference in the legislature's intended treatment of a "person twenty-one years of age, who has graduated at, and holds a diploma from, a university or college authorized to grant diplomas in dental surgery by the laws of any one of the United States" and a "graduate of a regular college of dentistry."

> We think the Act does mean to distinguish, for the purpose of examinations, between "a college or university authorized to grant diplomas in dental surgery," and "a regular college of dentistry." In the former, dentistry may be but an adjunct to the course, and there is no such assurance of thoroughness of instruction and practical application, as must be presumed in a regular dental college where the whole time of the students and instructors is given to the theory and practice of dental science.[17]

Thin? Maybe, but one ought not find the legislature to have acted unconstitutionally unless there is no alternative.[18] Thus

> we have no hesitation in holding that the only discretion conferred, is to waive an examination, when the applicant is a graduate of a regular college of dentistry and that in all other cases covered by the Act, examinations must be granted when application is made ...[19]

and Knowles' short-lived victory vanished in the court's remand for trial.

Notice what was required for Parry #17, *viz*, the determination of different legislative purposes for the two different uses of the term in question. The court had to work hard to find it, but at stake was the prevention of the unlicensed practice of dentistry, and the constitutionality of

---

and review the history of their development, we are constrained to conclude that they do not mean to leave room for the play and action of purely personal and arbitrary power.")

[17] *State v. Knowles*, 90 Md. at 654-55.

[18] This has become a popular substantive canon; *see* pp.55-56 above.

[19] *State v. Knowles*, 90 Md. at 656, 45 A. at 878.

the statute. The case does not illustrate Llewellyn's only criterion for abandoning Thrust #17, "consistency", but his was a rather impoverished version of Black's formulation.

Resolution:

One could find conflict between Thrust and Parry #17; the pair comes as close to a genuine conflict as any we have seen so far (*i.e.*, as close as Pair 5). But, like other canons, Thrust #17 is no more than a presumption, and no better than its justification. Of course a legislature, communicating control data to its denizens, will probably use words with constant, stable meanings. But if it has not, and it is clear that it has not or if a more powerful presumption, such as that the legislature acted constitutionally, consistently, rationally, sensibly, or intended its enactment to do something, then it would be to deny legislative purpose woodenly to insist on Thrust #17.

Given the ease with which it may be trumped, Thrust #17 would seem to be a rather weak presumption. It might be better expressed with Parry #17 as a prefixed "unless ...", as treatise writers prefer.

Pair 17 illustrates a persistent and pervasive problem with Llewellyn's method of producing his pairs and its resulting in a Manichean misconception of canons as universal rules, to be followed automatically or rejected. Treatise writers, of whom Black was Llewellyn's favorite source in creating the list, write section captions whose accuracy depends on their qualifications and exceptions. Without the "unless ..." clause the qualified generality would simply not reflect judicial practice or interpretative soundness. One might go so far as to say that a general exception of the form "unless the legislature clearly expresses a different intention" should be implied along with any canon.[20] Llewellyn's method of paraphrasing Black's captions by skipping qualifiers then separating the "unless ..." clause as parry produces, at the price of accuracy, only the most superficial of contradictions.

Canons of interpretation —like almost all generalities about human endeavors —are not universal rules that must either apply or be eternally abandoned. Canons are generalities that have been found wise, useful, and justified, but they are never an excuse for switching off one's brain. Pair 17 illustrates how Llewellyn's method of taking the obvious exception to a useful and justifiable generality and calling it a contradiction works only for a reader who does just that — switches off the brain.

---

[20] As the Supreme Court said in *United States v. Kirby*, 74 U.S. 482, 486 (1868); *see* Parry #12, above.

Pair Eighteen

THRUST: "Words are to be interpreted according to the proper grammatical effect of their arrangement within the statute."
PARRY: "Rules of grammar will be disregarded where strict adherence would defeat purpose."[1]

In addition to Black section 55, which he cites for both thrust and parry, Llewellyn cites Sutherland section 408 for Thrust #18 and section 409 for Parry #18. The source for both formulations appears to be the caption to Black's §55, with the usual changes to make aphoristic formulae, and as before, substituting "statute" for "act."

> GRAMMATICAL INTERPRETATION
> 55. Primarily, a statute is to be interpreted according to the ordinary meaning of its words and the proper grammatical effect of their arrangement in the act. But if there is any ambiguity, or if there is room for more than one interpretation, the rules of grammar will be disregarded where a too strict adherence to them would raise a repugnance or absurdity or would defeat the purpose of the legislature.

Both Sutherland and Black are less dogmatic than Llewellyn in their expression of this principle; for example both use the qualifier "primarily" in their versions of Thrust #18.

Thrust #18: "Words are to be interpreted according to the proper grammatical effect of their arrangement within the statute."

Statutes communicate to the governed; to do so they use language, words organized according to the rules of grammar. Thrust #18 is no more than a recognition of these simple facts. What other presumption could we make than that legislation uses conventional grammar? Litigated examples of Thrust #18 should, one hopes, be rare: our legislators tend to be well educated and to have well educated drafting assistance. Bad grammar, in contrast, is likely to generate interpretive questions for courts.

Llewellyn cites *Harris v. Commonwealth*,[2] a lovely case, but hardly an illustration of Thrust #18. The interpretation question was a scope ambiguity in Section 32 of Virginia's

---

[1] *Cannons* at 404.
[2] 142 Va. 620 (1925).

prohibition act, "The provisions of this act shall not be construed to prevent any person from manufacturing for his domestic consumption at his home ... wine or cider from fruit of his own raising ... ." Does "at his home" apply only to "his domestic consumption" or does it apply also to "manufacturing ..."? It mattered to Harris, who made wine on his farm in Brunswick county and was caught transporting it to his home in Greensville county. The opinion recites a version of Thrust #18, but obviously it is of no help; the scope of "at home" is intractably ambiguous in section 32. Instead of "technical grammatical rules," the court used two interpretive arguments and affirmed Harris' conviction. First, was a slippery slope *reductio*: the intent of the whole act was "was to break up and to prevent the use of ardent spirits as a beverage"; to allow manufacture of wine in one place and consumption in another would subvert that intent. Second, another section, section 12, specifically prohibited lawfully acquired "ardent spirits" anywhere other than one's home. Were "at his home" in section 32 be given narrow scope, permitting manufacture elsewhere provided storage and consumption were domestic, the two sections would clash.[3] It is instructive statutory interpretation, but neither needs nor advances the cause of Thrust #18.

Good appellate illustrations of Thrust #18 should be scarce, but one cited by Black, *viz Ohio National Bank v. Berlin*,[4] from the court of appeals for Washington, D.C. will serve. In 1901 the plaintiff bank won a judgment for Berlin's unpaid debt and sought a lien on an equitable interest Berlin inherited in real estate; the D.C. statute giving an automatic judgment lien was enacted in 1902. The appellant bank's argument that the automatic lien should date from its judgment in 1901 was a clear loser, but what about granting the same lien from the effective date of the statute, even though the judgment anteceded it? It would require going "beyond the letter of the statute," but there is no "apparent reason why the legislature should have made a distinction between future judgments and existing ones." However

> To hold that they give a lien to prior judgments from *the date of the enactment* is contrary to the grammatical construction and the plain, natural import of the words. There is no other language in the section warranting an inference that those words were intended to have any other than their literal and natural meaning. ... Undoubtedly, the lien given by the statute might wisely and justly have been extended to both classes of judgments, but the courts have no power to interpolate words necessary to accomplish that end. They have nothing to do with the motives actuating the legislature.[5]

It does use Thrust #18, and with it defeats a reasonable equitable argument for extending the scope of the statute, arguably consistently with legislative intent.

---

[3] Id, 142 Va. at 623-24 ("Construing sections 32 and 12 together, in view of the manifest purpose of the act, we are of opinion that the wine in question was not manufactured by Harris either *at* or *in* his *bona fide* home, and hence was unlawful. His possession of it being unlawful, his transportation thereof was also unlawful.") It was a criminal statute, and Harris was fined $300: Might he not have had a shot at lenity, "construe ambiguities in favor of the accused?"

[4] 26 App. D.C. 218 (1905)

[5] Id, 26 App. D.C. at 222.

Parry #18 is much more interesting.

Parry #18: "Rules of grammar will be disregarded where strict adherence would defeat purpose."

Both Black and Sutherland spend their textual efforts on Parry #18, the exception to the default cliché, Thrust #18. The justification is legislative supremacy, but that requires legislative intent to be both clear and not adequately expressed by the literal words of the statute. Examples should be rare.

Llewellyn cites *Fisher v. Connard.*[6] It is an excellent illustration, not just for its fine rhetoric but because it actually depends on Parry #18. Remember *Harris v. Commonwealth*, where poor Harris feloniously carried home the wine he'd made at his farm?[7] The statute in *Fisher v. Connard* was similar, but it had a comma, absent in *Harris v. Commonwealth*'s key statute, removing the scope ambiguity. But what then? Is the court obliged to reach a conclusion contrary to the manifest intent of the legislation? No way.

The facts as presented are unreadable; here are the essentials. Daniel B. Fisher owned premises in the city of Reading. On May 29th, 1877, the city solicitor filed a lien against the property for "city tax for 1876, $39.94, survey twenty-five cents, - $ 40.19" and registered the lien in the City Lien Docket on May 29th, 1877. On June 1st 1877 Fisher mortgaged the property to Thomas Jackson, for $ 2,000; the mortgage was recorded on June 9th 1877. When Thomas Jackson died, the mortgagee's interest passed to Henry Connard, Jr., and Henry H. Jackson, his personal representatives, now the plaintiffs. On November 3d 1879, a third party creditor, coincidentally a relative, *David* B. Fisher won a judgment against Daniel B. Fisher for $3,308.28 to satisfy which he had the property sold at a sheriff's sale on December 13th 1879, buying it himself for $40 unencumbered by the city's lien (which was satisfied out of the proceeds of other property sold at the sheriff's sale.)[8] What about the mortgage?

Under prior law a sheriff's sale cut off the interest of the mortgagee, even if recorded. This of course was an expensive source of insecurity for mortgage lenders, so the legislature came to the rescue with section 3 of "The Act of 23d of March 1867, P. L. 43":

> When the lien of a mortgage upon real estate is, or shall be prior to all other liens upon the same property, except other mortgages, ground rents, purchase money due to the Commonwealth, taxes, charges, assessments and municipal claims, whose lien, though afterwards accruing has by law priority given it, the lien of such mortgage shall not be destroyed, or in any way affected by any judicial or other sale whatsoever, whether such judicial sale shall be made by virtue or authority of any order, or decree of any Orphans' or other court, or any writ of

---

[6] 100 Pa. 63 (1882).
[7] 142 Va. 620 (1925), above.
[8] *Fisher v. Connard, supra*, 100 Pa. at 67-68.

> execution, or otherwise howsoever: *Provided*, that this section shall not apply to cases of mortgages upon unseated lands, or sales of same for taxes.[9]

But did it succeed? Defendant David Fisher "argued with much learning and ability ... that the proper antecedent of the word "lien" is "municipal claims," and that it is to such claims only that the words "whose lien though afterwards accruing has by law priority given it," applies." It was to this argument that the court replied with the oft-quoted passage.

> The grammatical construction of a statute is one mode of interpretation. But it is not the only mode, and it is not always the true mode. We may assume that the draftsman of an Act understood the rules of grammar, but it is not always safe to do so. The Act of 1867 was evidently passed with reference to preceding Acts in regard to taxes. In many of these Acts the words "taxes, charges, assessments and municipal claims" had been used together, and in connection with the word "lien." ... Our best judgment is that "taxes, charges, assessments and municipal claims" in the Act of 1867, were all intended as antecedents of the word "lien," and if this makes good law, the grammatical construction is not so important.[10]

As the protection of prior recorded mortgagees was one of the primary purposes of the legislation, about which no reader could reasonably have been in doubt, this makes very good sense.

Resolution:

Thrust #18 would thus seem to be rather weak. Sutherland says the "presumption gives way" if context or the statute as a whole indicates an intent different from the strict grammatical reading: "It is better always to adhere to a plain common-sense interpretation of the words of a statute, than to apply to them refined and technical rules of grammatical construction."[11] Properly recognized as a presumption and a relatively weak one, Thrust #18 reflects only a natural starting point, a commonplace with a commonplace justification: legislatures communicate in language, and language is rule-governed, in both semantics and syntax. But where clear, legislative intent is not to be denied by accidents of expression, even in the rules of grammar: Parry #18. You could call this a contrary, but only if you refused to recognize the realities of legislative governance and the democratic principle of legislative supremacy.

---

[9] Id, 100 Pa. at 68-69.

[10] Id, 100 Pa. at 69.

[11] Sutherland at §408, 793 & §409, 794 quoting the 1870 Pennsylvania supreme court, *Gyger's Estate. Eshleman's Appeal*, 65 Pa. 311, 312 (1870).

Pair Nineteen

THRUST: "Exceptions not made cannot be read."
PARRY: "The letter is only the 'bark.' Whatever is within the reason of the law is within the law itself."[1]

Although Llewellyn cites only one secondary source for Thrust #19, 25 R.C.L. *Statutes* §230, the source appears to have been 59 C.J. *Statutes* §643, the introductory paragraph of which ends "Where the terms of a statute are positive and unambiguous, exceptions not made by the legislature cannot be read into the act."[2] Canons, as well used wise saws, are not usually expressed in metaphors, so as one might expect the poetic expression of Parry #19 is not a commonplace; I have not yet been able to discover an occurrence of the "bark" metaphor other than on Llewellyn's list. It remains a curiosity. But once started, the metaphor should be continued in the contrast, for example, "The reason is the heart timber of the law" or "The bite of the law is its reason," not the abandonment we see here, leaving the "bark" dangling.

Thrust #19: "Exceptions not made cannot be read."

Among his secondaries, Llewellyn cites only 25 R.C.L. *Statutes* §230, a short section captioned "Express Exceptions": "It is well settled that an exception in a statute amounts to an affirmation of the application of its provisions to all other cases not excepted and excludes all other exceptions."[3] It does not give a justification.

Thrust #19 is simply a special case, and an especially clear case, of the paradigmatic canon "*Expressio unius est exclusio alterius*," Thrust #20, and has the same justification. The compilers of Corpus Juris give it, *inter alia*, just such a form: "...it is a general rule that an express exception excludes all others."[4] Black mentions it in the section on *expressio unius* ...as a special case:

---

[1] *Canons* at 404.
[2] 59 C.J. *Statutes* §643b. ("Exceptions."), at 1092.
[3] 25 R.C.L. *Statutes* at §230, 983; *see also* C.J. *Statutes* at §643b., 1093.
[4] 59 C.J. *Statutes* at §643b, 1092.

> Another case in which this maxim may almost invariably be followed is that of a statute which makes certain specific exceptions to its general provisions. Here we may safely assume that all other exceptions were intended to be excluded.[5]

Thrust #19 is especially clear because the general rule to which the exception is excepted is laid down with it and, indeed, reinforced by it. It is not, therefore, subject to the conditions on its application that plague the more general form.

Llewellyn's cited illustration, *Lima v. Lima Cemetery Ass'n*,[6] works well. Lima, a city in Ohio, had assessed the Lima Cemetery Association proportionally to its frontage on a city alley for grading and paving the alley. But "by Rev. Stats. §§ 2732, 3571, 3578 ..." burying grounds —cemeteries —are exempted from "taxation." "It is insisted that this exemption embraces assessments." All the court needed to defeat that insistence is first to distinguish an assessment from a tax and, second, to recite Thrust #19. First, taxes are to raise revenue, assessments to pay the costs of special improvements benefiting those assessed. Second,

> applying the well settled rule for the construction of provisions exempting property from such burdens, that is, that they are to be strictly construed ...we are required by the clear weight of authority to hold, that the exemption in our statutes of burying grounds from taxation (Rev. Stats. §§ 2732, 3571, 3578), has relation to taxation for revenue purposes, and does not extend to an assessment for a local improvement like that in question here.

There followed cites to forty-seven cases in nineteen states and only two exceptions, both from Wisconsin.[7]

Parry #19: "The letter is only the "bark." Whatever is within the reason of the law is within the law itself."

"[T]here are two opposing canons on almost every point."[8] How does Parry #19 oppose Thrust #19? They are at different levels of generality, not sufficiently closely related to be opposed. Even Llewellyn's chosen secondary source, C.J.*Statutes* §573, comes under the general sub-headings "Intention of legislature," "Construction to Effect Legislative Purpose," and "Spirit or Letter"[9] and Thrust #19 comes some one hundred and twenty-eight pages further on under the sub-headings "Provisos, Exceptions, and Saving Clauses – Exceptions."[10] One can readily subscribe to Parry #19 and still use Thrust #19 in interpreting a particular exception. Indeed that is the point of canons such as Thrust #19: they are devices for ascertaining and implementing the intent, or "reason of the law."

---

5 Black §72 ("EXPRESS MENTION AND IMPLIED EXCLUSION"), 219, at 222 .
6 42 Ohio St. 128 (1884).
7 Id, 42 Ohio St. 129-131.
8 *Canons* at 401.
9 59 C.J.Statutes at 943, 961 and 964.
10 Id at 1087 and 1092.

In support of Parry #19 Llewellyn might have gone to the Supreme Court's infamous *Church of the Holy Trinity*: "a thing may be within the letter of the statute and yet not within the statute, because not within its spirit, nor within the intention of its makers."[11] But instead he cites *Flynn v. Prudential Ins. Co.*,[12] a case decided on the basis of Thrust #19, but which could illustrate Parry #19 or, perhaps better, Parry #12. New York Insurance Law at the time said, at §55:

> No policy or agreement for insurance shall be issued upon the life or health of another or against loss by disablement by accident except upon the application of the persons insured; but ... and a person liable for the support of a child of the age of one year and upward may take a yearly renewable term policy of insurance thereon, the amount payable under which may be made to increase with advancing age and which shall not exceed the sums specified in the following table, the ages wherein specified being the age at time of death, and which, after the age of thirteen, may become an ordinary life policy for an amount not exceeding the sum specified in the table: ... Between the ages of seven and eight years, one hundred and sixty-eight dollars.[13]

Plaintiff Flynn had taken maximum policies with Metropolitan Life Insurance Company and defendant Prudential on his late daughter's life. After Metropolitan paid, Prudential refused, citing the above statute. The Appellate Division found for Flynn; the Court of Appeals reversed.

The purpose of the legislation was clear, namely to prohibit profiting on the misfortune of one's child and even to inhibit neglect of a child to gain such profit, and the Appellate Division's construction (arguing that the statute was in derogation of the common law and thus to be construed strictly) would subvert that intent rendering the statute "simply absurd." Two rules of construction mandated reversal. First, "Every interpretation that leads to an absurdity should be rejected." Second, such a reversal is permitted:

> In the interpretation of statutes, the great principle which is to control is the intention of the legislature in passing the same, which intention is to be ascertained from the cause or necessity of making the statute as well as other circumstances. A strict and literal interpretation is not always to be adhered to, and where the case is brought within the intention of the makers of the statute, it is within the statute, although by a technical interpretation it is not within its letter.[14]

And that, no doubt, is why Llewellyn cited *Flynn v. Prudential Ins. Co.* Parry #19 is a general permission to interpret the words of the statute liberally in order to effectuate legislative intent.

Resolution:

---

[11] *Church of the Holy Trinity v. United States*, 143 U.S. 457, 459 (1892).
[12] 207 N.Y. 315 (1913).
[13] *Flynn v. Prudential Ins. Co.*, *supra*, 207 N.Y. at 317-18.
[14] Id, 207 N.Y. at 319 (quoting "*People ex rel. Wood* v. *Lacombe*, 99 N. Y. 43, 49.")

Parry #19's bark has no bite, at least not against Thrust #19. Llewellyn's cited case, *Flynn v. Prudential Ins. Co.*, shows that, explicitly relying on Thrust #19 within the permission of Parry #19 as its ground of decision.

Parry #19 is another of the disappointments of Llewellyn's list. Perhaps it was scratched up simply because Thrust #19 is so unexceptionable, as Black says, "almost invariably … followed," so "safely assumed."[15] But in that case, it would have been better to have left both off the list or to have posted Thrust #19 as an exception.

---

[15] Black at §72, 219 at 222.

Pair Twenty

THRUST: "Expression of one thing excludes another."
PARRY: "The language may fairly comprehend many different cases where some only are expressly mentioned by way of example."[1]

Llewellyn's Thrust #20 is a straightforward translation of "*Expressio unius est exclusio alterius*." His Parry #20 appears to be from Sutherland:

> The maxim does not apply to a statute the language of which may fairly comprehend many different cases, in which some only are expressly mentioned by way of example merely, and not as excluding others of a similar nature.[2]

Thrust #20: Expression of one thing excludes another.

"*Expressio unius est exclusio alterius*" is probably the best known of all canons of construction. Not surprisingly therefore, it is also a favorite target of those who would deny the usefulness of canons. Reed Dickerson, for example: "[it is] a rather elaborate, mysterious sounding, and anachronistic way of describing the negative implication. ... Far from being a rule, it is not even lexicographically accurate … ."[3] However, like most canons it is generally susceptible to attack only when taken to claim more absolute authority and a universal scope beyond its justification, and not simply as an aid to determining legislative intent.[4] Secondary authorities are much more circumspect about it than Llewellyn's Manichean enterprise requires. Black, for example, begins "The maxim "expressio unius est exclusio alterius" is of very important, though limited, application in the interpretation of statutes."[5]

As a paradigm canon facing widespread hostility "*expressio unius* ..." stands in more need of justification than most. Black says "It is based upon the rules of logic and the natural

---

[1] *Canons* at 405.
[2] Sutherland §495, 924; quoted by Black at 222.
[3] Reed Dickerson, THE INTERPRETATION AND APPLICATION OF STATUTES 234 (1975); similarly, "The rule that the expression of one thing is the exclusion of another is in direct contradiction to the habits of speech of most persons." Max Radin, *Statutory Interpretation*, 43 HARV. L. REV. 863, 874 (1930).
[4] Michael Sinclair, TRADITIONAL TOOLS OF STATUTORY INTERPRETATION, 130-37 (Vandeplas Publishing, 2013).
[5] Black at §72, 219, and continues: "[I]t is not to be taken as establishing a Procrustean standard to which all statutory language must be made to conform."

workings of the human mind,"[6] which is fair enough for 1911, and certainly it is natural to our thought processes. But we no longer classify its justification as logic, confining that to deductions made on the syntax and semantics of propositions. The justification of "*expressio unius* ..." is in the relationship of the statutory language to the context of its enactment, the subject we now call "pragmatics,"[7] "the study of linguistic acts and the contexts in which they are performed."[8]

> Suppose that A and B are talking about a mutual friend, C, who is now working in a bank. A asks B how C is getting on in his job, and B replies, *Oh quite well, I think; he likes his colleagues, and he hasn't been to prison yet.* At this point, A might well inquire what B was implying, what he was suggesting, or even what he meant by saying that C had not yet been to prison. ... It is clear that whatever B implied, suggested, meant in this example, is distinct from what B said, which was simply that C had not been to prison yet.[9]

Ordinary interpersonal conversation requires cooperation, and the conditions of that cooperation, *felicity* conditions, explain our conversational reliance and our feelings of deception when they are violated. In Grice's introductory example we understand that B would not say, felicitously, that C had not been to prison yet unless she knew something in C's background suggesting he was dishonest, or somesuch. That background presupposition is, in the jargon, called a pragmatic *implicature* of her *saying* "he hasn't been to prison yet."[10] What she said was not untrue, but unless that implicature was true it was certainly deceptive, misleading, infelicitous. Felicity conditions always depend on the context of the conversation in question. Usually the contextual presuppositions of a conversation are obvious and go unspoken, unnoticed even, except in their violation. In a courtroom cross-examination there would be no reasonable expectation of felicity.[11]

---

6 Id.

7 Or "speech act theory."

8 Robert Stalnaker, *Pragmatics*, 22 SYNTHESE 272, 275 (1970). The source usually cited as the origin of the three part classification, syntax, semantics, and pragmatics, is Morris, *Foundations of the Theory of Signs*, 1 INTERNATIONAL ENCYCLOPEDIA OF UNIFIED SCIENCE 79, 87 (1938). *See also* Geoffrey Leech, PRINCIPLES OF PRAGMATICS 19-45 (1983).

9 Paul Grice, STUDIES IN THE WAY OF WORDS 24 (1989). For the application of this theory to law *see, e.g.* Sinclair, *Law and Language: The role of Pragmatics in Statutory Interpretation* 46 U.PITT.L.REV. 373 (1985); Geoffrey Miller, *Pragmatics and the Maxims of Interpretation*, 1990 WISCONSIN L. REV. 1179 (1990).

10 Other familiar examples: "Have you stopped beating your wife?" would only felicitously be asked by a person with reason to believe that the addressee used to or still does beat his wife; absent such a pre-supposed reasonable belief the question is an infelicitous verbal trap. "What is the sound of one hand clapping?" would only be asked felicitously by a person who reasonably believed in affirmative answers to the prior questions as to whether one hand could clap and if so whether it made a sound; asking without such a believe is infelicitous verbal gamesmanship. "She was poor but she was honest" is felicitous only against the contextual background of general dishonesty of the poor; that is the force of "but".

11 *See United States v. Bronston*, 409 U.S. 352, 354, 357-59 (1973); Sinclair, *Law and Language*, *supra*, 46 U.PITT.L.REV. at 383-84.

A legislature speaks only through statutes.[12] Statutes communicate the legislature's intended controls to the governed. But unlike ordinary conversation, we do not have to contemplate the possibility of violation of felicity conditions; we *have* to presume that a legislature will, in its statutes, not lie, cheat, or deceive, nor even be infelicitous.[13] That is, we can always presume that a legislature has acted felicitously in its statutes. This lies behind the pragmatic justification of many linguistic canons of construction.

Like conversation, legislative speech always takes place in a context with a legal background. The legislature in enacting the statute in question must be presumed to be aware of it. To ignore it in interpreting the statute will almost guarantee missing significant evidence of legislative intent.

Because we may assume the felicity of legislative speech, "*expressio unius...*," like all pragmatically justified interpretation, is more reliable than in general conversation. If the statute imposes a new restraint on otherwise familiar behavior —trading on inside information, keeping all of ones pay —then it should be interpreted to cover no more than it explicitly says. Other offenses may not be added by implication; the legislature gets to limit only the exact behavior listed. But if it was, say, merely giving structure to the old law —as for example does much of Article 2 —then that wouldn't hold.

That the Founding Fathers understood the operation *expressio unius...* is shown by their inclusion in the bill of rights of the Ninth Amendment: "The enumeration in the Constitution, of certain rights, shall not be construed to deny or disparage others retained by the people." This works to negate an *expressio unius...* argument that might be made on the enumerated rights to the exclusion of legal recognition of any others. But for the fundamental validity of Thrust #20, it would not have been necessary.

The ubiquity of the canon often goes unnoticed. Consider, for example, the basic "*who may*" of wills law:

> An individual 18 or more years of age may make a will.[14]

Can a person under the age of 18 make a will? Of course not. But the statute does not *say* that; we infer it by "*expressio unius ... .*" And it requires the contextual background that death severs a

---

[12] "The Legislature speaks; its officers act." *United States v. Reese*, 92 U.S. (2 Otto) 214, 252 (1875); Dickerson, THE INTERPRETATION AND APPLICATION OF STATUTES, 9-11 (1975). Of course members of a legislature speak, and at the federal level and in some states their speech is recorded in legislative histories, but a member is not the legislature. But the United States Constitution empowers the federal legislature to enact statutes, nothing more. U.S.CONST. Art.1 Sec.1.

[13] For an expansive account of the similarities and differences between legislative speech and interpersonal conversation see Sinclair, *Law and Language*, *supra*, 46 U.PITT.L.REV. at 385-90.

[14] This is Uniform Probate Code '2-501, but something equivalent is found in all wills statutes.

person from his property, a staple of our legal culture.[15] *Expressio unius*..., like all pragmatically based rules, depends on the background, which you must always establish if you are to justify using the canon.

Thrust #19 is a special case of *expressio unius*..., and especially reliable because it always works on such a clear and indisputable contextual background, *viz*, the statute itself in its main provision, from which the exception is carved out. The legislature, acting felicitously — that is, saying all and only what it intended —has enacted a rule and the exception(s) it allows; by *expressio unius*... we may safely infer that no other exceptions are intended. This was all intuitively obvious to judges and commentators without the aid of modern pragmatics: "Another case in which this maxim may almost invariably be followed is that of a statute which makes certain specific exceptions to its general provisions. Here we may safely assume that all other exceptions were intended to be excluded."[16]

Thrust #2, the maxim that statutes in derogation of the common law should be construed narrowly, is another special case. The legal context is the common law, of which all have notice as it embodies the prevailing norms of society. The legislature in enacting an exception to that contextual background needs to do so clearly to be effective and should be held to have said only as much as its audience will not misunderstand. Similarly the ancient rule of lenity, that criminal statutes are ordinarily to be construed narrowly —a surprising omission from Llewellyn's list — is, in the land whose default ideology is liberty, a special sub-case of *expressio unius* ... .

Clearly the same rationale, and therefore the maxim, will also apply to the creation of a new right or power.[17] Similarly, if a statute prescribed a mode of exercise of that new right or power, that mode too should be exclusive; *expressio unius* ... .[18] This example was in frequent use at the end of the nineteenth century when the Married Women's Property Acts were granting

---

[15] Thomas Jefferson, 7 JEFFERSON'S WORKS 454 (Monticello ed. 1904): "The earth belongs in usufruct to the living; the dead have neither powers nor rights over it. The portion occupied by any individual ceases to be his when he himself ceases to be, and reverts to society." (Letter to James Madison, dated September 6, 1789.) Thus: "Rights of succession to property of a deceased, whether by will or intestacy, are of statutory creation, and the dead hand rules succession only by sufferance." *Irving Trust Co. v. Day*, 314 U.S. 556, 562 (1942). This is implicitly denied by those who campaign against estate tax by characterizing it as a "death tax,"

[16] Black at 222.

[17] Sutherland at §495, 916-17 ("The maxim is applicable to a statutory provision which grants originally a power or right. In such cases the power or right originates with the statute, and exists only to the extent granted."

[18] Id at 919; Black at 221 ("Particularly when a statute gives a new right or a new power, and provides a specific, full, adequate mode of executing the power or enforcing the right given, the fact that a special mode is prescribed will be regarded as excluding, by implication, the right to resort to any other mode of executing the power or of enforcing the right.")

women rights over property and against their husbands;[19] thus they figure prominently in the early twentieth century treatises used by Llewellyn.

Llewellyn cites as decisional support for Thrust #20 *Detroit v. Redford Twp.*[20] The city of Detroit, Michigan, had annexed part of Redford Township and, in addition to real property, wanted a proportional share of the township's personal property; the trial court denied it and the Michigan supreme court affirmed. First, the legal context of the statute under which the annexation took place: "We may start with the established legal proposition that, in the absence of express statutory provision, annexation of territory from another municipality does not result in a right to a division of and a participation in the personal property of such municipality."[21] The statute, the "Home-Rule Act," in relevant part provided

> And whenever part of a city, village or township is annexed to a city, the *real* property in the territory annexed which belongs to the city, village or township, from which it is taken shall be sold * * * and that portion of the proceeds of such sale shall be paid to the city acquiring such territory which shall be in the same ratio to the whole amount received as the assessed valuation of the taxable property in the territory annexed bears to the assessed valuation of the taxable property in the entire city, village or township from which said territory is taken.[22]

This is straightforward and unambiguous and does not grant the annexing city a share of the township's personal property. "The statute obviously and plainly provides for a division of real property and of real property only."[23] The opinion doesn't say that it is using *expressio unius* ..., which it had mentioned earlier in the opinion in a gratuitous list of canons of construction, but that is exactly the argument it is making. It is a good illustration, made better by having its justification attached: "It would be over presumptuous to assume that it was a mistake or an oversight on the part of the legislature … ."[24] To assume such an oversight would be to directly contradict the democratic principle of legislative supremacy.

Thrust #20, *expressio unius...* , is often applied to lists, especially to lists of exceptions. "Where a statute enumerates the persons or things to be affected by its provisions, there is an implied exclusion of others … ."[25] But lists are often put in statutes with a "such as …" prefix, or an "and similar …" suffix, so as not to exclude things outside the express list but within its intent. That is

---

19 *E.g. Miller v. Miller*, 44 Pa. 170 (1863)(" The legislature has undertaken to enumerate the cases in which she may sue, and all others are omitted; Expressio unius exclusio est alterius, is a sound legal maxim.")

20 253 Mich. 453 (1931).

21 Id, 253 Mich. at 455 at 218.

22 "Section 14 of the home-rule act (section 2250, 1 Comp. Laws 1929)." Id.

23 Id, 253 Mich. at 455.

24 Id, 253 Mich. at 456.

25 Sutherland at §493, 921; Black at 220.

Parry #20: The language may fairly comprehend many different cases where some only are expressly mentioned by way of example.

One could posit two sub-categories to Parry #20, those where the exemplary role of the examples is express, and those where it is not. The former kind is so obvious as to require no explanation. Take an example familiar to us all and to Llewellyn in the years before 1950, U.C.C. 2-314(b).

> 2-314. Implied warranty of Merchantability.
>
> ...
>
> (2) Goods to be merchantable must be at least such as:
>
> **(a)** pass without objection in the trade under the contract description; and
> **(b)** in the case of fungible goods, are of fair average quality within the description; and
> **(c)** are fit for the ordinary purposes for which such goods are used; and
> **(d)** run, within the variations permitted by the agreement, of even kind, quality and quantity within each unit and among all units involved; and
> **(e)** are adequately contained, packaged, and labeled as the agreement may require; and
> **(f)** conform to the promises or affirmations of fact made on the container or label if any.

Of course there may be other possible ways for goods to be less than merchantable; that is the point of "*at least* such as." Equally obvious are statutory lists with an "and similar ..." suffix or the equivalent —*see* Thrust #22, *ejusdem generis*. Any such statute on its face precludes the application of *expressio unius* ... . This was the kind contemplated by Sutherland in the section from which Llewellyn copied Parry #20.

More subtle are the examples in which the statute mentions one or more particular cases without an express preclusion of Thrust #20. Llewellyn's illustration is *Springer v. Philippine Islands*, from the 1928 Supreme Court.[26] It is about the powers of the governor of the Philippine Islands, but there is a lot going on in the case involving separation of powers and the like. The law by which the United States exercised imperial power over the Philippine Islands, "referred to as the 'Organic Act',"[27] included in the powers granted the governor in §21 "a specific provision that the Governor-General shall appoint such officers as may now be appointed by the Governor-General, or such as he is authorized by this act to appoint, or whom he may hereafter be authorized by law to appoint." The *expressio unius ...* argument rejected is "that the effect of this is to confine the Governor-General's powers of appointment within the limits of this enumeration."[28] But there is much too much else in the statute for this to persuade, including the

---

[26] 277 U.S. 189 (1928).
[27] Id, 277 U.S. at 200-01, "... enactment of August 29, 1916, c. 416, 39 Stat. 545."
[28] Id, 277 U.S. at 206.

"general supervision and control of all of the departments and bureaus of the government in the Philippine Islands,"[29] a power which would include the power to appoint officers, were that not expressly mentioned. Thus:

> Where a statute contains a grant of power enumerating certain things which may be done and also a general grant of power which standing alone would include these things and more, the general grant may be given full effect if the context shows that the enumeration was not intended to be exclusive. ...Applying these principles, we are unable to accept the contention that the enumeration here in question is exclusive in the face of the general provisions already quoted and particularly of that one which declares that all executive functions are vested directly in the Governor-General or under his supervision and control.[30]

But that particular provision regarding the appointment of officers was itself in a proviso to §22; doesn't Thrust #19, *supra*, the most authoritative and general sub-case of *expressio unius* ..., require its limiting interpretation?

> But an analysis of the section ... shows, though not wholly beyond doubt, that the power given to the legislature is itself a proviso. In other words, both the grant of power to the legislature and the grant of power to the Governor-General are in form provisos to the general provisions of § 22 which precede them. It is difficult to assign to either proviso the general purpose of that form of legislation, which is merely to qualify the operation of the general language which precedes it. We think rather that both provisos are to be construed as independent and substantive provisions.[31]

This looks like wriggling. Wouldn't it be more effective to point out that §22 is about legislative power, as against the executive, and that an exception to it is thus to be interpreted as exclusive as a limitation on that legislative power, not as in any way a limitation on the governor's executive power? That is why it was stated particularly in §22 when already subsumable under the governor's §21 powers.

Thus the case is about a background general power granted the governor in §21, and, in §22, a power in the legislature to change that general power with the proviso that it may not take away the power granted the governor to appoint certain officers. It would be easy to see this, not as a counter-example to Thrust #20 with respect to §21 but rather as an example of it with respect to §22, even though the Supreme Court said *expressio unius* ... did not apply.

A better example is in *Ford et al. v. United States*,[32] from the 1927 Supreme Court, although it is about the interpretation of a treaty rather than a statute. George Ford and a number of others had been convicted of running alcoholic beverages into the United States from a ship in international waters off San Francisco during Prohibition, even though they were British

---

[29] Id, 277 U.S. at 200.
[30] Id, 277 U.S. at 206-07.
[31] Id.
[32] 273 U.S. 593 (1927).

nationals. The relevant section of the governing Treaty permitting the United States to search for and seize such contraband in international waters and its villainous carriers was

> (2) If there is reasonable cause for belief that the vessel has committed or is committing or attempting to commit an offense against the laws of the United States, its territories or possessions prohibiting the importation of alcoholic beverages, the vessel may be seized and taken into a port of the United States, its territories or possessions for adjudication in accordance with such laws.[33]

This is about the vessel, here the steamship Quadra, not about its officers and crew. Could it be statutory synecdoche? Legislatures and treaty makers are not supposed to indulge in literary figures. But if not, then isn't this inroad into the freedom of the seas to be confined to its express terms?

> It is urged that the principle of interpretation, *Expressio unius est exclusio alterius*, requires the implication from the reference to the adjudication of the vessel alone. This maxim properly applies only when in the natural association of ideas in the mind of the reader that which is expressed is so set over by way of strong contrast to that which is omitted that the contrast enforces the affirmative inference that that which is omitted must be intended to have opposite and contrary treatment. But here, as we have already pointed out, the obvious and necessary association of the seizure and the taking to port of the cargo and those on board with that of the vessel naturally carries the same association with the step of adjudication. This destroys the idea of contrast so that the inference based on the maxim can not here be drawn. The ship, on the one hand, and those on her and her cargo, on the other, are not, in the natural reading of the words, set over against each other.[34]

Perhaps that is synecdoche, but by whatever name, it is a fine example of Parry #20. It also makes very good sense.[35]

Resolution:

In Pair #20, once again there is only a clash between thrust and parry if the thrust is given a universal and mandatory role neither justifiable nor contemplated for it or any other canon. As the Supreme Court said in *Springer v. Phillipine Islands, expressio unius* ... "[l]ike other canons of statutory construction ... is only an aid in the ascertainment of the meaning of the law and must yield whenever a contrary intention on the part of the law-maker is apparent."[36]

Perhaps this explains Llewellyn's choice of Parry #20, avoiding the many quotable and more direct contraries of Thrust #20. For example he might have quoted Sutherland's simple and

---

[33] Id, 273 U.S. at 608.
[34] Id, 273 U.S. at 611.
[35] As the opinion later expounded; *Ford et al. v. United States*, 273 U.S. at 612-13.
[36] *Springer v. Phillipine Islands*, 277 U.S. at 206.

general "[not] when the context shows a different intention."[37] But this would have made the non-categorical, context-dependent nature of Thrust #20 all too clear, spoiling the hypothesized opposition. Even so the formulation of Parry #20, "The language may fairly comprehend many different cases *where some only are expressly mentioned by way of example*," [emphasis added] itself depletes the possibility of inconsistency.

Sutherland also gives in illustration: "[W]here the words used by the legislature are general and the statute is only declaratory of the common law, it will extend to other persons and things besides those actually named."[38] The editors of both C.J. and R.C.L. say "A statute may include and operate upon new cases and subjects which come into existence after its enactment and which are clearly within the mischief intended to be prevented."[39] Both illustrate the interaction of statute and context in determining the applicability of Thrust #20, *expressio unius est exclusio alterius*, and its inapplicability, something like Parry #20.

Thrust #20 remains one of the most useful, even essential of the canons, but one that must be used only with an understanding of its justification and the limits that justification imposes. The Supreme Court in *Ford et al. v. United States* quoted sage cautions from venerable Law Lords:

> The maxim of interpretation relied on is often helpful, but its wise application varies with the circumstances. [citations omitted] Broom's Legal Maxims, 7th Ed., p. 653, says:
>
> "It will, however, be proper to observe, before proceeding to give instances in illustration of the maxim, *Expressio unius est exclusio alterius*, that great caution is requisite in dealing with it for, as Lord Campbell observed in *Saunders* v. *Evans*, it is not of universal application, but depends upon the intention of the party as discoverable upon the face of the instrument or of the transaction; thus where general words are used in a written instrument, it is necessary, in the first instance, to determine whether those general words are intended to include other matters besides such as are specifically mentioned, or to be referable exclusively to them, in which latter case only can the above maxim be properly applied."
>
> Lord Justice Lopes says of the maxim in *Colquhoun* v. *Brooks*,[[40]]:
>
> "It is often a valuable servant, but a dangerous master to follow in the construction of statutes or documents. The *exclusio* is often the result of inadvertence or accident, and the maxim ought not to be applied, when its application, having regard to the subject-matter to which it is to be applied, leads to inconsistency or injustice."[41]

---

37 Sutherland at §495, 924.

38 Id.

39 25 R.C.L. *Statutes*, §229 at 983; *sim*. 59 C.J. *Statutes*, §582, 985.

40 *Colquhoun* v. *Brooks*, 21 Q.B. D. 52, 65.

41 *Ford et al. v. United States*, 273 U.S. at 611-12.

But so it is for all canons. In the simile usually applied to statistics, a canon of construction is useful as a lamp post is useful, for the purpose of holding up a light, not for the purpose for which a drunk might use it, and even less a dog.

Pair Twenty-One

THRUST: "General terms are to receive a general construction."
PARRY: "They may be limited by specific terms with which they are associated or by the scope and purpose of the statute."[1]

Pairs 21 through 23 return to the theme of Pairs 13 through 15, canons designed to help interpreters identify the meaning behind particular words or terms of a statute.

Llewellyn's source for the wording of Thrust #21 is in either of his cited secondary sources, Black §68: "General terms in a statute are to receive a general construction, unless restrained by the context or by plain inferences from the scope and purpose of the act,"[2] or C.J. *Statutes* §580:

> **(4) General and Specific Words—(a) In General.** General words in a statute should receive a general construction; but they must be understood as used with reference to the subject matter in the mind of the legislature, and strictly limited to it. Their meaning may, if necessary, be expanded, as may that of narrower words, or their meaning may be restricted, and they should be so limited in their application as not to lead to injustice, oppression, or an absurd consequence.[3]

As usual, both are considerably more cautious than Llewellyn; C.J. *Statutes* shows even more concern for the exception, Parry #21 (commonly known as *noscitur a sociis*.)

Llewellyn's source for Parry #21 appears to be Black §69: "General terms or provisions in a statute may be restrained and limited by specific terms or provisions with which they are associated."[4] He also cites Sutherland §347, which is around the point, but he might better have cited Sutherland's §414:

> § 414 (262). Effect of context and association of words and phrases — Maxim noscitur a sociis.— Not only are words and provisions modified to harmonize with the leading and controlling purpose or intention of an act, but also by comparison of one subordinate part with another; that is to say, the sense of particular words or phrases may be greatly influenced by the context, or their association with other words and clauses.[5]

---

1 *Canons* at 405.
2 Black at § 68, 196.
3 C.J. *Statues* at §580, 980 (footnotes omitted); *see also* R.C.L. *Statutes* at §223, 970.
4 Baack at §69, 196.
5 SUTHERLAND at §414, 803.

As Parry #21 is the only appearance of *noscitur a sociis* in the list, Sutherland's § 414 would have been the appropriate cite.

Thrust #21: "General terms are to receive a general construction."

Thrust #21 is no more than the "Plain Meaning Rule" (Thrust #12) applied to general terms, which is to say, simply reading words in a statute for what they are, but omitting limitation to the subject matter of the legislation most authors and all reasonable readers would presuppose. (In general we should be justified in assuming a legislature sticks to its topic.) In a statute prohibiting kite flying, one would not extend the generality of the word "kite" to the bird of prey commonly known as the "Black-shouldered Kite."

Llewellyn's cited case is *De Witt v. City of San Francisco*.[6] Undoubtedly due to the California Gold Rush of 1848, by 1852 the City of San Francisco was one of the most thriving locales on the Western front. The newly wealthy residents resented the city's taxation, and when the common council passed an ordinance to purchase the Jenny Lind Theatre and Parker House property to convert into a city hall, they balked.[7] The plaintiff taxpayers sought, and at first received, an injunction preventing the board of supervisors from purchasing the property. Appealing the district court's decision, the board of supervisors relied on section 7 of the Act of May 2, 1852:

> The board of supervisors shall have power, with the consent of a majority of all its members, to purchase or receive any property for the use of the county; to erect or lease a court house, jail, and such other buildings as may be necessary for the use of the county.[8]

The district judge had interpreted the words "purchase or receive any property necessary for the use of the county" and "erect or lease a court house, jail, and such other buildings" as belonging to "separate and distinct" sentences, thus conferring upon the board of supervisors the separate and distinct powers of (1) "purchas[ing] personal property as should be necessary for the county in its ordinary business" and (2) "erecting or leasing such buildings [i.e., court house, jail, etc.]."[9] The 1852 Supreme Court of California found the "very opposite":

> [H]aving given the board [of supervisors] the power to purchase any property, together with the further power of erecting a court house, jail and other buildings,

---

[6] 2 Cal. 289 (1852).

[7] The ordinance passed by the common council allowed the city treasurer to draw warrants upon the city treasury for the sum of $100,000. The plaintiffs' complaint alleged, in part, that such an expense would exceed the city's annual revenue by more than $50,000. *De Witt*, 2 Cal. at 289. It became known as "Jenny Lind Swindle."

[8] *De Witt*, 2 Cal. at 294.

[9] Id, 2 Cal. at 295–96.

> the conclusion would appear to be that it was intended to confer the power to purchase, at least the land on which to erect the court house, etc. And the fact that the words . . . are used in separate and distinct sentences, tends rather to establish than destroy this conclusion.[10]

Justice Wells reasoned that the authority to erect a court house or jail included the power to purchase the land on which to build such edifices; to hold otherwise would imply the *non*-ownership of the building's stone and mortar as well. Thus, it was understood that the board of supervisors was given the broad power to purchase *all* property, i.e., both *real* and *personal*. The general term "property" receives a general construction; Thrust #21.

Parry #21: "They may be limited by specific terms with which they are associated or by the scope and purpose of the statute."

Noscitur a sociis: a word "is known from its associates," or, prettily, "words of a feather flock together."[11] Justification is quite simple: stick to the subject. In ordinary discourse we try to stay on topic, not to make irrelevant excursions, so we may —indeed we must —presume that the legislature did too.

Llewellyn cites *People ex rel. Krause v. Harrison* from the 1901 Illinois Supremes.[12] Prior to 1889, the village of Hyde Park was independent of the city of Chicago. Within the boundaries of Hyde Park was a district known as the "prohibition district," with a number of restrictions concerning alcohol. The entrepreneurial spirit of one Felix F. Krause, a realtor acting on behalf of the people, spurred the ensuing litigation.

Hyde Park was annexed to Chicago on June 29, 1889. Pursuant to section 18 of the Annexation Act:

> When a part or the whole of an incorporated town, village or city is annexed, under the provisions of this act, to another city, village or incorporated town, and prior to such annexation an ordinance was in force prohibiting the issuing of licenses to keep dram-shops within said territory so annexed, or any part thereof . . . then such ordinance shall continue in full force and effect, notwithstanding such annexation. ...
>
> It is intended by this section to continue in full force and effect, all ordinances of any municipality, the whole or part of which is annexed to another city, incorporated town or village, whereby the licensing of dram-shops is prohibited or regulated within said city, village or incorporated town, or any part thereof, without the voters of the territory so affected consent, as hereby provided, to the

---

[10] Id, 2 Cal. at 296.
[11] *Advertiser Publishing Co. v. Fase*, 279 F.2d 636, 640 (9th Cir. 1960).
[12] 191 Ill. 257 (1901).

repeal of such ordinance by the city, village or incorporated town to which the territory is annexed.[13]

Krause, who had been operating a "meat market and grocery business" for the previous seven years, introduced alcohol to his inventory, section 18 of the Annexation Act notwithstanding. Interpreting section 18 to perpetuate only those ordinances regulating "dram-shops" —defined by Hyde Park's Revised Municipal Code to be "a place where spirituous or vinous or malt liquors are retailed in *less quantities than one gallon*" —Krause applied for a license authorizing him to sell "malt liquors in *quantities of one gallon or more* at a time."[14]

The Supreme Court of Illinois disagreed. Adopting the Branch Appellate Court's opinion verbatim, the court paid special attention to the fact that the particular prohibition portions of the Hyde Park Revised Municipal Code were amended and reaffirmed not more than five days prior to the annexation.[15] "Now, is it reasonable to suppose that the legislature intended by section 18 of the Annexation [A]ct to sweep away all these provisions, except so far as the regulation and enforcing of the keeping of a saloon or dram-shop is concerned?"[16]

In addition to its commonsensical approach the court also relied on the wording of section 18 of the Act itself, specifically, the word "whereby." "The word 'whereby,' there employed, is not intended to limit the effect of the saving clause of the section to dram-shops, as such, alone, but means all ordinances entitled 'Dram-shops.'" The court cited chapter 43 of Hyde Park's Revised Statutes, entitled "Dram-shops," where the term refers to "all matters there enacted with reference to licensing and regulating the evils arising from the sale of intoxicating liquors."[17]

The underlying reasoning is canonically logical: a word or phrase will be construed so as to comport with the scope and purpose of the statute. However, the purpose of the exercise was to illustrate, Parry #21. Had Llewellyn stumbled upon Sutherland's §414, perhaps *Muir v. Keay* would have been cited instead.[18] William Muir, like Felix Krause, was in the food and beverage business; from his house on Lower Temple Street, Birmingham, he operated a "refreshment house" called "The Café". Pursuant to the Refreshment Houses Act of 1860, "'all houses, rooms, shops, or buildings, *kept open for public refreshment, resort, and entertainment,*' during certain hours of the night, are to be deemed refreshment houses and require a licence." And when

---

[13] Id. at 261–62.
[14] Id. at 257–60 (emphasis added).
[15] "The amendatory ordinances of [the Hyde Park Revised Municipal Code], which are of particular applicability to the subject, were passed May 8, 1889, and June 24, 1889. Annexation took place June 29, 1989." Id. at 264.
[16] Id. at 264. (Pair 12: ". . . [except] when literal interpretation would lead to absurd or mischievous consequences or thwart manifest purpose.")
[17] Id at 265 (Thrust #17: "The same language used repeatedly in the same connection is presumed to bear the same meaning throughout the statute.")
[18] L. R. 10 Q.B. 594 (1875).

constable Charles Fletcher strolled by The Café at 11:30 p.m. on December 19th, 1874, Mr. Muir did not have the requisite license.[19]

Was Mr. Muir's place a "refreshment house" within the statute? He argued not: "It is objected that the words are 'refreshment, resort, *and* entertainment;' and that the entertainment intended must be a musical entertainment or other entertainment of a like nature . . . ." Justice Blackburn's response:

> . . . but this is not so. The word "public" must be read with each of the three words that follow it; and, notwithstanding what was said in the Court of Exchequer in the case cited, I do not think that entertainment need be something in the nature of refreshment. It is rather the correlative of resort—the reception and accommodation of the public who resort to the place in question. It is not a useless word. It does not apply to the mere giving of refreshment, nor to the mere fact of persons coming in; it means public reception.[20]

Noscitur a sociis.

Resolution

Canons of construction are established wise saws of sufficiently frequent use in the past to give them familiarity, reliability, and validity independent of the reasoning on which they rest. If there are very few appearances of an interpretive proposition, then that proposition should not be called a canon. In the list, Llewellyn had a habit of taking canons in their commonplace form and splitting them apart for the purposes of contrariety. Pairs 5, 12, 13, 14, 15, 17, and 18, for example, each consist of a canon divided within itself in order to support Llewellyn's thesis. Pair 21 follows suit. In all four of Llewellyn's secondary sources —Black, C.J. *Statutes*, Sutherland, and R.C.L. *Statutes* —Pair 21 is presented as a unified proposition, one contemplation. Neither of the divided parts occurs alone. Llewellyn's proposed contradiction exists only in his list.

---

[19] Id. at 595. On the night in question, The Café had approximately seventeen females and twenty gentlemen present, supplied with and paid for cigars, coffee, and ginger beer. *Id.* at 595–96.

[20] Id. at 597 (emphasis in original).

Pair Twenty-Two

> **THRUST**: "It is a general rule of construction that where general words follow an enumeration they are to be held as applying only to persons and things of the same general kind or class specifically mentioned (*ejusdem generis*)."
> **PARRY**: "General words must operate on something. Further, *ejusdem generis* is only an aid in getting the meaning and does not warrant confining the operations of a statute within narrower limits than were intended."[1]

Ejusdem generis, like *noscitur a sociis*, tells us to presume that the legislature stays on the topic of the legislation.[2] Where *noscitur a sociis* requires a word within a statute to be interpreted according to scope of the whole, *ejusdem generis* says "when a statute sets out a series of specific items ending with a general term, that general term is confined to covering subjects comparable to the specifics it follows."[3] The justification is as for Pair 21: in felicitous conversation we don't change the subject without waving a flag, and we presume a legislature does not either. And if it does flag such a shift, we should pay attention.

Llewellyn attributes Thrust #22 to all four secondary sources, Black, Sutherland, C.J. *Statutes*, and R.C.L. *Statutes*,[4] but Black, yet again, seems to be his source for the language:

> 71. It is a general rule of statutory construction that where general words follow an enumeration of persons or things, by words of a particular and specific meaning, such general words are not to be construed in their widest extent, but are to be held as applying only to persons or things of the same general kind of class as those specifically mentioned.[5]

Parry #22, like parries number 1, 4, 6, 9, 12, 13, 15, 16, 17, 18, and 21, can be summarized ". . . unless the legislature intended otherwise." For example, Black continues the heading to §71 "But this rule must be discarded where the legislative intention is plain to the contrary."[6] It is

---

1 *Canons* at 405.
2 Michael Sinclair, TRADITIONAL TOOLS OF STATUTORY INTERPRETATION, 114-19 (Vandeplas Publishing, 2013).
3 *Hall Street Associates, L.L.C. v. Mattel, Inc.*, 552 U.S. 576, 586 (2008); *see also Harrison v. PPG Industries, Inc.*, 446 U.S. 578, 588 (1980), *United States v. Turkette*, 452 U.S. 576, 581 (1980).
4 *Canons* at 405 n.45 (citing BLACK at §71, 203; SUTHERLAND at § 422–34, 814–30; C.J. *Statutes* at § 581, 981; R.C.L. *Statutes* at §240, 996).
5 Black at §71, 203 (Llewellyn substitutes 'they' for 'of persons or things, by words of a particular and specific meaning, such general words are not to be construed in their widest extent, but' and adds '(*ejusdem generis*)'.)
6 Black at §71, 203.

legislative supremacy and plain meaning in operation. Again, Llewellyn cites all four secondary sources, but this time Sutherland §437 seems to be the closest :

> Qualifications and exceptions to the rule of ejusdem generis.— . . . This rule can be used only as an aid in ascertaining the legislative intent, and not for the purpose of controlling the intention or of confining the operation of a statute within narrower limits than was intended by the law-maker. It affords a mere suggestion to the judicial mind that where it clearly appears that the law-maker was thinking of a particular class of persons or objects, his words of more general description may not have been intended to embrace any other than those within the class.[7]

Thrust #22: "It is a general rule of construction that where general words follow an enumeration they are to be held as applying only to persons and things of the same general kind or class specifically mentioned (*ejusdem generis*)."

Hull Hospital v. Wheeler, Llewellyn's primary citation, is a good illustration.[8] In the summer of 1931, Ms. Ida Zimmerman entered Hull Hospital in Hull, Iowa, suffering from a brain tumor. At one point during her stay, hospital staff had to remove Ms. Zimmerman's rings because of swelling. Before she died, Ms. Zimmerman incurred a bill of $706.80, of which $406.80 had been unpaid. In an effort to recover the unpaid portion, Hull Hospital attempted to obtain an "innkeeper's lien" on Ms. Zimmerman's rings. Although the hospital was awarded judgment for the remaining balance, the request for the lien was denied.

At issue was the interpretation and application of the Hotel Lien Act:

> For the purposes of this chapter:
> 1. 'Hotel' shall include inn, rooming house, and eating house, *or any structure where rooms or board are furnished*, whether to permanent or transient occupants.
> 2. 'Hotel keeper' shall mean a person who owns or operates a hotel.
> 3. 'Guest' shall include boarder and patron, or any legal occupant of any hotel as herein defined.
> 4. 'Baggage' shall include all property which is in any hotel belonging to or under the control of any guest.
> 10349. A hotel keeper shall have a lien upon the baggage of any guest, which may be in his hotel, for:
> 1. The accommodations and keep of said guest.
> 2. The money paid for or advanced to said guest.
> 3. The extras and other things furnished said guest.[9]

---

7 SUTHERLAND at § 437, 832.
8 216 Iowa 1394 (1933).
9 Iowa Code of 1931 §§ 10348, 10349; Id. at 1395–96 (emphasis added).

Hull Hospital argued for the inclusion of "hospitals" within the broad language "any structure where rooms or board are furnished".

The Iowa Supremes did not agree. First it relied on dictionary definitions to distinguish the plain meanings of "hotel" and "hospital,"[10] then, without explicitly mentioning *ejusdem generis*, followed it to hold in favor of Ms. Zimmerman's estate:

> [I]t is quite apparent that the legislature of Iowa in sections 10348 . . . did not intend to include a hospital in its definition of hotel. In subdivision 1 of section 10348, above quoted, the legislature, when using the phrase "any structure where rooms or board are furnished, whether to permanent or transient occupants", intended to restrict its meaning to businesses like hotels, rooming houses, and eating houses.[11]

Parry #22: "General words must operate on something. Further, *ejusdem generis* is only an aid in getting the meaning and does not warrant confining the operations of a statute within narrower limits than were intended."

Llewellyn cites two primary sources: *Texas v. United States*[12] and *Grosjean v. American Paint Works*.[13] *Texas v. United States* provides an instance of legislative intent's trumping *ejusdem generis*, but only after several layers of meandering Supreme Court-style reasoning. In 1933, the Interstate Commerce Commission authorized the Kansas City Southern Railway Company ("Kansas Railway"), a Missouri corporation, to acquire by lease the Texarkana & Fort Smith Railway Company, a Texas corporation. Kansas Railway decided to shutdown Texas Railway's company headquarters, it being more efficient to have one headquarters rather than two. The Texans did not take kindly to this.

Counsel for the State of Texas argued, in part, that, pursuant to §11 of Title 1 of the Emergency Railroad Transportation Act of 1933, "'Nothing in this title shall be construed to relieve any carrier from any contractual obligation which it may have assumed, prior to the enactment of this Act, with regard to the location or maintenance of offices, shops, or roundhouses at any point.'" To the contrary, the Court reasoned:

> [Section 11] refers explicitly to what is contained in Title I of the Act, with respect to "emergency powers," dealing with the authority of the Federal Coordinator of Transportation and kindred matters, and does not by its terms

---

[10] "It is said in the Encyclopedia Americana, vol. 14, p. 436, that a hotel is 'an inn or public tavern'. Webster's New International Dictionary defines a hotel to be: 'A house for entertaining strangers or travelers; an inn.'" Id. at 1396.

[11] Id at 1396–1398 (citations omitted).

[12] 292 U.S. 522 (1934).

[13] 160 So. 449 (La. App. 1935).

> apply to the provisions of Title II of the Act, in which are found the [provisions relevant to the issue at hand, i.e.,] consolidations, purchases and leases.[14]

In fact Title II had an immunity clause of its own. Justice Hughes:

> Title II of the Emergency Railroad Transportation Act, 1933, . . . carries its own provision as to immunity from state requirements . . . . Subdivision (15) of § 5 as amended, reads:
> "The carriers and any corporation affected by any order under the foregoing provisions of this section shall be, and they are hereby, relieved from the operation **of the antitrust laws . . . , and of all other restraints or prohibitions by or imposed under authority of law,** State or Federal, insofar as may be necessary to enable them to do anything authorized or required by such order."[15]

Here counsel for the State of Texas argued that subdivision 15 of §5 of Title II of the Emergency Railroad Transportation Act of 1933 operated to impute immunity only from those laws that fell within the category of "antitrust laws." Justice Hughes thought this interpretation "too narrow":[16]

> The rule of "*ejusdem generis*" is applied as an aid in ascertaining the intention of the legislature, not to subvert it when ascertained. The scope of the immunity must be measured by the purpose which Congress had in view and had constitutional power to accomplish. As that purpose involved the promotion of economy and efficiency in interstate transportation by the removal of the burdens of excessive expenditure, the removal of such burdens when imposed by state requirements was an essential part of the plan.[17]

As an illustration it is painful: the Court in *Texas v. United States* does mention *ejusdem generis*, but only briefly and buried in a heap of other more significant reasoning.

Llewellyn's second primary source, *Grosjean v. American Paint Works*, is a better illustration for Parry #22. Miss Alice Lee Grosjean, Louisiana's Supervisor of Public Accounts (a.k.a. the "taxman"), filed an action against American Paint Works alleging that, in light of Act No. 15 of the First Extraordinary Session of the Legislature for the year 1934, American Paint Works was $100 delinquent in tax and other penalties over 8,000 gallons of kerosene. American Paint Works claimed not to owe the tax: as the kerosene was being used as paint solvent, and not "illuminating oil, heating oil, or motor fluid," the legislature did not intend for it to be taxed.[18]

The district court employed *ejusdem generis* in ruling for American Paint Works but the appellate court held to the contrary, favoring legislative intent over a narrow interpretation. The controlling language was Act No. 15 of the First Extraordinary Session of the Legislature for the year 1934:

---

[14] Id. at 533.
[15] Id. at 534 (emphasis added).
[16] Id.
[17] Id. at 535–36 (citations omitted).
[18] *Grosjean*, 160 So. at 450.

> Be it enacted by the Legislature of Louisiana, That in order to provide a revenue for the purpose set forth in this Act and in order to carry out the same, there is hereby levied a tax of one cent per gallon on all kerosene sold, used, consumed, distributed or handled in the State of Louisiana for domestic consumption.
>
> The term "kerosene" as mentioned in this Act is intended to include **and shall include what is commonly known as coal oil, furnace oil, lamp oil, tractor fuel, distillate, burning oil, stove oil, or by any other similar name**, and is defined as follows:
>
> A refined petroleum product having the following properties to-wit: gravity 34 to 48 … .[19]

To the district court, because the Act's definition enumerated several specific common names for kerosene —"coal oil, furnace oil…etc" —and paint solvent is not of a like genus, *ejusdem generis* dictated that Act No. 15 did not apply to American Paint Works' kerosene. Quite the contrary, said the court of appeals. "It is … elementary that the doctrine of ejusdem generis is only a rule of construction, to be applied as an aid in ascertaining the legislative intent, and cannot control where the plain purpose and intent of the Legislature would thereby be hindered or defeated."[20] There was a clear statement of purpose having nothing to do with combustibility in the preamble and a scientific definition of "kerosene" in paragraph 3; *ejusdem generis* was simply unnecessary and unintended.

> It will be seen that, although paragraph 2 does contain certain terms, such as coal oil, furnace oil, lamp oil, etc., paragraph 3 is a chemical or scientific formula specifying particular properties and certain mathematical limitations. It will be noted at the outset that a product or fluid either falls within or without that scientific definition. The statute does not say that kerosene is defined as coal oil, furnace oil, lamp oil, etc., and all other similar fluids, thus making the doctrine of ejusdem generis applicable. [21]

Resolution

Again Llewellyn has manufactured contrariety. In all four secondary sources thrust and parry appear as one with the exception for contrary legislative intent clearly stated, as we saw above in Black's heading: " this rule must be discarded where the legislative intention is plain to the contrary."[22] For example, C.J. *Statutes*:

> [§581] **(b) Doctrine of Ejusdem Generis.** By the rule of construction known as "ejusdem generis," where general words follow the enumeration of particular classes of persons or things, the general words will be construed as applicable only to persons or things of the same general nature of class as those enumerated . … The doctrine of ejusdem generis, however, is only a rule of construction, to

---

[19] Id at 452–53 (emphasis added).

[20] Id at 453 (citing C.J. *Statutes* at § 581, 982).

[21] Id. at 453.

[22] Black at §71, 203.

> be applied as an aid in ascertaining the legislative intent, and cannot control where the plain purpose and intent of the legislature would thereby be hindered or defeated … .[23]

Yes, one might see a contradiction in between the thrust and parry of Pair 22, but who ever took either Thrust #22 or Parry #22 alone as a canon? So dominated are they by the overarching goal of statutory interpretation ("It is too well settled to be fortified by the citation of authorities that the prime purpose of statutory construction is to determine and ascertain the intention of the lawmaking body" said the Louisiana court in *Grosjean.*[24]) that no authority recites Thrust #22 without an exception more general than but inclusive of Parry #22. As with the majority of the pairs examined previously, conciliation is the status quo.

---

[23] C.J. *Statues* at § 581, 981–83 (footnotes omitted); *sim.* SUTHERLAND at § 422, 814 and § 437, 832, R.C.L. *Statutes* at § 240, 996–97.

[24] *Grosjean*, 160 So. at 453.

Pair Twenty-Three

THRUST: "Qualifying or limiting words or clauses are to be referred to the next preceding antecedent."
PARRY: "Not when evident sense and meaning require a different construction"[1]

Both Thrust and Parry #23 are paraphrased from Llewellyn's favorite textual source, the captions in the Black treatise. Black section 73:

> RELATIVE AND QUALIFYING TERMS
> 73. As a general rule, relative, qualifying, or limiting words or clauses in a statute are to be referred to the next preceding antecedent, unless the context, or the evident meaning of the enactment, requires a different construction.[2]

Apart from omitting "As a general rule, relative," "in a statute," and a comma, Llewellyn's Thrust #23 tracks Black §73's caption down to the "unless…" clause. Parry #23 tracks the remainder, substituting "not when" for "unless the context, or" and omitting "of the enactment," but adding "sense" to "meaning" as sources, if evident, of exceptions. The choice of words is neither formulaic nor necessary; for example C.J.Statutes, also cited by Llewellyn, is clearer and would be more easily split into thrust and parry:

> [§ 583] **(6) Relative and Qualifying Terms and Relation to Antecedents.** [R]elative and qualifying words, phrases, and clauses are to be applied to the words or phrase immediately preceding, and are not to be construed as extending to or including others more remote. This rule is, however, merely an aid to construction and will not be adhered to where extension to a more remote antecedent is clearly required by consideration of the entire act.[3]

Thrust #23: "Qualifying or limiting words or clauses are to be referred to the next preceding antecedent."

When you have words in a sentence modifying other words in the same sentence or, as in pronominalization, deriving their meaning from them, how do you tell which are the correct antecedent words? Grammarians call this the "control problem;" it has no general solution.[4] The

---

[1] *Canons* at 405.
[2] Black at § 73, 223–26.
[3] C.J. *Statutes* at § 583, 985.
[4] Robert P. Stockwell, Paul Schachter and Barbara Hall Partee, THE MAJOR SYNTACTIC

popular approximation —the "last antecedent" rule —is a weak reed indeed, hardly reliable enough to claim the status of a rule. Still it is the prima facie rule of ordinary English and a fair justification for Thrust #23. Black: "It is a rule of grammar, and a statute is presumed to be grammatically expressed." But as in ordinary discourse, so too in statutory interpretation: "But this will not be held in the face of the apparent and rational interpretation of the act."[5] Thus it is not surprising that the treatise writers should emphasize its frailty, that is, Parry #23.

Llewellyn cites only one case in support and illustration, *Dunn v. Bryan*,[6] from the 1931 Utah Supreme Court. The Utah statute at issue was:

> The county auditor shall prepare and publish during the month of January of each year, in some newspaper having general circulation in the county, a detailed statement of the financial condition of the county and all receipts and expenditures for the previous year ending December 31st, showing:
> (1) The total receipts of the county, stating particularly the source of each portion of the revenue;
> (2) The amount of cash on hand at the date of the last report;
> (3) The amount of sinking fund and how invested;
> (4) The number, date, and amount of every bond issued or redeemed and the amount received or paid therefor;
> (5) The indebtedness of the county, funded and floating, stating the amount of each class and the rate of interest borne by such indebtedness or any part thereof;
> (6) A concise statement of all property owned by the county with an approximate estimate of the value thereof, and the amount of cash in the county treasury and its several funds;
> (7) Each warrant issued, to whom and on what account; provided, that if more than one warrant has been issued to one individual on the same account during the year, the aggregate amount shall be shown in the statement as one warrant; and, provided, further, that various items paid out to individuals that are charges on the county shall not be published, but the same may be stated as a total, and the itemized statement of the same shall be on file in the auditor's office.[7]

Defendant Fred Bryan, County Clerk and Ex-Officio Auditor of Tooele County, took the last proviso, "provided, further, that various items paid out to individuals that are charges on the county shall not be published, but the same may be stated as a total, and the itemized statement of the same shall be on file in the auditor's office," as applying to all items on the list of required publications, publishing only the aggregates for each category. Plaintiff A. F. Dunn sought a writ of mandate that items (1) through (6) be published in full detail arguing that only item (7) came within the scope of the final proviso. Not surprisingly, challenger Dunn prevailed. The opinion is dominated by legislative intent and the modifying language's being in a proviso:[8]

STRUCTURES OF ENGLISH 164–202 (1973).

5 Black at §73, 224.

6 77 Utah 604 (1931).

7 1927 Utah Laws § 1555.

8 Thrust #27, *Canons* at 406.

> [I]t is not likely that the Legislature would, by a proviso, leave it optional with a local officer to completely emasculate the statute and destroy the force and effect of the main proposition which the proviso modifies. ... Since the intent of the law, expressed in plain language, requires the publication of a detailed statement, an application of the rules of construction do not permit the proviso to be construed and applied to mean that nothing but totals are required.

However Thrust #23 played a significant role, being quoted in near verbatim form from an encyclopedia, and debated.

> Another canon of construction is that "relative and qualifying words, phrases and clauses are to be applied to the words or phrases immediately preceding, and are not to be construed as extending to or including others more remote." 36 Cyc. 1123. The phrase "that are charges on the county" must be held to modify the immediately preceding noun "individuals" and not as descriptive of the remotely antecedent noun "items."

Clerk Bryan's counsel fought back, with a semantic argument that might well have prevailed had the legislative intent not been quite so apparent.

> Counsel for defendant suggests that this construction is not available because "it is hardly probable that a presumably literate Legislature would have used the ambiguous relative that to refer to an antecedent signifying persons when it had at hand the more definite who, which in common grammatical usage is always used with reference to persons rather than things."

But the Court responded that "lexicographers and grammarians give their sanction to the use of the relative pronoun 'that'" for such personal referents, and quoted three dictionaries with examples, including a rather inapt Biblical quote, Proverbs 9: 7: "'He that reproveth a scorner.'" Thus:

> It would seem, therefore, that the word "that" was properly used in introducing the phrase "that are charges on the county" as a defining relative phrase modifying the immediately preceding noun "individuals." The pronoun has reference to "individuals that are a charge on the county," rather than to "items that are a charge on the county."[9]

The case makes a fine illustration, suitably tenuous, grammatically.[10]

Parry #23: "Not when evident sense and meaning require a different construction."

The justification for this equivocation is simply the lack of generality, authority, and conviction of the "last antecedent" rule. In ordinary English the "rule", so called, gives way to common sense, and in statutory interpretation it gives way also to apparent legislative intent.

---

[9] *Dunn*, 77 Utah, all at 609–10.

[10] One wonders how closely Llewellyn read this case; its analysis might have induced him to change the shape of U.C.C. §2-202, the usual reading of which is overly influenced by the lay-out on the page.

Secondary sources, including those Llewellyn relied on, usually build it into their statements of Thrust #23.

Llewellyn's illustrative case is *Myer v. Ada County*,[11] from the 1930 Idaho Supreme Court. Plaintiff, John H. Myer, was a justice of the peace who wanted more pay, six dollars rather than three, in seventeen cases he had worked. The governing statute, cited as "C. S., sec. 3710," was:

> For all services and proceedings before a justice of the peace in a criminal action or proceeding on examination, when an examination is not waived, or trial upon an issue of fact . . . $ 6.00.
> When an examination is waived or there is a plea of guilty . . . $ 3.00.

Myer's argument is quoted as "Appellant contends that the words 'all services and proceedings' were intended by the legislature as an omnibus clause and include cases dismissed without examination or trial."[12] It isn't transparently clear, but by applying Thrust #23, regardless of common sense or the rule that one ought not so to interpret a statute as to reduce another part of it to irrelevance,[13] Myer argued that "on examination" should apply only to a "proceeding" and not reach "a criminal action." That is, the language should be read as "a criminal action, or (proceeding on examination)", not as "a (criminal action or proceeding) on examination . . . ."[14] The Court rejected the argument on historical grounds, going through the previous versions of the statute and their progressive modifications to the current version to demonstrate legislative intent. What about Thrust #23, the foundation of Myer's thesis?

> A reading of the context of the act of 1864, and the act as amended, convinces us that . . . the qualifying phrase, "on examination," in the present act refer[s] to the clause "all services and proceedings" and not solely to the last antecedent. The rule that a qualifying clause refers solely to the last antecedent is of no great force, and a slight indication of a contrary legislative intent may overturn it.[15]

It is a pity Llewellyn did not choose to cite the wonderfully titled *Sixty Pipes of Brandy*, from the Supreme Court of the United States, 1825.[16] The statute, cited as "§43 of the Revenue Law," was:

> . . . [A]nd if any casks, &c. containing distilled spirits, &c. which, by the foregoing provisions, ought to be marked and accompanied with certificates, shall be found in possession of any person, unaccompanied with such marks and certificates, it shall be presumptive evidence that the same are liable to forfeiture, and it shall be lawful for any officer of the Customs, or of Inspection, to seize

---

[11] 50 Idaho 39 (1930).
[12] Id at 41.
[13] Thrust #16. *Cannons* at 404 (Myer's argument would eliminate the $3 payment provision.)
[14] Yes, Myer's reading would require another article, "a", before "proceeding", but that didn't come up in the opinion.
[15] *Myer*, 50 Idaho at 42 (citing SUTHERLAND at § 420, 812.)
[16] *Sixty Pipes of Brandy v. Kennedy & Maitland*, 23 U.S. (10 Wheat.) 421 (1825). A pipe of brandy is 114 gallons.

> them as forfeited; and if, upon the trial, in consequence of such seizure, the owner or claimant of the spirits, &c. seized, shall not prove that they were imported into the United States according to law, and the duties thereupon paid or secured, they shall be adjudged to be forfeited.

The casks in which the liquor had been imported were properly marked and certificated, but it seems that the revenue agents thought the contents of the casks might not be quite what they once were, that they had been at least in part substituted with locally produced spirit. Under the statute, what had "to be marked and accompanied with certificates"? On Thrust #23, blindly applied, it would be only "distilled spirits, &c.", and not "any casks, &c. containing distilled spirits, &c." and even less the remote "any casks, &c." alone. But how, one wonders, at the beginning of the 19th century without chemical and DNA identification techniques now available, would one mark and accompany with a certificate the liquid contents and not the cask?

> The words are, "if any casks containing distilled spirits, which ought to be marked and accompanied with certificates," &c. That these words must necessarily be confined to the cask, and cannot extend to its contents, results, we think, from requiring the article to be marked, as well as accompanied with the certificate; a requisition, absurd in terms, if applied to the distilled spirits contained in the casks.[17]

Supreme authority for the virtues of common sense and obvious intent in statutory interpretation.

Resolution

Thrust #23 is rather a rule of grammar than a canon of construction, and a very weak one at that.[18] You might call it a rule and say that Parry #23, expressing its weakness, was its opposite,[19] but that would hardly accord with reality, or ordinary understanding. The Idaho Supreme Court said it well in *Myer v. Ada County*: "The rule that a qualifying clause refers solely to the last antecedent is of no great force, and a slight indication of a contrary legislative intent may overturn it."[20] In all four of Llewellyn's secondary sources —Black, C.J. *Statutes*, Sutherland, and R.C.L. *Statutes* —Pair 23 is presented as a unified proposition. Thus Pair 23 needs no resolution, as Llewellyn's proposed contradiction does not exist outside his list. Once again Llewellyn has split apart a generality of interpretation to make two pseudo-canons, neither part of which can stand alone, and a pseudo-contrariety.

---

17 *Id.* at 423.

18 "weak one" what? rule of grammar or canon of construction?

19 *Canons* at 401: "[T]here are two opposing canons on almost every point."

20 50 Idaho at 42 (citing SUTHERLAND at §420, 812).

Pair Twenty-Four

THRUST: "Punctuation will govern when a statute is open to two constructions."
PARRY : "Punctuation marks will not control the plain and evident meaning of language."[1]

Llewellyn's source for the language of Pair 24 is not clear, although Black is the best candidate. The pair is a curiously strained attempt to create a conflict, but it fails on its face. Thrust #24 covers only those situations in which the statute has two constructions,[2] and Parry #24 covers those situations in which it has one only "plain and evident" construction, that is, situations precluded by Thrust #24.

The source of the uncertainty about punctuation as an interpretive aid is historical. British statutes used to be enacted without any punctuation at all. The punctuation that appeared in published versions was inserted by others —editors, publishers' clerks —so was not authoritative. Accordingly, judges treated punctuation with skepticism, leading treatise writers to make a version of Parry #24 the primary position, with punctuation as "a last resort." For example C.J. *Statutes* (at 1932 the most recent of Llewellyn's four secondary sources) is adamantly hostile:

> [§590] **d. Punctuation**. Punctuation is no part of a statute and cannot control its construction against the manifest intent of the legislature, and the court will punctuate or disregard punctuation as may be necessary to ascertain and give effect to the real intent.[3]

Of course! To give effect to the punctuation would be to grant interpretive authority to a publisher's clerk. Judges are and should be more respectful of their own power than that.

None of that history continues into this age of statutes. Even the United States Supreme Court has hung its constructive hat on a comma, for which *United States v. Ron Pair Enterprises,*

---

[1] *Canons* at 405.
[2] Why not "two or more"? The caption of the cited section of Black, §88, begins "If the statute is equally open to two constructions, ..." Black at § 88, 263.
[3] C.J. *Statutes* at § 590, 989–90. R.C.L. *Statutes* (the fourth of Llewellyn's secondary sources) in 1919, at "§ 220. Punctuation" was a little less hostile: "It seems to be well settled that punctuation is a fallible standard of the meaning of a statute, and the last resort as an aid in its interpretation, though it may be resorted to as such aid when the meaning of the statute is doubtful."

Inc.[4] is justly renowned. Yet among commentators the skeptical attitude to punctuation persists. McKinney's Consolidated Laws of New York tells us, remarkably, "The members of the Legislature are not necessarily charged with a knowledge of the grammatical rules of the English language, … In other words, legislators are not presumed to be good grammarians, and inaccurate grammar must yield to the legislative intent."[5] That may be so, but if the particular statute in question has a normal grammatical reading, what choice have we but to take it? Just as the legislature is presumed —unless it specifies otherwise —to be using words in their normal meanings, so too it must be presumed to be using ordinary grammar, of which punctuation is a part. What other presumption is viable? In other words, Thrust #24 may not have reflected the prevalent judicial attitude to punctuation at the middle of the twentieth century, but it ought to now.

Thrust #24: "Punctuation will govern when a statute is open to two constructions."

Thrust #24 is not an accurate statement of prevalent interpretive practice at any point in our interpretive history; the distrust of punctuation was more pervasive and certainly did not endorse its resolving an under-determinacy. Justice Baldwin for the 1837 Supreme Court:

> Punctuation is a most fallible standard by which to interpret a writing; it may be resorted to when all other means fail; but the Court will first take the instrument by its four corners, in order to ascertain its true meaning: if that is apparent on judicially inspecting the whole, the punctuation will not be suffered to change it.[6]

Today we have to trust punctuation unless other evidence undermines the apparent interpretation, so Thrust #24 is still not accurate, but for different reasons. As of 1950 when *Canons* was published we were in transition from disregard through *prima facie* but fragile trust to the present default position described above. Nor do Llewellyn's secondary sources support giving primacy to punctuation when "a statute is open to two constructions." That is, Thrust #24 has never been accurate so it can hardly count as a canon.

In support of it, Llewellyn cites *United States v. Marshall Field & Co.*,[7] a curious choice for that purpose as it simply fails, although it does address punctuation.

> The individual items are separated by commas and the complete clause is followed by a semicolon. While punctuation is not a controlling element in the interpretation of a statute, *Barrett* v. *Van Pelt*, 268 U.S. 85, 69 L. Ed. 857, 45 S. Ct. 437, nevertheless punctuation marks do have their place in ascertaining the meaning of language and in determining the legislative intent. *Markell* v. *United States*, 16 Ct. Cust. App. 518, T. D. 43239.

---

4 489 U.S. 235 (1988).

5 1 McKinney's Consolidated Laws of New York, Ch.6, §K, §§ 251–54 (1971) (footnotes omitted).

6 *Ewing v. Burnet*, 36 U.S. 41, 54 (1837).

7 18 C.C.P.A. 228 (Court of Customs and Patent Appeals, 1931).

The case was about the import duty on "wool-felt rugs, or small-sized carpets, used to cover the floors of what are known as children's play yards, these 'yards' being small portable enclosures with wooden floors upon which the articles are spread." Was it to be 30% because they were mere "mats or druggets" under

> PAR. 1117. ... All other floor coverings, including mats and druggets, not specially provided for, composed wholly or in chief value of wool, 30 per centum ad valorem.

or were they more luxurious carpets or rugs under

> PAR. 1116. Oriental, Axminster, Savonnerie, Aubusson, and other carpets and rugs, not made on a power-driven loom; carpets and rugs of oriental weave or weaves, produced on a power-driven loom; ... 55 per centum ad valorem.

to be taxed at 55%? The court made a very thorough analysis of PAR. 1116, with punctuation providing a boost, but the grounds for decision were independently ascertainable legislative intent.

> Had Congress intended that "other carpets and rugs" should constitute a class by themselves without reference to the state of the materials of which composed, provided they were not made on a power-driven loom, it seems to us, the word "and" now appearing after "Aubusson" would have been omitted and a semicolon inserted in its stead, or that some other wording would have been chosen for this, evidently carefully studied, paragraph.
>
> The phrase "not made on a power-driven loom" either relates back to each type of carpet mentioned before it--"Oriental, Axminster, Savonnerie, Aubusson, and other"--or else it was presupposed that the first four types were, in fact, not made on power-driven looms, and, in order to render it certain that all similar types, even though some new name should arise in the trade and be applied, would be included, the words "other ... not made," etc., were inserted.

But there was artillery of a heavier weight on which to rely. "It is not necessary to determine here which alternative is correct, because in either event, we feel sure, from the context, that Congress must have there had in mind other *woven* rugs, not made on a power-driven loom." First there was an argument using the canon *noscitur a sociis* (without explicitly saying so) as all the items listed in PAR. 1116 by name other than "rugs, not made on a power-driven loom" are hand made, luxurious, and very expensive, whereas the "mats and druggets" of PAR. 1117 are inexpensive, like the non-woven felt mats in question. Second, all this was stated expressly in the legislative history.[8]

Tedious, yes, but thorough, exemplary statutory interpretation. Nevertheless it's poor support for Thrust #24. Still, as Thrust #24 is and always has been inaccurate as a capsule of case law, there was little by way of support to be found.

---

[8] *Marshall Field & Co.*, 18 C.C.P.A. at 229–36.

Parry #24: "Punctuation marks will not control the plain and evident meaning of language."

The sense of Parry #24 is well expressed in the caption of Black's §86[9] and probably comes closest to a concise general rule, if one could be properly be posited:

> The punctuation marks in the published copies of an act are not allowed to control, enlarge, or restrict the plain and evident meaning of the legislature as disclosed by the language employed.[10]

Notice the words "in the published copies," reflecting the ancestral difference between the unpunctuated version enacted and subsequently promulgated versions with editorially inserted punctuation. The difference has long since disappeared, but the attitude lingers on. Parry #24, not a very dramatic claim, unlike Thrust #24 was and is empirically accurate.

In support Llewellyn cites *State v. Baird*,[11] from the 1930 Arizona Supreme Court, in which the plaintiff-appellant's argument rested solely on punctuation. Dilworth Baird, T. A. Bailey, Hugh E. Laird and J. L. Felton, members of the council of the town of Tempe, in Maricopa County, voted themselves a pay increase. In another civil action that pay increase was found to be *ultra vires* and the recipients repaid the town. But that wasn't enough for George T. Wilson, the county attorney; he wanted them also to be ousted from their positions on the council. The statute was:

> No alderman or councilman of any town, organized hereunder, shall, during the term for which he shall have been or shall be elected, accept, take or receive to his own use, from the town of which he shall be an alderman or councilman, any sum of money or other thing of value, other than that which is, by this chapter provided to be paid to such alderman or councilman, for his services as such alderman or councilman; and every person who shall violate the provisions of this section, shall be deemed guilty of a misdemeanor and upon conviction thereof, in any court of competent jurisdiction, shall be fined not less than one hundred dollars, nor more than three hundred dollars, such fine to go to the school fund of the county in which such town shall be located; and he shall also cease to be an alderman or councilman, as the case may be, of such town.[12]

County attorney Wilson argued that the semicolon before the ouster clause, "and he shall also cease to be an alderman or councilman, as the case may be, of such town", marks it as independent of the requirement of conviction precedent to a fine. "This contention of the independence of the penalties is predicated exclusively upon the fact that a semicolon separates the two penalties." To this the defendant aldermen reply that "the penalties are conjunctively and

---

[9] Not the cited § 87, which reads:

> If there is no doubt as to the meaning of the legislature, other than such as is created by the defective or erroneous punctuation of the statute, the courts will disregard the punctuation marks and read the statute as correctly punctuated.

Black at § 87, 263.

[10] Black at § 86, 263.

[11] 36 Ariz. 531 (1930).

[12] Id. at 533 (cited as "paragraph 1889 of the Civil Code of 1913, . . . Section 405, Rev. Code 1928.").

not disjunctively stated." Before getting to the grammatical argument, the court gives history and policy and cases not only from Arizona but also from Massachusetts, Nevada, Iowa and Virginia to the effect that a criminal conviction is always a condition precedent to ouster, as intended in this statute. The punctuation argument gets an appropriately abrupt dismissal:

> As we see it, the separation of the two penalties by semicolon does not affect the legislative intention in the least. As punctuated, the meaning is the same as it would be in the absence of all punctuation. The division of the sentence by semicolon doubtless was made because of the insertion of the clause appropriating fines to the school fund and not to indicate that the penalties might be enforced by different proceedings. The rule is that punctuation will not be resorted to except when the meaning is doubtful. At best it is a most fallible standard by which to interpret a writing. 3 Bouvier's Law Dictionary, 3d Rev., p. 2769.[13]

And the defendants' demurrer was affirmed. It is a quite satisfying as an illustration of Parry #24,[14] and an endorsement of judicial disregard of punctuation.

Resolution

There is no need for resolution of Thrust and Parry #24 as they do not conflict. Each, by its own terms, addresses a different situation.

The pair is unfortunate in other ways. Thrust #24 should not find its way onto any list of canons today let alone in 1950. Llewellyn's cited authorities do not support it, and the two treatises he relies on but does not cite here are affirmatively to the contrary. We might hope for something like it in the future, and that such a development in judicial attitude will cause legislatures to take as much care with punctuation as they do with their choice of words, but until that day arrives there is no supportable generality like Thrust #24. Justice Baldwin is still correct, "punctuation is a most fallible standard by which to interpret a writing."[15]

---

[13] *Id.* at 533-36.
[14] Better, and easy enough to find, would be *Hammock v. Loan and Trust Co.*,105 U.S. 77 (1882) from the 1882 Supreme Court, *per* Justice Harlan, with a key decision requiring ignoring a comma.
[15] *Ewing*, 36 U.S. at 54.

Pair Twenty-Five

> **THRUST**: "It must be assumed that language has been chosen with due regard to grammatical propriety and is not interchangeable on mere conjecture."
> **PARRY:** "And" and "or" may be read interchangeably whenever the change is necessary to give the statute sense."[1]

We must assume that the legislature followed the conventional rules of English grammar; what choice do we have? Just as the legislature is presumed —unless it specifies otherwise —to be using words in their normal meanings, so too it must be presumed to be using ordinary grammar.

But Llewellyn's opening of Thrust #25 is not intended as a restatement of this platitude. If it were, the second half's saying that "the language … is not interchangeable" would not make sense. For Thrust #25 Llewellyn cites Black's Section 75, which is, like Parry #25, about 'and' and 'or': it comes under the caption "CONJUNCTIVE AND DISJUNCTIVE PARTICLES" and has the bold heading:

> The word "and," in a statute, may be read "or," and vice versa, whenever the change is necessary to give the statute sense and effect, or to harmonize its different parts, or to carry out the evident intention of the legislature.[2]

In other words, Parry #25, for which he cites not Black but Sutherland and R.C.L.Statutes. Four pages on in Black, at the end of the section is a subsection, "*Limitations of Rule*," after emphasizing that "'and" and 'or' are in no sense interchangeable terms, but, on the contrary, … are used in the structure of language for purposes entirely different", Black writes:

> It must be assumed that the language of a statute is chosen with due regard to grammatical propriety. And therefore the courts are not at liberty to treat these words as interchangeable on mere conjecture or according to their own notions of expediency or policy.[3]

Obviously, this is the source of Thrust #25, just as the section's heading is the source of Parry #25. It is a rare instance of Llewellyn's using text, not caption as his source.

---

[1] *Cannons* at 406.
[2] Black at 228.
[3] Id at 231.

Thrust #25: "It must be assumed that language has been chosen with due regard to grammatical propriety and is not interchangeable on mere conjecture."

One ought not read a statute so as to produce an absurd or unworkable result. "[A] statute authorizing a city to provide for the "health, safety, and convenience" of the inhabitants does not require that its ordinances should have relation to all three of these objects at once."[4] That is, Parry #25; what sort of decision might be to the contrary? what sort of decision might illustrate Thrust #25?

Llewellyn's cited example, *Hines v. Mills*,[5] from the 1933 Arkansas Supreme Court, offers support for Thrust #25 but hardly helps his cause of contrariety of thrust and parry. Mills, as trustee of a veterans' home, had invested a government grant in certain securities, as permitted by law. Hines sought to have him disgorge those funds as he had not first obtained the permission of the probate court. The statute in question read "Every guardian shall invest the funds of the estate in such manner or in such securities, in which the guardian has no interest, as allowed by law or approved by the court."[6] Were "as allowed by law or approved by the court" to read "as allowed by law *and* approved by the court", Hines would be correct. But why should it?

> The language of the act is unambiguous, and, as written, has one meaning only. It says and means that a guardian may invest his ward's funds in securities "allowed by law or approved by the court." ... It is only permissible to use the words "or" and "and" interchangeably in statutes where the context requires that it be done to effectuate the manifest intention of the Legislature or where not to do so would render the meaning ambiguous or result in an absurdity. It is not necessary to substitute the conjunctive "and" for the disjunctive "or" in the statute to prevent either a dubious meaning or an absurd one. There is nothing in the context to indicate that the Legislature intended in the enactment to use the word "and" in the place of the word "or." ...The word "or" was used without rendering the meaning either dubious or absurd. It would not be permissible for this court to substitute the word "and" for "or" to effectuate a change in the intention of the Legislature. Such a change would amount to an encroachment upon legislative prerogatives.[7]

Not exactly rousing, but support nevertheless for Thrust #25.

Parry #25 "And" and "or" may be read interchangeably whenever the change is necessary to give the statute sense."

Llewellyn's cited secondary sources, Sutherland and R.C.L. *Statutes*, take a decidedly more cavalier attitude towards 'and' and 'or' than does Black, or, for that matter, his fourth

---

4 Black at §75, 228-29, citing *City of Red Wing v. Guptil*, 72 Minn. 259 (1898).
5 187 Ark. 465 (1933).
6 "§ 12 of act 36 of the General Assembly of 1929", Id at 466.
7 Id.

secondary source, C.J. *Statutes*. Sutherland and R.C.L. *Statutes* must have coordinated their accounts as they begin identically:

> The popular use of "or" and "and" is so loose and so frequently inaccurate that it has infected statutory enactments. While they are not treated as interchangeable, and should be followed when their accurate reading does not render the sense dubious, their strict meaning is more readily departed from than that of other words, and one is read in place of the other in deference to the meaning of the context. Whenever it is necessary to effectuate the obvious intention of the legislature the courts have power to change and will change "and" to "or" and vice versa.[8]

Fulghum v. Bleakley,[9] the case Llewellyn chose to illustrate Parry #25 is rather more subtle than necessary. Remember "Guest Statutes"? In cases of automobile accidents they relieved the driver of liability to his non-paying guests for his ordinary negligence. South Carolina's was an exact copy of the first, Connecticut's:

> No person transported by the owner or operator of a motor vehicle as his guest without payment for such transportation shall have a cause of action for damages against such automobile, its owner or operator for injury, death or loss, in case of accident unless such accident shall have been intentional on the part of said owner or operator or caused by his heedlessness or his reckless disregard of the rights of others.

The problem lies in the exception, the "unless … " clause.

> If the phrase 'or caused by his heedlessness' is to be taken as strictly disjunctive as by itself constituting an exception to the general rule of nonliability, and 'heedlessness' is held to be synonymous with 'negligence,' the entire statute is nugatory and effects no change whatever in the law as it existed before its enactment.

Plaintiff Fulghum argued that "the wording of the Act is plain and unambiguous and should not be changed in order to give the statute a different interpretation", but the South Carolina Supreme Court was not prepared to let the evident intent of the legislature go for nought.

> The framers of the statute undoubtedly used the noun 'heedlessness' in place of the adjective 'heedless' and the word 'or' for 'and.' The phrase 'or caused by his heedlessness or his reckless disregard of the rights of others' meets the legislative intention when it is construed to read 'or caused by his heedless and his reckless disregard of the rights of others.'

Thus was saved the intention of the legislature to require for a driver's liability to his guest "something more than the mere failure to exercise the care of a reasonably prudent man which is

---

[8] Sutherland at §397, p.756, R.C.L. *Statutes* at §226, p.977.

[9] 177 S.C. 286 (1935)(Plaintiff Fulghum was represented by J. Strom Thurmond).

the familiar definition of negligence."[10] It did not matter to the ultimate outcome, however, as the Court then found the evidence sufficient to support a finding of recklessness.

Resolution

Thrust #25, as written by Llewellyn —and construed to be intelligible —says no more than that the legislature enacting a statute in English may be presumed to have used English semantics and syntax. This is hardly a canon so much as a condition on communication, a presupposition of all applications of statutes. And, as Parry #25 implicitly concedes, it is a strong presumption, not to be abandoned unless "necessary to give the statute sense."[11] This writing itself, as does the reader's reading of it, rests on the same presumption.

Thrust #25 is not a canon, but Parry #25 is a generalization often quoted in one form or another to justify an interpretation preserving legislative intent and effectiveness, that is, a canon. But it is no more in conflict with Thrust #25 than any other commonplace of statutory governance; to the contrary, like all English sentences it depends on Thrust #25. As is plain to all English speakers, 'and' and 'or' have different meanings, different relations with the words they conjoin. But sometimes in a statute an 'and' may function as an 'or' or an 'or' as an 'and' if the statute is to be meaningful or serve a sensible, governing role.[12] The plain meaning rule —Pair 12 —and the principle of legislative supremacy have more interpretive weight than any claimed universal rule of linguistic usage.

---

[10] Id at 289-91. The entire argument here was quoted from the Connecticut Supreme Court decision *Silver v. Silver,* 108 Conn. 371 (1928). One wonders why Llewellyn didn't use the original rather than the copy.

[11] *Cannons* at 406, quoting Black at 228.

[12] A working hypothesis is that where 'and' functions as 'or' or vice-versa there will be a negation or at least a negative polarity over the whole clause.

Pair Twenty-Six

> **THRUST**: "There is a distinction between words of permission and mandatory words."
> **PARRY**: "Words imparting permission may be read as mandatory and words imparting command may be read as permissive when such construction is made necessary by evident intention or by the rights of the public."[1]

Thrust #26 is obviously not a canon; it is a truism about language. But Thrust #26 is a presupposition of Parry #26, which would make no sense were there no such distinction; *i.e.* but for Thrust #26 there would never be an occasion for asserting Parry #26.

Pair 26 appears to have originated in Black's caption to §151 (which Llewellyn cites for Parry #26):

> But words in a statute importing permission or authorization may be read as mandatory, and words importing command may be read as permissive or enabling, whenever, in either case, such a construction is rendered necessary by the evident intention of the legislature or the rights of the public or of private persons under the statute.[2]

C.J.*Statutes* §631, Llewellyn's alternate cite, simply presumes that mandatory and permissive words will be used in statutes in their ordinary sense and concentrates on the exceptions, "when necessary to effect legislative intent."[3]

Thrust #26: "There is a distinction between words of permission and mandatory words."

Of course there is a distinction between words of permission and mandate; if there weren't then communicating a permission or a command as such would not be possible in words. We have to take Llewellyn's Thrust #25 as a careless expression of what he needs here, *viz*:

> The words "may," "authorized," "shall," "must" and the like, as employed in statutes, are first of all to be presumed to have been used in their natural and ordinary sense, …[4]

---

1 *Cannons* at 406.
2 Black at §151, 520 (Substituting 'imparting' for 'importing' is a bit lame, don't you think? But 'made' for 'rendered' is an improvement.)
3 C.J.*Statutes* at §631, 1073.

What other presumption could one make? It is rather like Thrust #25 in saying merely that if the legislature is using English it must presume the governed will understand its words and their grammatical concatenations as English.

Llewellyn cites *Koch & Dreyfus v. Bridges*,[5] in which the 1871 Missouri Supreme Court enforced a 'shall' as mandatory. It may have been an easy case, there being little to suggest that compliance with the statute was problematic, but it does contain a wealth of wisdom on statutory interpretation and is, perhaps, the source of Llewellyn's unfortunate formulation of Thrust #26.

A foreclosure sale of real estate had been held not on the county courthouse steps but at "the market house in the town of Summit [which] is not a legal place for a sheriff's sale of land." The statute

> provides that "all sales by any sheriff or other officer, by virtue of any execution or other process, shall be made at the courthouse of the county, except when personal property, too cumbersome to be removed, shall be levied on, which may be sold at the place where the same may be found, or at any other convenient place, ... and such sales may be made on the first Monday of every month, or on the first Monday or Tuesday of each term of the circuit court of the county." Rev. Code, 528, art. 277.

There appears no leeway for treating this as permissive, but the appellant argued that it was "directory," meaning the same thing, and thus that the sale was valid. The opinion does not rest formalistically on the language of the statute, but rather that it was "evidently intended to secure certainty and uniformity as to the place of sale of land by the sheriff under execution or other process at law. ... To our minds it is obvious at least, that the surest if not the only way of effectuating that intent, and guarding against the evils at which it was aimed, is to hold the requisition of the act imperative." Thus the petitioner's argument would require judicial subversion of legislative intent, in defiance of legislative supremacy:

> This mode of getting rid of a statutory provision by calling it directory is not only unsatisfactory, on account of the vagueness of the rule itself, but it is the exercise of a dispensing power by the courts, which approaches so near legislative discretion that it ought to be resorted to with reluctance, only in extraordinary cases, where great public mischief would otherwise ensue, or important private interests demand the application of the rule. There is no more propriety in dispensing with one positive requirement than another; a whole statute may be thus dispensed with when in the way of the caprice or will of a judge.

There is more too, a veritable textbook of statutory interpretation with many other canons brought into play. For Llewellyn's and our purpose, suffice it to say that "the appellant acquired no title to the property in controversy at the sheriff's sale in the town of Summit."[6]

---

4 Black at §150, 520.
5 45 Miss. 247 (1871).
6 Id at 257-63.

Parry #26: "Words imparting permission may be read as mandatory and words imparting command may be read as permissive when such construction is made necessary by evident intention or by the rights of the public."

Black lists the captions to §§150 and 151 together at the beginning of his commentary on the topic of these words; §151 spells out the exception to §150's generality that the legislature intended its words in their normal sense, "unless it is necessary to carry out the purpose of the legislature, effect justice, secure public or private rights, or avoid absurdity."[7] *Corpus Juris*, Llewellyn's other chosen secondary source for Parry #26, emphasizes the primacy of giving effect to legislative intent.[8]

Llewellyn cites two cases in support of Parry #26, but neither is helpful. The first, *Jennings v. Suggs*,[9] from the 1935 Georgia Supreme Court, gives neither the statute in question (governing the notice a municipality must give of a meeting to change zoning) nor how it involved permissive or mandatory words. It does however quote formulaically from two prior cases,[10] suggesting that some issue involving the strictness of the required compliance was involved. The second, *Ewing v. Union Central Bank*,[11] from Kentucky in 1934, is a pedestrian illustration of Thrust #26 (as recontrived, above.) The cite must have crept in by mistake.

Illustrative cases are not hard to find, especially given the prolific footnotes of treatises. *Supervisors v. United States, ex Relatione*,[12] from the 1867 Supreme Court is a good example, with genuine reasoning to legislative intent. It was a writ of mandamus to force the county supervisors to levy a tax. The statute, superficially, was permissive, but the Supreme Court found it mandatory.

> That act declares that "the board of supervisors under township organization, in such counties as may be owing debts which their current revenue, under existing laws, is not sufficient to pay, may, if deemed advisable, levy a special tax, not to exceed in any one year one per cent. upon the taxable property of any such county, to be assessed and collected ..." .[13]

The taxpayer argued that this clearly gave the supervisors discretion. But, after expounding English and United States precedents, the Court continued:

> The conclusion to be deduced from the authorities is, that where power is given

---

[7] Black at §150, 520.

[8] C.J.*Statutes*, §631, 1072 at 1073-74.

[9] 180 Ga. 141 (1935).

[10] ""The true rule for the construction of the word *may* in a statute is, that when such statute concerns the public interest, or affects the rights of third persons, then the word *may,* shall be construed to mean *must or shall.*" *Birdsong* v. *Brooks,* 7 Ga. 88. "In the construction of statutes, *may* is held to mean *shall* in two cases, viz., where the thing to be done 'is for the sake of justice, or for the public benefit.'" *Weems* v. *Farrell,* 33 Ga. 413, 419." 180 Ga. at 141-42.

[11] 254 Ky. 623 (1934).

[12] 71 U.S. 435, 4 Wall. 435 (1867).

[13] Id at 445.

> to public officers, in the language of the act before us, or in equivalent language -- whenever the public interest or individual rights call for its exercise -- the language used, though permissive in form, is in fact peremptory. What they are empowered to do for a third person the law requires shall be done. The power is given, not for their benefit, but for his. It is placed with the depositary to meet the demands of right, and to prevent a failure of justice. It is given as a remedy to those entitled to invoke its aid, and who would otherwise be remediless.
>
> In all such cases it is held that the intent of the legislature, which is the test, was not to devolve a mere discretion, but to impose "a positive and absolute duty. [14]

Resolution

It is a mistake to expect generalities about law to have the universal truth, the absolute vulnerability to counter example that we expect of laws of science. Law is a human artifact, and as with all human practices is subject to willful and accidental variation, to subversion and to error. In statutory governance, the fundamental principle of legislative supremacy requires deference to legislative intent rather than to judicial preference.

Sometimes a legislature slips up in expressing its intent, sometimes grossly, for example by writing "less" where it meant "more"[15] or omitting a "not,"[16] sometimes more subtly, as in using "shall" when "may" better reflects its intent.[17] And, as illustrated above in *Supervisors v. United States, ex Relatione*,[18] when public or individual rights are at stake and the statute governs the behavior of a public official, permissives may routinely be read as mandatory. This is exactly as in Black's caption, paraphrased as Parry #26.

Thrust #26, had it been written as a pseudo-canon and potentially contrary to Parry #26 —for example, paraphrasing Blacks §150 caption, "Permissive and mandatory terms are presumed to have been used in their natural and primary signification, and should not be interpreted otherwise..." —would not have been an absolute, universal rule but a generality subject to exceptions —as Black continues, "unless it is necessary to carry out the purpose of the legislature … ."[19] Pair 26 is similar to Pair 25 in this respect: they are no more conflictual than any other commonplace of statutory governance. They are also similar in that neither is canonical.

---

[14] Id at 446-47.

[15] *See Amalgamated Transit Union Local 1309 v. Laidlaw Transit Services, Inc*. (Amalgamated II), 448 F.3d 1092, 1094 (9th Cir. 2006)(Bybee, J., dissenting).

[16] *See Johnson v. United States Gypsum Co.,* 217 Ark. 264, 229 S.W.2d 671 (1950); *see* Hart & Sachs, THE LEGAL PROCESS 1187-88 (William N. Eskridge, Jr., & Philip P. Frickey, ed.s, 1994)

[17] *See* e.g. *The People of the State of Illinois v. Frank G. Heilman Company*, 263 Ill. App. 514 (1931).

[18] 71 U.S. 435, 4 Wall. 435 (1867).

[19] Black at §150, 529.

Pair Twenty-Seven

THRUST: "A proviso qualifies the provision immediately preceding."
PARRY: "It may clearly be intended to have wider scope."[1]

Scope uncertainties are a rich source of interpretive problems, be they about adverbs or adjectives, restrictive clauses, exceptions, or the referential antecedents of pronouns. Pair 27 is about the scope of exceptions stated in statutes.

Llewellyn cites *C.J.* Statutes §640 and Sutherland §352 for Thrust #27; Sutherland:

> The natural and appropriate office of the proviso being to restrain or qualify some preceding matter, it should be confined to what precedes it unless it clearly appears to have been intended to apply to some other matter.[2]

As it is in ordinary English, so it must be in statutes.

Thrust #27: "A proviso qualifies the provision immediately preceding."

As with all regularities of language, Thrust #27 "is not an arbitrary rule to be enforced at all events" but a presumption of what the speaker/writer —here lawmaker —intended.[3] Nor is it a very strong presumption; *C.J.* Statutes,gives it only one short paragraph, most of which is devoted to making an exception "where necessary to effectuate legislative intent," Parry #27.

Llewellyn cites *State* ex rel *Higgs v. Summers*,[4] from the 1929 Nebraska Supreme Court, a poor choice as support for Thrust #27, but an interesting explication of alternative meanings for "Provided …" as a statutory connector.

> As a general rule the office of a proviso is to modify the operation of that part of the statute immediately preceding the proviso, or to except something from the operation of the statute which would otherwise have been within it, but it is often used in other senses, such as here, where we are dealing with an addition by way of amendment made under new circumstances to a form of words adopted many years before. It is a common practice in legislative proceedings, on the consideration of bills, for parties desirous of securing an amendment to them to precede their proposed amendment with the term "provided," so as to declare that

---

1 *Cannons* at 406.
2 Sutherland at 673; Black, §130 (cited for Parry #27) is similar.
3 *C.J.* Statutes at 1090, §640.
4 118 Neb. 189 (1929).

> notwithstanding existing provisions the one thus expressed is to prevail, thus having no greater signification than would be attached to the conjunction "and" or "but" in the same place, and simply serving to separate or distinguish the two different paragraphs or sentences. … .[5]

It is a good practical wisdom, but doesn't help or illustrate Thrust #27.

A simple illustration is *Clay Center State Bank of Clay Center, Neb., v. McKelvie*, from the 8th Circuit, 1927.[6] The statute in question was

> Nothing in this chapter shall be so construed as to exempt any property in this state from execution or attachment for clerk's, laborer's, or mechanic's wages, for money due and owing by any attorney at law, for money or other valuable consideration received by said attorney for any person or persons, nor shall anything in this chapter be construed to exempt from execution or attachment property of the value of more than five hundred dollars for any debt contracted by any person in the purchase of the actual necessaries of life for himself or family or for any person or persons who were, at the time of contracting such debt, dependent upon such person purchasing the same for support; *provided*, that where the debt contracted therefor shall be deemed the debt of both husband and wife; and provided further, that nothing herein contained shall be construed to exempt in the aggregate more than five hundred ($500.00) dollars' worth of personal property to both husband and wife.

The debate was exactly on the application of Pair 27. The debtor, naturally seeking to maximize the exemption, argued that the last proviso applied to the whole of the statute ("section 9040"), *i.e.*, Parry #27; the creditor argued for Thrust #27, "that this proviso applies only to the language which immediately precedes it… ." The court, finding no motivation in the legislation to do otherwise and some support in parallel statutes, opted for the default, Thrust #27.

> … we think it is clear the proviso was here employed for its usual purpose, namely, to limit the language which immediately preceded it to one exemption of $500, and prevent it from being interpreted to give one exemption to the husband of $500, and another exemption to the wife of $500.[7]

Parry #27: "It may clearly be intended to have wider scope."

Llewellyn did not cite the section of *C.J.* Statuteshe cited for Thrust #27, but might well have as it states the proposition comprehensively and succinctly:

> But where necessary to effectuate the legislative intent, a proviso will be construed as applying to other sections, either preceding or subsequent, or to the entire act in which it appears.[8]

---

5 Id at 192-93.
6 19 F.2d 308 (8th Cir., 1927)
7 Id at 309-10.
8 *C.J.* Statutes, §640, 1090.

Thrust #27 is not an overwhelmingly strong grammatical generality, and the treatises therefore devote more time to the varieties of exception. There is nothing mysterious in the justification: that's how it is in ordinary English, and on the other hand, legislative supremacy is a powerful imperative. *State* ex rel *Higgs v. Summers,*[9] Llewellyn's case cite for Thrust #27 is an example.

Illustrations abound. Nevertheless, in *Reuter v. San Mateo County,*[10] from the 1934 California Supreme Court, Llewellyn has found a case about a proviso that does not illustrate Parry #27. It is about a complicated inter-relationship between California's Constitution, the county charter, and general state laws, interesting in its own right, and informative about the interpretation of provisos in constitutions and their interaction with other law, but not an example of Parry #27.

One of Black's illustrations, *Mayor and Councilmen of the City of Cumberland v. Magruder,*[11] from the 1871 Maryland Supreme Court, is more apt. The mayor and Council of Cumberland had contracted for a new bridge over the Potomac, $24,000, for which they were "preparing to issue coupon bonds of the city, [pledging] the faith and credit of the city … to an amount far exceeding $10,000, without first submitting the question to the decision of a majority of the legal voters of the city… ." They claimed power to do this under and 1867 act, but an 1864 amendment to the city charter included a proviso that plaintiffs Magruder *et al* argued limited that power to a maximum of $10,000.

> Its fourth section contains grants of certain powers usually conferred upon municipal corporations, including the power to levy a tax not exceeding fifty cents in the hundred dollars and then concludes thus: "*provided* that they" (the Mayor and Councilmen) "*shall not have* power to close or alienate any public street or alley, *or* pledge the credit and faith of said city for any sum exceeding ten thousand dollars without first submitting the question to the voters of said city, after twenty days public notice, and a majority of the legal voters assenting thereto."

The mayor and his council, no doubt envisaging their names on the beautiful new bridge, argued Thrust #27, the proviso limits only the power granted in the immediately preceding section. But the Maryland Supreme Court would have none of it.

> [W]hatever may be the ordinary office of a proviso in excepting something from the enacting clause, or qualifying or restraining its generality, or excluding some possible ground of misinterpretation, in our judgment no such narrow interpretation ought to be placed on this provision. It is engrafted upon the effective part of the charter of a municipal corporation, and no matter by what phrase it may be preceded, is in terms an absolute and unqualified negation of all power to close or alienate any of the public streets, and an equally comprehensive and definite restriction upon the exercise of any power to pledge the faith or

---

9 118 Neb. 189 (1929).
10 220 Cal. 314 (1934).
11 34 Md. 381 (1871).

> credit of the city beyond the limited sum. Its language is too plain to be misunderstood, too imperative to be disregarded, and the result it seeks to attain too salutary and important to be defeated by any nice construction founded on the position in which it is placed, the connection in which it is found, or the technical word by which it is prefaced. In respect to position and connection it is equally potent as if enacted in a separate section.

The justices also approved the policy of the proviso as a "most wholesome and wise restriction, intended to protect in some degree the citizens and tax payers" from profligate administrative expenditures. Without "the previous sanction of a majority of the legal voters" the city father's were without the power to proceed, and plaintiffs won their injunction.[12]

Resolution

Llewellyn did not choose the words for his thrusts and parries with care. Pair 27, for example, are on their face about different modalities, Thrust #27 being an empirical generality — "A proviso qualifies the provision immediately preceding" —and Parry #27 being a possibility of an intention —"It [a proviso] may clearly be intended to have wider scope [than the provision immediately preceding]." Both Thrust #27 and Parry #27 could thus be true, the legislature (the deleted agent of the passive voice parry) having failed in its intention. But had he been more careful, would it have helped?

Conform both to the form of Parry #27 by making Thrust #27 about legislative intention and under the modality "may": "A proviso may be intended to qualify the provision immediately preceding." There would be no incompatibly, but Thrust #27 as modified would be such a timid understatement as to be of no value at all.

Conform both to the form of Thrust #27 by making Parry #27 an empirical generalization: "It [a proviso] qualifies not only the immediately preceding provision but also has wider scope [than the provision immediately preceding]." Now the two would conflict, but Parry #27 would be obviously false.

So we need to treat the two with charity even to start a conversation.

The whole problem is in treating the default interpretive principle, Thrust #27, as rule-like or commanding. It is not, either in everyday English or in statutes, but it is the presumed scope, the default, or "unmarked" case. As with all defaults/presumptions/unmarked cases, all Thrust #27 does is throw the burden of justification on one who would claim an exception. In this case that burden is not specially heavy. Perhaps that is why neither Thrust nor Parry #27 would count as a canon on most people's lists.

---

[12] Id at 385-88.

Pair Twenty-Eight

THRUST: "When the enacting clause is general, a proviso is construed strictly."
PARRY: "Not when it is necessary to extend the proviso to persons or cases which come within its equity."[1]

It is nice to see a canon again, at last, and to end the list with one. Thrust #28 is usually listed as a subsidiary case of *expressio unius est exclusion alterius*, Thrust #20. In Llewellyn's list Thrust #28 put in an earlier appearance in a variant form as Thrust #19, "Exceptions not made cannot be read."[2] It will naturally come with similar justification and exceptions. However, Thrust #28 is usually considered stronger than *expressio unius* ... as the background law has been expressed so immediately in the preceding provision. Exceptions to it will accordingly be more difficult to find and justify; hence the circumspection with which Parry #28 is expressed ("when it is necessary...", "within its equity...").

Thrust #28 appears to have come from the caption to Black's §131: "A proviso in a statute, where the enacting clause is general in its terms and objects, must ordinarily be construed strictly." Llewellyn cites this section for both Thrust and Parry #28 and also Sutherland §322,[3] although this is clearly a mistake and should be §351.[4] It is surprising that he did not also cite *C.J.* Statutes as in the sections adjacent to the section cited for Thrust #27, *i.e.* §§639 and 641, the same thesis is advanced very clearly with a similar exception.

The source of Parry #28 comes three pages into the text of Black §131:

> But this rule is not invariably applicable. There are cases in which a proviso to a statute should be liberally construed. This is the case when it is necessary to extend the proviso to persons or cases which come within its equity, though not its strict letter, in order to effectuate justice or secure the benefits or remedies

---

[1] *Cannons* at 406.

[2] *Cannons* at 404 (where it came with the lame parry "The letter is only the "bark." Whatever is within the reason of the law is within the law itself.").

[3] Sutherland at 756 ("A private statute is one confined to a special case. An act "to enable the Bishop of Canton to make a lease to A.B." is a fair example of a private statute.").

[4] Sutherland at 676-77 ("A proviso is ... used for the purpose of taking special cases out of a general class .... The general intent will be controlled by the particular intent subsequently expressed. ... An exception is strictly construed.")

> which the proviso had in contemplation, and especially when the statute is penal in its nature.[5]

(It is surprising how familiarity inures one to the copying and omission of the appropriate citation.)

Thrust #28: "When the enacting clause is general, a proviso is construed strictly."

25 R.C.L. *Statutes* §230: "It is well settled that an exception in a statute amounts to an affirmation of the application of its provisions to all other cases not excepted and excludes all other exceptions."[6] As a special case of the canon "*Expressio unius est exclusio alterius*," Thrust #20, Thrust #28 has a similar justification.

We can presume that the legislature was setting all and only the controls it intended. If the legislation imposes a change on the background law, that is, it changes the legal or cultural norms, by enacting a prohibition against a prior freedom, or permission on a social or legal prohibition, then it will be confined strictly to the words enacted. But, for example, were the statute merely giving structure to the old law, or codifying part of common law (like much of Article 2 of the Uniform Commercial Code, for example) then *expressio unius* ... wouldn't hold, the statute could be interpreted liberally. Like all pragmatically based rules, this justification depends on the background, which one must always establish if one is to justify using the canon.

But an exception or a proviso always has a clear and simply ascertainable background, namely, the statute in its main provision. The immediate presence of the rule out of which the exception is carved, and that it is an exception, strengthen Thrust #28 as a special case of *expressio unius*... . The legislature, acting felicitously –*i.e.* saying all and only what it intended – has enacted a rule and the exception(s) it allows; by *expressio unius*... we may safely infer that no other exceptions are intended.[7]

The 1841 Supreme Court, quoted by Black, expressed the concept clearly:

> [W]e are led to the general rule of law which has always prevailed, and become consecrated almost as a maxim in the interpretation of statutes, that where the enacting clause is general in its language and objects, and a proviso is afterwards introduced, that proviso is construed strictly, and takes no case out of the enacting clause which does not fall fairly within its terms. In short, a proviso carves special exceptions only out of the enacting clause; and those who set up

---

5 Black at 436.

6 25 R.C.L. *Statutes* §230, 983.

7 Black at 222 ("Another case in which this maxim may almost invariably be followed is that of a statute which makes certain specific exceptions to its general provisions. Here we may safely assume that all other exceptions were intended to be excluded.")

> any such exception, must establish it as being within the words as well as within the reason thereof.[8]

In *Montgomery v. Martin,*[9] from the 1928 Pennsylvania Supreme Court, Llewellyn has chosen an extraordinarily complicated example, but also one with a remarkably strict reading of a proviso, not in a statute but in the state's constitution. The Pennsylvania constitution had a general prohibition on state debt, article IX, section 4:

> No debt shall be created by or on behalf of the State, except to supply casual deficiencies of revenue, repel invasion, suppress insurrection, defend the State in war, or to pay existing debts; and the debt created to supply deficiencies in revenue shall never exceed, in the aggregate at any one time, one million of dollars.

By amendment in 1918 and again in 1923 (raising the amount) a proviso was added to facilitate highway construction:

> Provided, however, that the General Assembly, irrespective of any debt, may authorize the State to issue bonds to the amount of [one hundred millions of dollars] for the purpose of improving and rebuilding the highways of the Commonwealth.

The state duly issued bonds in the sum of one hundred million dollars, but redeemed or repurchased a total of $3.7million. At that the Governor "directed defendants to prepare and print highway bonds in the amount of three million dollars, for issuance under authority of that statute, to replace like securities purchased and cancelled;" this suit sought to enjoin that printing. Under the proviso, did the state government have the power to issue new bonds to replace those retired and repurchased? The Pennsylvania Supreme Court answered that it did not!

> In this country the legislature of a state represents the sovereign will of a sovereign people, and, in the absence of constitutional restrictions, can authorize the state to borrow any amount of money for any purpose it sees fit …; therefore section 4 of article IX of our Constitution must be viewed as a restrictive measure, and the proviso with which we are particularly dealing must be treated as part of the general provision to which it is attached. In other words, the main purpose of the section in question is to limit the inherent right of the State to borrow money, and the proviso, by qualifying this restriction, becomes part of it. The office of a proviso is to "qualify, restrain, or otherwise modify the general language of an enacting clause." A proviso "is to be strictly [not liberally] construed" …, and "can have no existence separate and apart from the provision which it is designed to limit or qualify." These are not technical but common sense rules, applicable to the interpretation of any written instrument; they govern the construction of constitutional provisions as well as of statutes.[10]

Yes, but still isn't this a remarkably narrow interpretation? That the state had authorized one hundred million dollars in bonds and could therefore not authorize any more, even though less

---

[8] *United States v. Dickson*, 40 U.S. (15 Pet.) 141, 165 (1841).

[9] 294 Pa. 25 (1928).

[10] Id, at 29-30, citations ommitted.

than one hundred million dollars of those bonds were outstanding? It took about seven more pages of explanation, some of it sparkling but most densely abstruse to reach the conclusion. It is indeed to construe the proviso narrowly, a most convincing illustration of the canon if not reliant upon it.

Parry #28: "Not when it is necessary to extend the proviso to persons or cases which come within its equity."

C.J. Statutes offers a clear statement resting on legislative intent:

> But where from the language employed it is apparent that the legislature intended a more comprehensive meaning, it [the proviso] must be construed to enlarge the scope of the act, or to assume the function of an independent enactment.[11]

Of course, like any interpretive principle or canon of construction, if Thrust #28's justification does not apply then it will not apply either. Take for example Llewellyn's poorly chosen illustration for Thrust #27, *State* ex rel *Higgs v. Summers*.[12] The statute originated in 1897 as

> When for a continuous period of one year a district shall have less than two legal voters residing therein, the county superintendent may, in his discretion, annex the district to one or more adjoining districts upon petitions signed by a majority of the legal voters of such adjoining district or districts.[13]

But ten years later, in 1907, the legislature added

> Provided, if any school district shall, for two consecutive years, fail to maintain a public school, as required by law to do, it shall be the duty of the county superintendent of the county in which such district lies to attach the territory of such district to one or more adjoining school districts.[14]

precisely to provide for circumstances such as those at issue, *viz*, where a district had more than two legal voters but not enough children to operate a school. The "Provided …" clause does not, as plaintiffs argued, signal an exception to be read narrowly, but an addition to the original enacting clause, and so the Nebraska Supreme Court found.

Given the strength of Thrust #28, good examples of Parry #28 are hard to find. Llewellyn uses Black's prime example, *Forscht v. Green*,[15] from the 1866 Pennsylvania Supreme Court. "The evil of betting on elections was very great prior to the Act of 1839," so the act declared that monies bet on an election shall be forfeit "to the authorities in charge of the poor of the district where such bet on an election shall be made," but subject to a proviso: "*provided,* … suit is brought within two years from the time of making such bet."

---

11 *C.J.* Statutes at 1091, §§641.
12 118 Neb. 189 (1929).
13 Id at 192.
14 Id.
15 53 Pa. 138 (1866).

Forscht lost his bet of $220 to Donell "on the result of the Congressional election, in the York, Cumberland and Perry district, in 1862" but told defendant Green, the stakeholder, not to pay Donell. Green, however, paid Donell, subject to indemnification. Forscht then waited two years for the directors of the poor to claim the money, and when they did not, brought this suit for it. Nobody doubted that the enacting clause required forfeiture of any stake illegally bet on an election; thus it is quasi criminal in nature and, by the maxim of lenity, to be strictly construed. The trial judge, however, held the proviso to be a statute of limitation on suit for the forfeited money and thus held for the defendant. The Supreme Court reversed, finding the proviso be a condition precedent to the directors of the poor's right to the stake, a more liberal reading.

> The proviso is not a statute of limitation, but a conditional limitation on the right to recover the money. Where the right is not exercised, the money or thing bet stands, as to ownership, where it did before the enactment of the section. It is in this respect in the nature of a *qui tam* liability, where property or money may be forfeited if sued for within a certain specified period, but which remains unaffected as to ownership if not so claimed or sued for.

Who, then, gets the money? The point of the statute, remember, was to remedy the evil of gambling on elections.

> It is our duty, therefore, to construe the statute so as to advance the remedy and suppress the mischief, and I know of no more effectual way to do this than to hold, in cases like the present, where the poor directors fail to do the duty imposed by the statute, namely, to sue and recover money or property bet on elections, that the losing party's right to recover from the stakeholder remains and may be asserted. This we think is not only the best policy, but the only construction of which the statute of 1839 is susceptible.[16]

The trial court therefore was reversed and Forscht, who lost the bet, recovered the $220 from the stakeholder defendant (who, one hopes, recovered from Donell, who won the wager.)

Construing the proviso as a condition is more liberal than construing it as a statute of limitations, but not by a whole lot. When one's best illustration rests on so thin a difference, the pickings are clearly slim.

Resolution

There is only a clash between Thrust #28 and Parry #28 if the thrust is given a universal and mandatory role never contemplated for it or any other canon or rule of grammar. As the Supreme Court said, a canon of statutory construction "is only an aid in the ascertainment of the meaning of the law and must yield whenever a contrary intention on the part of the law-maker is apparent."[17] Justifications for canons derive from legislative intent and the requirements for

---

[16] Id at 139-41.

[17] *Springer v. Phillipine Islands, supra*, 277 U.S. 189, 206 (1928).

successful communication, so when the justification does not apply nor should the canon. This is not a conflict, merely sensible and appropriate interpretation.

The justification for Thrust #28 is unusually solid, allowing of few exceptions. The burden on one arguing Parry #28 is correspondingly heavy. Not surprisingly, it does not yield many instantiations. One might insist that those instantiations demonstrate the opposition between Thrust #28 and Parry #28, but that would only be on a mindlessly superficial reading.

CONCLUSION

Karl Llewellyn's famous attack on canons of construction, an "arranged selection … appended" of twenty-eight pairs of "dueling" canons, is designed to support his claim that "there are two opposing canons on almost every point."[1] In the sixty years since its publication, the argument has been highly praised, not only for its demonstration of the radical indeterminacy of canons of construction but as a landmark of legal realist scholarship. So dominant has been Llewellyn's thesis and its supporting list that academic research into canons virtually ceased for the second half of the twentieth century.[2]

Yet the argument does not stand up to scrutiny. As we have seen, the list fails to produce contrariety in its pairs, fails to deconstruct canons of construction as legitimate tools of statutory interpretation, often even fails to list genuine canons —it simply fails to support Llewellyn's thesis.

… rules, rules

One comes to suspect that underlying Llewellyn's compilation of formulae as canons is a quite common fallacy. Einer Elhauge expresses it well: "[W]here the meaning of a duly enacted statute is unclear, then judges have no choice but to make some decision about what default rule to choose to resolve that unclarity."[3] Wrong. The judge facing an issue under an unclear statute has no choice but *to decide that issue*. She does not have to adopt some default rule and does not have the power to create such a rule. To say the reasoning by which the judge reaches a decision is equivalent to adopting a default rule is pure hypostatization, redundant, and misleading. Only the rules of reasoning govern reasoning, and they come with no authority but themselves.

---

1 *Canons* at 401.

2 *See* Introduction, above, or, for sutably impressive quotables, Daniel A. Farber, "*The Inevitability of Practical Reason: Statutes, Formalism, and the Rule of Law*," 45 VAND.L.REV. 533, 535 (1992); John F. Manning, "*Legal Realism and the Canons' Revival*," 5 THE GREEN BAG 2nd 283, 283-84 (2002); James J. Brudney and Corey Ditslear, "*Canons of Construction and the Elusive Quest for Neutral Reasoning*," 58 VAND.L.REV. 1, 8 (2005).; Frederick Schauer, "*Llewellyn on Rules*," http://law.bepress.com/uvalwps/uva publiclaw/art131 (2010) at 12.

3 Einer Elhauge, "*Preference-Estimating Statutory Default Rules*, 102 COLUM.L.REV. 2027, 2104 (2002).

If you thought of canons as universal, binding rules, formula to be followed mechanically at any opportunity,[4] then you could find inconsistency in some of the pairs of formulae on Llewellyn's list. But very seldom is a law in operation precisely determinate and mechanically applicable, not even those statutes with numbers, like speed limits. How much less Manichean are the wise saws formulated to aid, not dictate, interpretation. Yet most general criticisms of canons treat them this way —as fixed, unconditional, formulaic rules of universal applicability.

The conception of all law as hard-edged, universal, and unconditional rules to be applied mechanically is quite common. One sees it, for example, imposed on common law in the IRAC model of case analysis, which takes any judicial decision as a rule to be applied thereafter until rescinded. Such a superficial conception will generate equally superficial inconsistencies; canons taken in this way might indeed be at odds. But our law has never been so woodenly unreasoned, and had it been it surely would have lacked the resilience to survive, methodologically intact, through the social upheavals and revolutionary changes of the last two hundred and thirty years. Reason built on knowledge and experience,[5] in common law, the application of statutes, and even in the interpretive use of canons, has distinguished the judicial decision-making of our tradition from the totalitarian exercise of power.

A canon gets its status from the regularity of occurrence of its conditions of application and the robustness of the reasoning associated with it, as well as its prolonged acceptance by the judiciary. One might think of a canon as a conduit: it collects a set of applicable conditions and focuses them, producing a conclusion. If the applicable conditions do not obtain, then the canon will not apply. To think of two canons as contradictory because their underlying conditions of application are different is to misconceive their nature. It is this mistake that often produces the appearance of antipathy between otherwise compatible canons.

Isaiah Berlin —always perspicuous —wrote, "nothing very clear, simple, & obviously true can be said, without enfeebling qualifications."[6] To think of an ordinary exception, when split from its main clause, as a contrary is simply to misconceive the nature of generalities about human practices and in particular, canons of construction. Yet fully half the pairs on Llewellyn's list —pairs 2, 4, 5, 7, 12, 13, 15, 16, 17, 18, 21, 23, 27, and 28 —were constructed by splitting an "*unless* ..." from an acceptable generality and claiming each to be an independent canon. Eminent legal historian Willard Hurst summed up the role of canons succinctly: "A rule of construction was only an aid to fulfilling the legislative intent; as such it was always rebuttable by more specific matter from the statutory text or from legislative history."[7]

---

[4] *See, e.g.*, Dickerson, THE INTERPRETATION AND APPLICATION OF STATUTES 234 (1975).

[5] *Pace* Justice O.W.Holmes, Jr.

[6] Isaiah Berlin, ENLIGHTENING: LETTERS 11946-1960, 45 (Henry Hardy and Jennifer Holmes, ed.s, 2009).

[7] James Willard Hurst, DEALING WITH STATUTES (1982).

Un-canonical canons?

Too many of Llewellyn's thrusts and parries have little legitimate claim to being counted as canons of construction. The fourteen pairs concocted by splitting the exception out of a reasonably acceptable generalization, often a canon, could not create a canon in either thrust or parry. Add to those either the thrust or the parry (or both) in pairs 1, 3, 5, 8, 9, 10, 11, 24, and 26 yields twenty-three of the twenty-eight pairs of dubious canonical stature. Some, such as Thrust #5 and Thrust #24, seem to have been created on no authority whatsoever simply to contradict their opposing pairs, and lack both theoretical and judicial support. When one realizes that the origins of so many thrusts and parries on the list are merely the captions of sections in treatises (mostly Black's *Construction and Interpretation of Laws*), one can hardly be surprised at this.

Some, for example Pairs 25, 26, and 27, are merely restatements of general grammatical rules, adapted from one or other of the four secondary sources on which Llewellyn relies, most often Black. A legislature must use language to communicate control data to those governed; if that were to make every rule of grammar a canon of construction, then we would not only have a great many more canons than we hitherto thought, we would lose much of the distinctively legal quality of the concept of a canon of construction. As grammatical rules characterize statutory communication no differently than they do other careful communication in language, there seems little to be gained by calling them "canons of construction." Therefore, pairs Pairs 25, 26, and 27, like other simple rules of grammar —syntax and semantics —are mischaracterized as canons. This, however, is a minor quibble when compared with the other problems with the list as support for Llewellyn's thesis.

Scholarship

Llewellyn's *Canons* may have inhibited scholarship on canons for most of the latter part of the twentieth century,[8] but over the last twenty-five years, along with the growing academic interest in statutes, interest in and debate about canons has picked up —not, however, as a critique of Llewellyn's thesis or his list of "contrary" pairs. Recently some scholars (curiously they tend to be conservative) of statutory construction have argued for an increase in rigidity, in formalism in the use of canons. Adrien Vermeule argued that every judge should adopt and follow a fixed interpretive doctrine;[9] Gary O'Connor argued for a restatement as an authoritative formulation of permissible rules of interpretation;[10] and in the extreme, Nicholas Quinn

---

[8] Jonathon R. Macey & Geoffrey P.Miller, "*The Canons of Statutory Construction and Judicial Preferences*," 45 VAND.L.REV. 647, 647 (1992.

[9] Adrien Vermeule, "*Interpretive Choice*," 75 N.Y.U.L.REV. 74 (2000); *see* Sinclair, "*The Proper Treatment of "Interpretive Choice" in Statutory Decision-Making*," 45 N.Y.L.S.L.REV. 389 (2002)(on the fallacies in Prof. Vermuele's reasoning.).

[10] Gary E. O'Connor, "*Restatement (First) of Statutory Interpretation*," 7 N.Y.U.J.OF LEGISLATION & PUBLIC POLICY 333 (2003-04).

Rosenkranz argued for the adoption of statute-like rules of interpretation.[11] Such views are mistaken. A legislature might enact a formula, say "*expressio unius est exclusio alterius*," as interpretive law, but it could not prevent a court from looking to legislative intent and grounds for inferring it —even the reasons underpinning the enacted canon —and not applying the formula when it was to the contrary. This book should, *inter alia*, have demonstrated that any attempt to rigidify or formalize canons and their use is fundamentally misguided. Canons rest on reasoning; their canonical quality functions more as an assurance of the validity of a mode of reasoning than as an independent command. Any attempt to rigidify canons into rules of law must fail: reasons and reasoning are beyond judicial or legislative control.

One cannot properly sum up this protracted examination of Llewellyn's attack on canons without mentioning again the method by which he obtained so many of the thrusts and parries, namely his paraphrasing or copying from treatises, especially Black's *Construction and Interpretation of Laws*, sometimes with unfortunate word substitutions (for example, "statute" for "act", "imparting" for "importing"). The exact source of a verbal formula would not matter if it really were a canon. After all, a wise saw of sufficient familiarity and frequency of use to count as a canon should have a fairly stable verbal form: any instance of it will look like a copy or close derivative of most of the prior occurrences. That was not the case with most of the thrusts and parries on Llewellyn's list, suggesting a larger problem with the whole enterprise. Too often, too, the cited cases failed to support, or even relate to, the thrust or parry.[12] Llewellyn's iconic stature in twentieth century jurisprudence may exacerbate one's disappointment, but also suggests saying no more on the point.

But what does all this say about legal academia? Sixty years of acceptance,[13] of almost uniform reverence:[14] How could that be? It doesn't take the pages of pedestrian research and exposition you've seen above to show that there are and always were serious problems with this "classic critique" [15] of canons. Thrust #5 is hanging out there bereft of even an exemplar, let alone the acceptance and familiarity of a canon. There's the conglomeration of titles, preambles, and section headings in Thrust #11, all of different value and propriety in statutory interpretation, obviously not a candidate canon nor subject to unitary contradiction. Merely reading the list makes such examples jump out. Indeed, the stability and longevity of many canons suggest that

---

[11] Nicholas Quinn Rosenkranz, "*Federal Rules of Statutory Interpretation*," 115 HARV.L.REV. 2085 (2002).

[12] For example, six of the seven cases cited for Pairs 25, 26, and 27 (there were two for Parry #26) were not supportive or simply irrelevant.

[13] *See generally* SYMPOSIUM: A REEVALUATION OF THE CANONS OF STATUTORY INTERPRETATION, 45 VAND.L.REV. 529 *et seq*. (1992)(in which *Canons* met with uniform approval.)

[14] Almost: Justice Scalia stands out as a critic; *see* Antonin Scalia, A MATTER OF INTERPRETATION, 26-27 (1997).

[15] James J. Brudney and Corey Ditslear, "*Canons of Construction and the Elusive Quest for Neutral Reasoning*," 58 VAND.L.REV. 1, 8 (2005).

they are well adapted to their tasks, that a sudden demonstration of their invalidity should be treated with suspicion.

In any other discipline one would expect every element of every pair in Llewellyn's list to be scrutinized closely, the justifications to be laid on the table for examination. Academic neglect was like adopting a theory in chemistry on the basis of an extraordinary experiment that nobody ever even tried to replicate. Llewellyn's eminence in the profession goes only part of the way to explaining the failure, and of course there is not much in the way of kudos to be had for repeating another person's research, and nor is secondary, derivative work likely to find a place in a leading journal. But still there seems to have been some misalignment of academic values at work. Happily, however, it was only academic law that suffered; judges continued much the same as before to make use of canons when they found them appropriate.

BIBLIOGRAPHY

A

Aquinas, Thomas, SUMMA THEOLOGICA, Question 90, Articles 1 and 3 (1273) 7

Aristotle, NICHOMACHEAN ETHICS, Bk.V, Ch.10, 1137b 29

—RHETORIC, Bk.1, Ch.13 29

B

Ballard, Frederick A., *Retroactive Federal Taxation*, 48 HARV.L.REV. 592 (1935) 58

Bentham, Jeremy, *Of Promulgation of the Laws*," 1 WORKS (Bowring, ed. 1859) 7

Berlin, Isaiah, *Logical Translation*, in Henry Hardy, ed., CONCEPTS AND CATEGORIES: PHILOSOPHICAL ESSAYS (1978) 63

—*Two Concepts of Liberty*, THE PROPER STUDY OF MANKIND 191 (Hardy and Hausheer, ed.s, 1997) 19

Black, Henry Campbell, HANDBOOK ON THE CONSTRUCTION AND INTERPRETATION OF LAWS (2nd ed., 1911) 8 *et seq.*

Blackstone, William, 1 COMMENTARIES ON THE LAWS OF ENGLAND (4th American edition, George Chase, ed., 1938) 7, 58, 106, 123

Braucher, Robert, *The Legislative History of the Uniform Commercial Code*, 58 COLUM.L.REV. 798 (1958) 31

Breitel, Charles, *The Lawmakers*, 65 COLUM.L.REV. 749 (1965) 20

Breyer, Stephen, *The Uses of Legislative History in Interpreting Statutes*, 65 S.CAL.L.REV. 845 (1992) 6

Brudney James J., and Corey Ditslear, "*Canons of Construction and the Elusive Quest for Neutral Reasoning*," 58 VANDERBILT LAW REVIEW 1 (2005) 1, 201

C

Cardozo, ,Benjamin N. THE NATURE OF THE JUDICIAL PROCESS (1921) 106

Carter, James C., THE PROPOSED CODIFICATION OF OUR COMMON LAW (New York Evening Post Job Printing Office, 1884) 63

Cole P., & J.Morgan, SYNTAX AND SEMANTICS, SPEECH ACTS (1975) 5, 17, 143

Cook, Walter W., LOGICAL AND LEGAL BASES OF THE CONFLICT OF LAWS (1942) 129

59 CORPUS JURIS (1932) 8 *et seq.*

Crawford, J., THE NEGOTIABLE INSTRUMENTS LAW (1897) 31

D

Demosthenes, *Speech against Timokrates*, XXIV DEMOSTHENES, 371 (350 B.C.E.)(J.H.Vince, trans., Loeb Classical Library, 1935) 7

Dickerson, Reed, THE INTERPRETATION AND APPLICATION OF STATUTES (1975) 3, 143, 145, 202

E

Elhauge, Einer, *Preference-Estimating Statutory Default Rules*, 102 COLUM.L.REV. 2027 (2002) 202

Eskridge, William N., Jr., *The Case of the Amorous Defendant: Criticizing Absolute Stare Decisis for Statutory Cases*, 88 MICH. L. REV. 2450 (1990) 106

—*DYNAMIC* STATUTORY INTERPRETATION (1994) 3, 6

F

Farber, Daniel A., "*The Inevitability of Practical Reason: Statutes, Formalism, and the Rule of Law,*" 45 VANDERBILT LAW REVIEW 533 (1992) ix,1, 201

FEDERALIST PAPERS, THE, (C.Rossiter ed. 1961) 106

Frank, Jerome, *Words and Music: Some Remarks on Statutory Interpretation*, 47 COLUM. L. REV. 1259, 1259 (1947) 36

Frankfurter, Felix, *Some Reflections on the Reading of Statutes*, 47 COLUM.L.REV. 528 (1947) 21, 63, 101, 116

Fuller, Lon L., THE MORALITY OF LAW (1964) 7

G

Grice, H. P., *LOGIC AND CONVERSATION*, (William James Lectures, Harvard University, 1967) 5, 17, 143

—STUDIES IN THE WAY OF WORDS (1989) 143

H

Hale, Sir Matthew, THE HISTORY OF THE COMMON LAW OF ENGLAND (1713)(Charles M. Gray, ed., U. Chicago Press, 1971) 106

Hart, H.L.A., THE CONCEPT OF LAW (1961) 63

Heydon's Case, 30 Co. 7a, 76 Eng.Rep. 637 (Exch. 1584) 19, 23, 30, 39, 47, 68

Holmes, Oliver Wendell, Jr., *The Theory of Legal Interpretation*, 12 HARV.L.REV. 417 (1899) 100

Hurst, James Willard, DEALING WITH STATUTES (1982) 9

I, J

Jefferson, Thomas, 7 JEFFERSON'S WORKS (Monticello ed. 1904) 146

K, L

Leech, Geoffrey, PRINCIPLES OF PRAGMATICS 19-45 (1983) 143

Leibniz, Gottfried Wilhelm . (1646-1716) MONADOLOGY ¶31 (1714) x

Llewellyn, Karl N., "*Remarks on the Theory of Appellate Decision and the rules or Canons of about how Statutes are to be Construed,*" 3 VANDERBILT LAW REVIEW 395 (1950) ix, 1 *et seq.*

—THE COMMON LAW TRADITION—DECIDING APPEALS (1960) 2, 111

Locke, John, SECOND TREATISE ON GOVERNMENT (1690) 7

M

Macey Jonathon R., & Geoffrey P.Miller, "*The Canons of Statutory Construction and Judicial Preferences*," 45 VANDERBILT LAW REVIEW 647 (1992) 1, 202

Manning, John F., "*Legal Realism and the Canons' Revival,*" 5 THE GREEN BAG 2nd 283 (2002) 1, 2, 98, 201

Manning, John F. and Matthew C. Stephenson, LEGISLATION AND REGULATION (2010) 1

Marshall, Lawrence C., *Let Congress Do It": The Case for an Absolute Rule of Statutory Stare Decisis*, 88 MICH. L. REV. 177 (1989) 106

—*Contempt of Congress: A Reply to the Critics of an Absolute Rule of Statutory Stare Decisis*, 88 MICH. L. REV. 2467 (1990) 106

McKeehan, Charles L., *The Negotiable Instruments Law*, 50 AM. L. REG. 437 (1902) 31

Mentschikoff,, Soia, *Highlights of the Uniform Commercial Code*, 27 MOD.L.REV. 167 (1964) 31

Miller, Geoffrey P., *Pragmatics and the Maxims of Interpretation*, 1990 WISCONSIN L. REV. 1179 (1990) 7, 143

Mooney, Eugene F., *Old Kontract Principles and Karl's New Kode: An Essay on the Jurisprudence of Our New Commercial Law*, 11 Vill. L. Rev. 213, 235 (1966) 25, 31

Morris, Charles W., *Foundations of the Theory of Signs*, 1 INTERNATIONAL ENCYCLOPEDIA OF UNIFIED SCIENCE 79 (1938) 5, 143

N, O

O'Connor, Gary E., *Restatement (First) of Statutory Interpretation*, 7 N.Y.U.J.OF LEGISLATION & PUBLIC POLICY 333 (2003-04) 173

P, Q, R

Rabelais, Francois, GARGANTUA AND PANTAGRUEL Bk.3, Ch.39 (1546) 4

Radin, Max, *Statutory Interpretation*, 43 HARV. L. REV. 863 (1930) 143

Rosenkranz, Nicholas Quinn, *Federal Rules of Statutory Interpretation*, 115 HARV.L.REV. 2085 (2002) 174

RULING CASE LAW *Statutes*, (1929) 8 *et seq.*

Ruud, Millard, *No Law shall Embrace More Than One Subject*, 42 MINN.L.REV. 389 (1958) 83

Ryle, Gilbert, THE CONCEPT OF MIND (1949) 77

S

Scalia, Antonin, A MATTER OF INTERPRETATION: FEDERAL COURTS AND THE LAW (Princeton U.P., Princeton, 1997) 4, 206

Frederick Schauer, "*Llewellyn on Rules*," http://law.bepress.com/uvalwps/uva publiclaw/art131 (2010) 201

Schnader, William A., *Pennsylvania and the Uniform Commercial Code*, 37 TEMP.L.Q. 265 (1964) 31

Sinclair, Michael .B.W., *Law and Language: The Role of Pragmatics in Statutory Interpretation* 46 U.PITT.L.REV. 373 (1985) 7, 143, 145

—*The Proper Treatment of "Interpretive Choice" in Statutory Decision-Making*," 45 N.Y.L.S.L.REV. (2002) 173

—"*Only a Sith Thinks Like That": Llewellyn's "Dueling Canons," One to Seven*, 50 NEW YORK LAW SCHOOL LAW REVIEW 919 (2006) i? *et seq.*

—"*Only a Sith Thinks Like That": Llewellyn's "Dueling Canons," Eight to Twelve*, 51 NEW YORK LAW SCHOOL LAW REVIEW 1003 SSRN: http://ssrn.com/abstract=902853 (2006-07) x

—"*Only a Sith Thinks Like That": Llewellyn's "Dueling Canons," Thirteen to Sixteen*, 53 NEW YORK LAW SCHOOL LAW REVIEW 953 SSRN: http://ssrn.com/abstract=1337057 (2008-09) x

—"*Only a Sith Thinks Like That": Llewellyn's "Dueling Canons," Seventeen to Twenty*, SSRN: http://ssrn.com/abstract=1387503, (2008) x

—"*Only a Sith Thinks Like That": Llewellyn's "Dueling Canons," Twenty-one to Twenty-four*, SSRN: http://ssrn.com/abstract=1557831, January, 2010 (with Adam Schlusselberg) x

—"*Only a Sith Thinks Like That": Llewellyn's "Dueling Canons," Twenty-five to Twenty-eight*, SSRN: http://ssrn.com/abstract=1682164, September, 2010 (with Adam Schlusselberg) x

—TRADITIONAL TOOLS OF STATUTORY INTERPRETATION (Vandeplas Publishing, 2013) 2, 6, 8, 20, 64, 70, 82, 159

Slawson, W. David, *Constitutional and Legislative Considerations in Legislative Lawmaking*, 48 CAL.L.REV. 216, 239 (1960) 58

Stalnaker, Robert , *Pragmatics*, 22 SYNTHESE 272, 275 (1970) 143

Stockwell, Robert P., Paul Schachter & Barbara Hall Partee, THE MAJOR SYNTACTIC STRUCTURES OF ENGLISH (1973) 165

Sutherland, J.G., STATUTES AND STATUTORY CONSTRUCTION (2nd ed., 1904) 8 *et seq.*

SYMPOSIUM: A REEVALUATION OF THE CANONS OF STATUTORY INTERPRETATION, 45 VANDERBILT LAW REVIEW 529 *et seq.* (1992) 1, 202

T

Thorne, Samuel E., A DISCOURSE ON THE STATUTES (1942) 6

U, V

Vermeule, Adrien, *Interpretive Choice*, 75 N.Y.U.L.REV. 74 (2000) 173

W

Wald, Patricia M., *The Sizzling Sleeper: The Use of Legislative History in Construing Statutes in the 1988-89 Term of the United States Supreme Court*, 39 AMERICAN U. L. REV. 277, 301 (1990) 6

Williston, Samuel, THE LAW GOVERNING SALES OF GOODS AT COMMON LAW AND UNDER THE UNIFORM SALES ACT (1909) 31

Wittgenstein, Ludwig, PHILOSOPHICAL INVESTIGATIONS (1953) 120

X, Y, Z

INDEX

A

academic evaluation of Llewellyn's pairs 1, 174-175

administrative interpretation 85-90

'and' and 'or' 153-156

Ashwander principle — avoid constitutional issues 55-56

B

brooding omnipresence in the sky 17

C

canon of construction

- definition 2–4
- general criticisms 3

captions (section captions) 71-73

D

definitions 51, 57-59

E

ejusdem generis 135-140

exceptions 115-118, 165-170

Expression of one thing excludes another 3

expressio unius est exclusio alterius 2, 3, 119-128, 165-170

F, G

general and particular 63

Goldbach's Conjecture 2

grammar 111-114

H

Heydon's Case 19, 23, 30, 39, 47, 68

hypothesis 1

I

ignoratio elenchi 3

implicature 15

interpretation clause 51, 56-59

J

judicial interpretation prior to enactment 81-84

jurisprudential pantheon 2

K, L

last antecedent rule 141-145

legislative intent 5-6

legislative supremacy 6-7

lenity 22, 80, 103, 122

linguistic canons 4

linguistics 5

M, N

necessity of notice 6-7

next preceding antecedent (last antecedent) rule 141-145

noscitur a sociis 129, 131-134

O

'or' and 'and' 153-156

ordinary *cf.* technical meanings 95-99

P

permissive and mandatory words 157-160

Plain Meaning Rule 7-8, 75-80

pragmatic implicature 15

pragmatics 5

preamble 68-71

precedent, doctrine of 85-90

provenance of the pairs on the list 91-94

punctuation 147-151

Q, R

retroactive law 7, 45-50

S

secondary sources 8

section captions 71-73

semantics 5

stare decisis 4, 85-88

stare dictis 4

statutes …

- declarative of common law 23-24
- displacing common law 25-28
- foreign origin and interpretation 29-38
- in derogation of the common law 17-22
- *in pari materia* 39-44
- interpretation clause 51, 56-59
- overruling judicial interpretation prior to enactment 81-84
- remedial 19-22

substantive canons 4

syntax 5

T

technical *cf.* ordinary meanings 95-99

titles 65-68

U

Use ordinary meanings 5

V, W

words of the statute control 13

X, Y, Z

www.ingramcontent.com/pod-product-compliance
Lightning Source LLC
LaVergne TN
LVHW082333200926
848481LV00012B/3330